Tribal Commonalities and Underdevelopment: *An Interface*

Tribal Commonalities and Underdevelopment: *An Interface*

NISHAKAR PANDA

SERIALS PUBLICATIONS
NEW DELHI (INDIA)

First Published - 2009

ISBN: 978-81-8387-270-6

Published by

SERIALS PUBLICATIONS
4830/24, Prahlad Street, Ansari Road
Darya Ganj, New Delhi-110002 (India)
Phone : 23245225 Fax : 91-11-23272135
E-mail: serials@satyam.net.in

For

ANUSUYA

CHANDAN & ANANYA

CONTENTS

Preface

India has the dubious distinction of having second largest concentration of tribal communities in the World. These scheduled tribes constitute 573 groups and sub-groups and are distributed in different proportions in most of the States and Union territories of this Sub-continent. There is a wide variation in their social system, economic organization and political structure. Though they have a common cultural chord displaying their group identity, their art and craft, music and song, language and literature, rituals and religion are diverse and dissimilar in different regions. But one conspicuous commonality with the Scheduled Tribes of India is their backwardness and underdevelopment. The present work is a modest attempt of an economist to discuss and dissect a hither to neglected community's economy, society, culture etc. and critically appraise, analyse and examine a number of issues overtly or covertly contributing to the present State of their underdevelopment.

In fact, this collection, initially it was planned, should precede my earlier book "Policies, Programmes and Strategies for Tribal Development: A critical Appraisal". Idea conceived was that the readers or researchers for that matter, could have a sequence of ideas and fusion of viewing process in gettingt a thumbnail picture of origin and evolution of scheduled tribes of India, their distribution and concentration in different regions of the Country, matters and aspects pertaining to tribal economy and their economic organization, their social system, political structure and cultural commonalities and most importantly, factors and forces responsible for their backwardness and underdevelopment (what have been attempted in the present work). And then, what has been done so far to address them, what are the policies envisaged, strategies conceptualized, projects executed and programmes implemented right from the ancient era and after more than half a century of planning and then to take stocks of things; what is their impact on them, where we stand now and how far we have succeeded in mitigating the miseries of these marginalized sections and fulfilling the coveted objective of mingling them in the mainstream(that had been presented in my earlier book as aforementioned). Having discussed all the issues, the obvious question would be; what is the proper planning, how should we proceed by surmounting the inherent inconsistencies and any suggestions for modifications in the models and approaches and policy recommendations. (To be focused on my forthcoming issue, a critique on "planning for tribal development: issues and implications", which is under preparation). All this was envisaged to maintain a perspicacious coherence in the all important issue of Tribal development, its genesis, present structure and future perspective. But it happened otherwise. As usual, execution stood apathetic to planning. With constant persuations of my academician friends, of course, with good reasons, second one preceded the first.

Be that as it may, in this issue I have attempted to present in a broader perspective what anthropologists said on the origin and evolution of scheduled tribes, their society and culture. I supplemented their views in a larger context. Such presentations, I feel, are quite necessary to have a complete and clear glance on the subject matter. To understand the present position in its entirety, I tried to focus on tribal economy and trace their economic organizations with some anecdotes and examples. In 'Tribal Backwardness and Underdevelopment' which forms the central theme of this work, I have identified sixteen critical parameters and pointers which have a direct bearing on the subject in question. Since these aspects require a transparent, sound and informed thinking in the present Juncture, I have analysed the matter with some updated data, facts and figures and made some general observations, wherever relevant. The issues and indicators broadly discussed are : Demographic Pattern, Primitive Tribal Groups, Diminutive/Lesser Tribes, Superstition and Sorcery, Gender Dimensions, Lack of Basic Minimum Services, Incidence of Poverty, Exploitation and Indebtedness, Literacy, Shifting Cultivation, Forest, Displacement, Land Reforms, Unemployment, Political Participation and last but not the least, Representation in Administration.

There are certain fundamental flaws in the general conception about salvaging the scheduled tribe communities. I have humbly tried to dispel those misinformation and misconception in the appropriate context. They are very much a sizeable section of our society, important stake holders of development and, therefore, form an integral part of the growth process. I have, therefore, preferred to reflect on the issues and indicators which need aggressive intervention. They are to be addressed not in routine or mundane manner but in a mission mode with pure human touch, if at all we are sensitive to the subject matter. The aforementioned points are illustrative and not exhaustive. There may, however, be many more aspects and areas which indirectly affect their impoverishment. There is scope of elaboration and elucidation which may trigger further brainstorming and detailed deliberations in the years to come.

Shree Gundicha, NISHAKAR PANDA
04.07.2008

Acknowledgements

At the outset, I convey my gratitude to the numerous readers of my earlier book for their innumerable letters and e-mails displaying their appreciation and compliments. I have loved to receive your letters ad e-mails. I owe a word of thanks to them all. Thanks must go to my friends and well wishers who have constantly supported and incessantly inspired me to bring out this volume. I greatly valued their suggestions and untiring encouragements. Special thanks to my colleagues for their assistance and cooperation in this work.

I also like to convey my thanks to the librarian and staff of different libraries at New Delhi, Hyderabad, Ranchi and Bhubaneswar for providing me scope to go through the relevant materials. I intend to make particular mention of State Planning Board Library, Government of Orissa for their personal support. Relevant inputs and required information were collected from Planning Commission and concerned Ministries of Government of India and different offices, agencies and institutions of Government of Orissa. Those data collected were collated and compiled for this book. I am extremely thankful to all of them for their cooperation.

My wife, Anusuya, is the moving force in my endeavour. Her untiring support and unstinted stimulation spurred me to complete the work in time. My son, Chandan and daughter Ananya are the constant sources of inspiration for me. They bore my negligence and tolerated my apathy. I express my heartfelt thanks to my wife and children for their contribution and record my gratefulness to them. My deeper sense of appreciation goes out to my parents Smt. Sabitri and Sri Chintamani Panda for all their love and affection for me. Finally, big thanks to my publisher for bringing out this book.

NISHAKAR PANDA

1 Introduction

The largest concentration of tribal communities in the world, next to Africa, is in India.[1] There are as many as 573 different tribal communities with several sub-groups and many overlapping communities in more than one States roughly constituting 8 per cent of the total population of India. A majority of scheduled tribes of India are economically, socially and educationally backward. Many of them are primitive and geographically isolated. These tribal communities in India live in around 15 per cent of area of the country most of which are hills and dales, forests and plateaus and therefore, under developed and inaccessible. In order to probe tribal problems thoroughly and deeply, it is necessary to take a broad view of the tribes stressing their commonalities and to go into the socio-economic background of different tribes of India. The economic, social and political organisations of Scheduled Tribes, their cultural traits, language and literature, art and craft, dance and music and their religion are vast and varied. But, the Indian tribes, barring a few exceptions, are backward and under-developed compared to the general population. They are still in a state of impoverishment and identify themselves as a distinct section of the society. It is worthwhile to trace their socio-economic and cultural commonalities in the perspective of their backwardness and underdevelopment.

REVIEW OF LITERATURE

Knowledge acquisition and accumulation is a continuous, gradual and endless process. It is built over a range of information and familiarity gained by experience. The works of scholars and researchers contribute significantly in the course of knowledge construction. Study findings and policy outlooks serve as a beginning for the future. The links that can be established between and among studies enrich knowledge and offer policy insights[2]. Extensive studies in the fields of economic, religion and socio-cultural patterns of the scheduled tribes have been made by anthropologists, sociologists, geographers and historians. Eminent economists have studied their economic patterns and problems and conducted evaluation studies on the programmes, policies and projects meant for the development of Scheduled Tribes.

A. Baines' in his 'Ethnography'[3] (Strassburg, 1912) has described the individual tribes and peoples of India very briefly. His presentation of the so-called 'hill-tribes' is, however, too short for their proper characterisation. Moreover, this book includes also the non-aboriginal peoples of India. In the context of the Indian tribes, H. Risley' in his book 'The People of India'[4] (Calcutta 1915), analysed on some races but not all the races of the Indian sub-continent. He highlighted mainly the problems of different castes. G. S. Ghurye's 'The Scheduled Tribes'[5] (Bombay 1959) contains certain features and problems of the Indian tribals. Some anthropological theories of the author are placed in the book. In 'Tribal Life in India' by N.K. Bose[6] (New Delhi 1971), there is general description of the tribals of India. In the same way, different anthropological aspects of Scheduled Tribes of India have been discussed in 'Tribal India' by K. L. Bhomick *et al*, and 'Indian Tribes' by Chakravorti and Mukherjee.

Stphen Fuchs in his book 'The Aboriginal Tribes Of India'[7] presents the general situation of the tribes in all the regions of India and also points out the special features of the individual tribes. He also gives a basic and concise description of the works of historians and anthropological survey on the living races and peoples of India. Thus, Fuchs (1973) has written a comprehensive account of the aboriginal tribes of the Indian subcontinent. Hudson (1922) has traced the complex historical evolution of various tribes of India.[8] Hulton (1941) has further analysed their conditions.[9] Dalton (1872) has provided an account of the tribal societies of north-eastern states.[10] Guha (1939-1951) has discussed the racial affinities of the Indian aborigines in different perspectives.[11] The major demographic structure of tribal India has been analysed by Mamoria.[12] Sengupta (1959) has studied the consumption and nutrition pattern of the aborigines.[13] Vidyarthi (1959-1978) has produced valuable studies on the socio-cultural-economic organisations of the Indian tribes.[14] Ghurye (1963) has depicted the historic development of the Indian tribes and made a chronicle of tribal development since independence.[15] Ambastha (1969) has studied the education system *vis-à-vis* the income and expenditure pattern of the tribes.[16] Bhowmick (1971) has dealt with the ethnographic structure and other characteristics of important tribes of India.[17] Bose has discussed the socio-cultural features of the Indian tribes.[18] Basu opines that development strategy of tribal communities has to be in tune with the development strategy of the nation.[19] Dube (1977) has examined the changing pattern of socio-cultural organisation of the tribes.[20] B.D. Sharma investigates into the impact of socio-cultural practices on the economic development of tribals.[21]

Having thus discussed the various works and studies made on tribal development of India in general, it is pertinent to have flashes of various government reports published and papers of seminars, symposiums, workshops, conferences and colloquiums on the subject. A good number of reports were published from time to time to highlight the tribal society, economy and tribal problems. These include: Annual Reports on Commissioner of Scheduled Castes and Scheduled Tribes, Report of the Backward Classes Commission, Report of the Study Team on Social Welfare and Welfare of Backward Classes (1959), Report of the Estimates Committee (1959), Report of the Committee on Special Multipurpose Tribal Blocks (1960) headed by Dr. Verrier Elwin, Report of the Scheduled Areas and Scheduled Tribes (1960-61) headed by U.N. Dhebar, Report of the Study Group on Welfare of the Weaker Sections of the Village Community, Study Team on Tribal Development

Programme (1966) headed by P. Shilu Ao, and Taskforce on Scheduled Tribes by Vidyarthi (1972) etc.[22]

Besides, various seminars and workshops on Tribal Development have been organised from time to time in different academies and institutes. Two such seminars relevant in this context need be mentioned here. A seminar on 'Tribal Development Problems' was organised at the H.C.M. State Institute of Public Administration, Jaipur in May 1975. The Centre for Tribal Development of the Manikya Lal Verma (MLV) Tribal Research and Training Institute in collaboration with the Tribal Area Development Department, Udaipur had convened a seminar on 'Tribal Development: Past Efforts and New Challenges' (December 1987). The observations and findings of the seminars have been compiled in the form of a book entitled *Tribal Development: Past Efforts and New Challenges* by J.P. Singh and N.N. Vyas. The authors are of the opinion that notwithstanding the substantial benefits accrued to tribal people over Plan periods, the results have not been commensurate with expectations.[23]

Let us now turn to tribal ethnography and geography, tribal economy and tribal development of different states and regions of the country. Studies on the tribes of different states were taken up by various anthropologists. Studies of ethnographic nature were undertaken by Dalton and Hunter in 1872-73; the later British ethnographers published only a few notes and papers on the tribes of eastern states in the *Journal of the Asiatic Society*.[24] S.N. Roy is believed to be the first Indian scholar to write on the tribes of Orissa. He wrote on the Savara tribe of Orissa in a descriptive paper published in "Man in India" in 1927 and later in 1935 he wrote the first full-length monograph on the Hill Bhuinya. Verrier Elwin discussed about the 'Bondo' tribe in his book *Bondo Highlands* (1950).[25] Srivastav too discussed about 'the educational problems of tribes.[26] The socio-cultural, religious and anthropological studies of Juang, Gadaba, Savara and Bhuinya tribes have been conducted by Bose, Chatopadhyaya, Sitapati and Mohapatra. N.C.A.E.R., New Delhi, made a study on the problems of Scheduled Tribes and suggested specific recommendations for their development.[27] Sinha and Mishra (1976) have investigated into the spatial distribution and socio-economic-cultural organisations of Orissan tribes.[28]

In the present study, however, it has been attempted to critically examine the stages of development and regional concentration of STs of India, their Socio-Political and economic-cultural commonalities and offer educative and informative insights on their backwardness and under development.

Need and Scope of the Present Work

As yet, no substantial and extensive literature is available on the evolution of Indian tribes, their distribution in Indian territories, their socio-economic and cultural aspects and analysis on the forces and factors contributing to their backwardness and underdevelopment. No systematic work has also been done on the analysis of Socio-Economic and Political Organisations, cultural traits of scheduled tribes of India, their marriage and religious practices etc. A very few literature available on region specific analysis of socio-cultural practices of individual tribes only touched the fringe of the subject. Moreover, different types of scheduled tribes of India and their classification, various stages of their development right from their evolution, their concentration and distribution in different regions of India need be analysed to have a complete and clear-cut idea on the genesis of Development of tribal communities in its entirety over the years. It is very fashionable and many people take a fancy in making stray remarks about the backwardness and under development of scheduled tribes. But hardly anybody concerned with their development have tried to delve deeper into the crux of the problem. Are the scheduled tribes of India really backward? Are they underdeveloped in true sense of the term? If it is in the affirmative, the obvious question then is; why? Are backwardness endemic to their socio-cultural traits, economic habits? Are any extraneous agencies or covert currents responsible for this sorry state of affairs? What are the forces and factors contributing to their backwardness? For proper perception of the problems of scheduled tribes of India, periodic planning, envisaging polices, implementing programmes and schemes and devising strategies for their development, the aforementioned issues need be highlighted and addressed with data and statistics as well as facts and figures.

A modest attempt has, however, been made in the present work to address all these issues. Therefore, it was extremely essential to discuss and dissect the issues pertaining to the evolution of scheduled tribes in India, their classification and concentration in different parts of the country, their society and social structure, their economy and economic organization, their political process and cultural chord, their language and religion, their marriage practices, their Art, music, dance, so on and so forth. Having focussed all these aspects and issues, it is also necessary to highlight on the causal connections of their backwardness and reasons of their under development. The present work is an humble move in this direction.

Approach and Structure

The Methodological approach adopted in the present work is purely an inductive method based on secondary sources of information supplemented with secondary data. The study is descriptive as well as quantitative and wherever possible anecdotes and illustrations have been cited. Secondary data have been collected from various connected Departments of Government of India, state Governments and the Planning Commission of India. A number of research studies, articles, papers presented in seminars/symposiums, conferences and colloquiums, various related reports and books in different libraries have been referred to for building up theoretical insights and ideas to support the study.

As regards structure of the book, it contains Six chapters. The first chapter introduces the subject. Prior to the description on the commonalities of scheduled tribes and their backwardness, this introductory chapter reviews the literature on the subject, reflects the need and scope of the present work and the approach followed and structure shaped. The Second chapter gives a brief account of the classifications and Regional distribution of Indian Tribes. A thumbnail picture of tribal economy and their economic organisations are presented in the Third chapter. The Fourth chapter offers a brief description on the tribal society and their social systems. It also contains a bird's eye view of the political structure of Scheduled Tribes of India since pre-independence period. The Fifth chapter discusses the tribal culture in its entirety. The last chapter provides a detailed analysis on the backwardness and under development of Scheduled Tribes of India with a concluding note.

Before highlighting commonalities of Scheduled Tribes of India from Socio-economic, cultural and political standpoints, it has been attempted to delve deeper into the genesis of their development. The queries and questions on what is a tribe, who are Scheduled Tribes, how are they classified into different groups and races and what are the stages of their development etc. have been addressed. Negritos are the earlier races and Proto-Australoids are the second oldest racial group. Then there are also Mongoloid races and oriental races. Brief discussions on these races and groups of Scheduled Tribes have been made and then various stages of their development have been traced. Concentration of Scheduled Tribes in different parts and regions of India since ancient and pre independence period have also been dealt with. The distribution of Scheduled Tribes in Northern India, Southern India, Western India, Eastern India and Southern India have been focused with specific references to southern Plateau, the central tribal land, eastern ghat region and coastal region of eastern part of the country.

In the economy and economic organizations, the basic economic activities and status of different individual tribes of India such as Hunters and food gatherers, shifting cultivators or primitive cultivators, Dependent labourers and food collectors, settled cultivators, peasants, Artisans, Industrial workers etc. and tribes of higher social status have been highlighted. The economy of Indian tribes centres round the activities such as agriculture, horticulture, sericulture, Animal

Husbandry, Fishery and Forest etc. Tribal society and their social structure is not uniform for all categories of tribes. Moreover their social structure is different in different areas and different parts of the Country. There are different sub-tribes and clans, their family structure are different, the shape and size of their house and dwelling units are radically different, their food habits are not uniform, the marriage pattern is also different from one community to another community and they claim different totemistic origin. Youth dormitory is an important organization in most of the tribal societies. It plays both as a cultural and recreation centre of the community.

The culture is an umbrella term with wide ramifications. It bears the identity of a clan or a community and their position in society. The culture of Scheduled Tribes differ from one group to another, it is also different from one region to another depending on their concentration. A nomadic and food gathering tribe has a separate culture and religion. A tribe living in a Jungle with shifting or settled cultivation follows a culture not akin to the culture of a tribe living in the plains. The rituals and festivals, dance, song and music, architecture and literature, art and craft and religion of different individual tribes in different parts of the Country have been reflected in separate sections under tribal culture.

Since time immemorial, even before evolution of any political system in any part of the World, the Scheduled Tribes had a strong, well organized and a neatly structured political system. Their political system was not, however, uniform for all the clans or communities though it is evolved over a period of time and metamorphosed to the present system and structure. Their political structure was different in ancient times. It underwent several changes in pre and post independence period with quite dissimilar political systems in different parts and regions of the country. Even different categories of tribes follow a different pattern in a same region. During the British Regime, they had a political structure and a system of Internal democracy. Some communities who are loyal to the britishers follow a system of autocracy and became loyal to a leader of their own group but the other tribal communities in India who opposed the britishers and supported independence movement had a system of clan committees and all the members had a opinion and voice to share. Active movements for a certain degree of political autonomy and self-rule started in different parts of the country. Jharkhand movement in Jharkhand, Santal movement in Orissa, Musuan movement in Nagaland are few such anecdotes. In post independence period, in the present political system of the country, though they had a different political structure and process varying from region to region like Northern, Southern, Central, Eastern and Western parts of the country, there is a clan democracy prevalent in almost all the tribal communities.

After addressing social, economic, political and cultural issues of STs of India, it is incumbent to discuss their backwardness and underdevelopment in general irrespective of their geographical concentration or clan classifications. They are backward and under developed and they keep themselves immune from the modernisation process and aloof from the rest of the communities of the country. Why after all they are backward and under developed in comparison to the rest of the population in this sub-continent? Various forces and factors have been analysed, discussed and dissected to ascertain if they contribute to this present state of affairs. Their demographic pattern is very much complex and presents a paradoxical picture. Primitiveness prohibits many tribal groups to assimilate themselves in the mainstream of national life. Some tribes are in the process of diminution and extinction. They are still known as lesser tribes even after six decades of development for their upliftment. The sex composition of Scheduled Tribes is different from the general population of the country. Their gender dimension has acted as a deterrent factor. Besides, tribal areas lack basic minimum services like health and housing, education, drinking water, electricity, supportive infrastructure etc. Massive unemployment or seasonal unemployment or disguised unemployment are widely prevalent among STs. An analysis has been made on their work participation rate and occupational status. Various data and figures provided in this section to substantiate that unemployment has a strong role to play for their under-development. Most of the tribal communities riddle in poverty. Low purchasing power and incidence of poverty has contributed positively for their backwardness. Instances of large scale indebtedness and exploitation by the usurious, unscrupulous and egregious money lenders are quite common. The literacy rate of Indian tribes is far below the literacy rate of the total population of India. Their high rate of illiteracy compelled them to remain subdued and sub-servient. Their excessive dependence on forest and their strong conviction that they are actual owners of the jungles and not other people or the government and stringent forest laws make them impoverished. Many of the Scheduled Tribes practice shifting cultivation. Absence of any modern scientific methods of cultivation and low fecundity of the soil and high rate of displacement from their home and land also contributed both directly and indirectly for their poverty and backwardness. In any mining operation and industrial projects or any new major or medium irrigation ventures for that matter, the Scheduled Tribes are worst sufferers so far as displacement and rehabilitation is concerned. Added to this, a cursory glance on their representation in various all India Administrative services or their political participant right from PRIs to the highest echelons of democratic structure like Loksabha or Rajya Sabha surmised the fact that they are still far back and lagging behind compared to other communities. Supportive statistics and data are presented to corroborate the fact. At the end, a concluding note has been presented.

NOTES AND REFERENCES

1. Verrier Elwin (1963), New Deal for tribal India, Government of India, New Delhi, p. 5.
2. Pawan K. Karma (1987), *Cooperative Management, Practices, Problems and Prospects*, New Delhi, Deep and Deep Publications, p. 12.
3. Baines (1912), A, *Ethnography*, Strassburg.

4. Risely H. (1915), *The People of India,* Calcutta.

5. Ghurye. G. S. (1959), *The Scheduled Tribes,* Bombay.

6. Bose. N. K. (1971), *Tribal Life in India,* New Delhi.

7. Fuchs. Stephen (1973), *The Aboriginal Tribes of India,* Macmillan India, New Delhi.

8. T.C. Hudson (1922), *The Primitive Culture of India,* The Royal Asiatic Society, London.

9. J.H. Hulton (1968), "Primitive Tribes", in O'Malley, L.S.S. (Ed.), *Modern India and the West,* Oxford University Press, London (First Edition, 1941 at Oxford), pp. 415-44.

10. E.T. Dalton (1872), *Descriptive Ethnology of Bengal,* Government of Bengal, Calcutta.

11. B.S. Guha (1951), "The Aboriginal Races of India", *Science and Culture,* Vol. 4, No. 12, 1939, pp. 677-83; B.S. Guha, "The Indian Aborigines and Their Administration", *Journal of Asiatic Society,* Vol. 17, No. 1, pp. 19-44.

12. C.B. Mamoria (1957), *Tribal Demography in India,* Kitab Mahal, Allahabad, 1957; C.B. Mamoria, "Tribes in India–Their Classification", *The Modern Review,* Vol. 150, No. 4, pp. 278-283.

13. P.N. Sengupta (1959), "The Aborigines, Their Nutrition and Welfare", *Bulletin of the Bihar Tribal Research Institute,* Vol. 1, No. 1, pp. 56-66.

14. (a) L.P. Vidyarthi (Ed.) (1959), *Anthropology and Tribal Welfare in India,* Council of Social and Cultural Research, Bihar.

    (b) L.P. Vidyarthi and B.K. Roy (1976), *The Tribal Culture of India,* The Concept Publishing Co., Delhi.

    (c) L.P. Vidyarthi (1978), *Rise of Anthropology in India* (two volumes), Concept Publishing Co., Delhi.

15. G.S. Ghurye (1963), *The Scheduled Tribes,* Popular Prakashan, Bombay, 3rd Revised Edition.

16. N.K. Ambastha (1969), *A Critical Study of the Tribal Education,* S. Chand, Delhi.

17. K.L. Bhowmick (1971), *Tribal India, A Profile in Indian Ethnology,* The World Press, Calcutta.

18. N.K. Bose (1972), *Tribal Life in India,* National Book Trust, New Delhi, 1971; N.K. Bose, *Some Indian Tribes,* National Book Trust, New Delhi.

19. Ashok Ranjan Basu (1985), *Tribal Development Programmes and Administration of India*, National Book Organisation, The Mail, Shimla.
20. B.D. Sharma (1978), *Tribal Development–Concept and the Frame*, Prachi Publications, New Delhi.
21. S.C. Dube (1977), *Tribal Heritage of India* (in 4 volumes), Vikash Publishing House Pvt. Ltd., New Delhi.
22. P.K. Bhowmick (1986), "Reports on Scheduled Tribes, An Appraisal", in L.P. Vidyarthi (ed.), *Tribal Development and Its Administration*, Concept Publishing Company, New Delhi, p. 49.
23. Harpreet Kaur (1995), *Tribal Development Administration*, Shiva Publishers Distributors, Udaipr, pp. 11-12.
24. Makhan Jha (1982), *Readings in Tribal Culture*, Inter India Publications, p. 1.
25. Elwin Verrier (1950), *Bondo Highlands*, Oxford University Press, Bombay.
26. L.R.N. Srivastav, A.C. Pal and P. Pal (1971), *Identification of Educational Problems of the Saoras of Orissa*, N.C.E.R.T., New Delhi.
27. N.C.A.E.R., "Techno-Economic Survey of Orissa: Appraisal Report on Tribal Areas", September, 1961.
28. B.N. Sinha and B.K. Mishra (1976), "Tribes of Orissa: A Geographical Analysis", *Geographical Review of India*, Vol. XXXVIII, No. 2, pp. 167-187.

2 Classification and Distribution

The scheduled tribes of India are of different categories and composition, they have been concentrated in different regions of the country in different proportions and they are in different stages of development.

WHAT IS A 'TRIBE'?

Before discussing the categories and concentration of Scheduled Tribes of the country, it is relevant to focus briefly on what precisely the term 'tribe' is and who are the 'Scheduled Tribes'. The English term 'Tribe' is derived from the Latin word 'tribus'[1] designating a particular kind of social and political organisation existing in all these societies. Originally it was used to imply three divisions among the early Romans. Later on it was used to mean the 'poor' or the 'masses'. In English language, the word appeared in the sixteenth century and denoted a community of persons claiming descent from a common ancestor. In India, the term 'tribe' has legal and administrative connotations. British census officials-cum-anthropologists first used the term 'tribe' for the purpose of enumerating social groups in India and the term was used from 1881 to 1931 censuses. The Government of India Act, 1935 used the term 'backward tribe'. The Indian Constitution has retained the terminology with slight modification using 'Scheduled' in place of 'Backward'.[2] But the Constitution does not contain a precise definition of the term.[3] The Constitution of India nowhere states explicitly how a 'tribe' can be recognised and how it can be distinguished from a caste. It did well not to try to give such a definition. The term 'tribe' can perhaps be better understood in contrast with the term 'scheduled caste'. It appears to be easier to define a 'scheduled caste'. For a caste to be 'scheduled', it has to be economically and culturally backward, exploited by the peoples of superior culture and treated as socially inferior. But it has also to be sufficiently numerous to make special protective measures worthwhile. 'Scheduled castes' share many aspects of culture with the Hindus, or in some cases, with the Muslims of India, but they are backward economically, exploited and socially degraded and for these reasons often kept apart ('untouchables'). Thus, they require special protection if they are to be brought up to the level of the rest of the population. On the other hand, the 'scheduled tribes', though often backward and exploited, are rarely socially degraded. This make the difference between the two social groups clear, the term 'self-sufficiency', proposed by U.R. Ehrenfels, may be relevant in this connection: the tribals are, or want to be, self-sufficient in their cultural life. This desire for self-sufficiency may be one of the main factors why they stay outside the mainstream of national life, why they hold on to their own traditions, culture and values although they are most often painfully confronted with the fact that these traditions and values are inadequate in modern life. Thus, while the majority communities in India marched on and progressed, at least in material culture, the tribals remained backward and were thus exposed to exploitation. Members of the 'scheduled castes', on the other hand, though they also may be a people set apart, backward and subject to severe exploitation, do not have that desire for 'self-sufficiency'. If they form a society apart and are backward, it is because they have been socially rejected by the majority of communities and, due to their social degradation and economic exploitation, do not have the physical and moral strength to rise up to the level of full-fledged members of the Indian nation. A 'tribal'(Girijan) is so because he belongs to a society with a particular frame of mind, while the 'Harijan', belonging to a 'scheduled caste', is, though in a peculiar cultural position, of one mind with majority communities and has no desire to be different from them.

According to the Oxford Dictionary, a tribe 'is a group of people in a primitive or barbarous stage of development acknowledging the authority of a chief and usually regarding themselves as having a common ancestor'. This is good enough as far as it goes; but it does not go far enough. The dictionary of Anthropology mentions a tribe as a social group, usually with a definite area, dialect, cultural homogeneity and unifying social orgnisation.[4] The term 'tribe' in that sense refers to a type of society and designates a stage of evolution in human society. As a type of society, the term signifies a set of characteristic features and as a stage of evolution, it connotes a specific mode of social organisation.[5] Anthropologists define tribe as a collection of groups of people who share patterns of speech, basic cultural characteristics, and in the traditional sense, a common territory.[6]

Lucy Mair defines a tribe as 'an independent political division of a population with a common culture'. G. W.B. Huntingford maintains that a tribe 'is a group united by a common name in which the members take a pride, by a common language, by a common territory, and by a feeling that all who do not share this name are outsiders, 'enemies' in fact.

An East Asian Consultation, held at Sagada (Philipines), defined a tribal community as forming a 'group of people generally constituting a homogeneous unit, speaking a common language, claiming a common ancestry, living in a particular geographic area, generally lacking in scientific knowledge and modern technology and having a social structure based on kinship.

According to Ghurye, 'the common features possessed by all the tribal groups are as follows: (1) They live away from the civilised world in the inaccessible parts in the forests and hills. (2) They speak the same tribal dialect. (3) They belong either to one of the three stocks–Nagritos, Avstroloid or Mangoloids. (4) They profess primitive religion known as animism in which worship of ghosts and spirits is the most important element. (5) They follow primitive occupation such as gleaning, hunting and gathering of forest products. (6) They are largely carnivorous. (7) They live either naked or semi-naked. (8) They have nomadic habits and love for drink and dance.[7] The assumptions of Lewis has been that ideally tribal societies are small in scale, are restricted in their spatial and temporal range of their social, legal and political relations and possess a morality of religion and world view of corresponding dimensions.[8] This definition, however, does not focus the essential characteristics of a 'tribe' and the scope of the definition is restricted to the ideas of tribal societies. Pathy was of the opinion that 'a tribe is a tribe which is included in the list of Scheduled Tribes'.[9] T.K. Naik, however, proposed seven criteria by which a 'tribe' can be recognised. They are: (i) functional interdependence within the community; (ii) economic backwardness; (iii) geographical isolation; (iv) common dialect; (v) politically a unit under a common tribal authority; (vi) own traditional laws and (vii) members are averse to change.[10] Vimal Chandra was of the view that primitiveness and backwardness are the tests applied for specifying a 'scheduled tribe'. The main characteristics common to all the Scheduled Tribes are: (1) tribal origin, (2) primitive way of life, (3) habitat in remote and less accessible areas, and (4) general backwardness in all respects.[11]

According to Stephen Fuchs, 'As far as Indian tribes go, the essentials seem to be only a comparatively simple and primitive economy combined with a certain degree of residential instability, a simple, though not always, classless social organisation.'[12] Tribe, as defined by Belleille is a collection of individuals sharing a common culture.[13] Bailey who has dealt with the tribal problem in his study of Kondhamal region of Orissa says that a tribal society consists in its (1) direct command over resources, (2) access to the products of economy by an independent status, and (3) its population strength in total region.[14] Suresh Chandra Rajora has attempted to cite some basic features of a tribal society like (1) Tribal society is a whole society, (2) Tribal oral system is a normative binding force, (3) Culture of silence, (4) Tribals have their own specific economic system, (5) Polygamy is an institution of prestige and glory, (6) Clan solidarity and (7) Liquor economy.[15] Thus, the term itself bears an ideology of self identification.[16] High hills, deep valleys, evergreen forests, untouched natural resources, invaluable minerals, embedded in the earth, abode of simple people–happy, unconcern about the 'morrow', moving about freely like gentle breeze–unbound, unfettered by dictates of the modern world.[17] The most accepted definition in the Indian context is given by Prof. Majumdar. To him, "A tribe is a social group with territorial affiliation, endogamous with no specialisation of functions, ruled by tribal officers, hereditary or otherwise, united in language or dialect, recognising social distance from tribes or castes. But without any stigma attached in the case of a caste structure, following tribal traditions, beliefs and customs, illiberal of naturalisation of ideas from alien sources, above all, conscious of a homogeneity of ethnic and territorial integration".[18]

However, there is no particular definition, which is universally accepted. There are diversities of views of each anthropologist. Nevertheless, certain characteristic features as discussed above, have been put forward for determining a 'tribe' or a 'tribal community'. With the advent of modernity, large scale deforestation, penetration of Hinduism and Christianity into interior tribal pockets, large scale transformation of subsistence economy into a market economy, the historical specificity of tribal society and their structural features have become more or less extinct. There are, now-a-days, only attributional aspects. In India their comments designate are '*Adivasi*' (original settlers), *Girijan* (hill dwellers), *Vanyajati* (forest caste), *Adimjati* (primitive castes), *Jan Jati* (folk communities), *Anusuchit Jan Jati* (Scheduled Tribes).

CLASSIFICATION OF RACES

The Scheduled Tribes of the country can be broadly classified into different classes and Categories on the basis of their history, origin and racial features. The evidences on the racial features, qualities and composition, origin and history of scheduled tribes available so far are rare and scanty. Also very little is known about the origin and routes of the living races of India. Anthropologists admit that their knowledge about the origin and subsequent history of the numerous aboriginal tribes is hazy. However, anthropological evidence shows that there is existence of distinct racial strata in each cultural region and this can be correlated, albeit to a smaller extent, to social strata. But, in no case one racial element is socially supreme always and everywhere. The social status of different races and groups do change from place to place and time to time. Anthropologists made different classifications of earlier races of India. A general classification is, however, adopted in the following paragraphs.

NEGRITOS; THE EARLIEST RACE

Some believe that the Negritos were one of the earliest racial element in India. Guha thinks that the Kadar, Irulas and Panyans of south India have a Negrito strain, though even he admits that they are not pure Negritos.[19] The German anthropologist E. von Eickstedt agrees with this contention. According to him, there is definitely a Negrito component in the Malid sub-group of the south Indian Veddids.[20] But D.N. Majumdar and S.S. Sarkar deny the existence of any Negrito strains in south India. The Small stature of these tribes, their dark skin colour, their occasionally frizzly hair with short spirals-admittedly Negrito elements-are found also in other races.[21] E.von Eickstedt, however, calls these Negritos as Proto-Negritos. Hutton believes that the existence of Negritos in Assam is fairly probable. Their former existence in this area reveals itself by the occasional occurrence of a strikingly 'Papuan' profile, a low stature, curly or even kinky hair and a dark complexion. He also asserts the survivals of many items of material culture showing Melanesian affinities. Some anthropologists have found traces of Negrito strains among the very primitive Maler, and similar features can perhaps be found among the many small vigrant tribes of India, who live the life of foodgatherers inspite of very adverse conditions, are generally of small stature and dark complexion. Curly hair is often found in these tribes.[22]

PROTO-AUSTRALOIDS; THE SECOND-OLDEST RACIAL GROUP

The second-oldest racial group, according to Guha, is that of the Proto-Australoids. A somatic study of the aboriginal population of India shows little marked differences in the shape of the head, form of the nose, projection of the face, skin colour, form and structure of hair.[23]In central and south India, there are many tribes which have physical features of well-developed supra-orbital ridges as well as a sunken nasal root. These tribes have been compared with the Veddas of Sri Lanka and the aborigines of Australia. The majority of central and south Indian tribes and tribes of western central India belong to this racial type.

E. von Eickstedt, however, has a different opinion. He does not agree with this classification of Guha's. He classifies Proto-Australoids differently: he distinguishes a Veddid race which he sub-divides into a southern Indain Malid race (from mala, meaning mountain) and a central Indian Gondid race. Then he distinguishes a Melanid race of Europo-Negroid character and origin. Its only difference from the Europid race of this type is that it has a very dark skin colour. He discovers this race in the Carnatic type of the highly civilised South-Dravidas (in Tamilnadu) and in the Mundas, Hos and Santals of Chota Nagpur and Orissa in the Kolid type of the primitive Austro-Asiatics.[24]

The tribes of northern, eastern and central India have been divided into three major groups Linguistically; one group speaking Mundarain tongue, another a Dravidian Dialects, and the third-the largest speaking an Aryan language. There are many among the Aryan-speaking group of tribes who have adopted their present form of speech quite recently. Besides, few of the most primitive tribes, which at the same time claim to be the oldest settlers in the region, also speak an Aryan language. Most linguists hold that the Munda languages are related to the Austro-Asiatic language group with the exception of the Korkus perhaps, all Mundari-speaking tribes are located in eastern and north-eastern central India. These are the Korwas, Cheros, Turis, Asurs, Kols, Mundas, Kharias,

Birhors, Bhumij, Kharwars, Mahlis, Hos and Santals. The Korkus, who also speak a Munda language, are now widely separated from the main Munda group and live in central Madhya Pradesh. Another group which can be found in the north-eastern region of central India speaks a Dravidian tongue. Some tribes of this group hold the tradition that in former times they had been living in south India. In fact, Gondi, Kurukhi, Malto and Kolami are grammatically more closely related to Kanarese than to their immediate southern Telugu-speaking neighbours. The Dravida-speaking tribes of Bihar, Madhya Pradesh and Orissa are the Maler, Oraons or Kurukh, Mannewars, Kaikaris, Gonds, Marias, Murias, Bhatras, Parjas, Kolams and Khonds or Kondhs. All the way from the south, in Andhra Pradesh, eastern Maharashtra, south-eastern Madhya Pradesh, Orissa and north-eastern Madhya Pradesh aboriginal tribes speaking Dravidian dialects remained back and settled down. Linguists have established a close connection of Ollari, Poya and Parji, spoken in southern Madhya Pradesh and Andhra, with Kolami and Naiki, spoken in northern Madhya Pradesh. All these five dialects have close affinities with Telugu.[25]

THE MONGOLOID RACES

Mongoloid races have settled in the sub-Himalayan, in Assam regions and in the lands adjoining the eastern frontiers and Burma. The Chaingpas are the pure Tibetan origin, who are found in the plateaus south-east of the Karakorum ranges adjoining Tibet. Distinct Mongoloid features like high cheekbones, epicanthic fold, as well as the racial strains of the Oriental race have been shown by the north-eastern Ladakhis and Baltis. The Mongoloid strain appears as the dominant element among the Lahoulis, the Limbus, the Lepchas and the Rongpas in the tracts of the chaingpa to the Bhuttan hills north of Assam. Medium to tall stature, a brachycephalic head and broad face, high cheekbones, a long flat nose, the epicanthic fold, little hair on the face and body, and a light-brown skin colour etc. are the chief characteristics of these tribes. The same type of tribes can be found in the east and north of Nepal but the basic type there is non-mongoloid element. A number of tribes and peoples are also there who can not be grouped in the above classification and whose anthropological position is not clearly defined. The Assamese of the plains, who form a mixed population of Shans and Bengalis are among them. The Chakmas of Tripura, and the Mog tribes of the Arakan-Yoma hills belong to brachycephalic Mongoloid type. It is believed that they came from Burma. However, anthropological study of a number of mountain tribes is very much fragmentary and limited and not much is known or recorded about them.

AN ORIENTAL TYPE

Both B.S. Guha and the German anthropologist E. Fischer, have the opinion that in north-east India, there is an Oriental type which, according to them, is represented by the Badakshis in Badakshan (north Afghanistan). It is quite dominant in north Afghanistan and from there spread from Dir to Kyber, and from Chitral to west Nepal. It is now found among the Ladakhis and Baltis and perhaps all along the sub-Himalayan regions. This race has a long and acquiline nose and also rosy white skin colour.

STAGES OF DEVELOPMENT

The tribes and sub-tribes in India can also be classified into different classes, groups depending upon their present state of development and other factors mainly, mode of living in forest, shifting villages, forest villages, community villages and revenue villages.[26] They have got a heterogeneous cultural pattern with variegated economic condition and activities largely based on ecological settings and ethnic environment. They are in varying stages of development and assimilation. They are categorised[27] into:primitive tribals, tribals in transition, assimilated tribals and economically developed tribals. The primitive tribals are living in the inaccessible, remotest corners of the forests. They are basically shifting cultivators who depend on hunting and collectional economy. They lead largely the communal life of their villages[28] and 'have little contact with non-tribals, except through markets and law courts.'[29] In this context primitiveness should not be confused with backwardness. The former referring distinctly to the earlier stages of economic evolution like hunting, food gathering and shifting cultivation and the later referring to the lower levels of economic structure like subsistence economy and living condition. A primitive tribe may have developed several wants, but may not necessarily be poor in the modern context. Following this premise the primitive tribal communities are not same as the backward tribal communities.

The tribal people under the second category live on the foothills. They are very much like those in the first category except that they have greater social contact with the non-tribals in the plains.[30] They also primarily depend upon 'podu' and live as hunters and food gatherers. The assimilated tribes live in the plains with the non-tribals. Assimilated as they are in the Hindu or Christian society, they have lost most of their original characteristics and imbibed modern cultural traits. They take to regular agriculture and allied occupations. Some of the tribals who are in the process of acculturation are employed in skilled and semi-skilled fields in the industrial and mining complexes.[31] The assimilated tribal and the non-tribal communities in Orissa have more or less identical problems. The economically developed tribal people lead a settled life. Significant development has already taken place in their social life as a result of Hindu or Christian influence.[32]

Regional Distribution

A most genuine civilisation on Indian Subcontinent, not an importation of any form by outsiders or foreigners settling on Indian soil, is probably, 'Indus valley civilisation' which flourished in a vast tract of land in northern India, particularly in two large towns, mahenjodaro and Harappa. High fecundity of soil of the Indus valley, favourable monsoon congenial ecological system caused massive concentration of people and consequent growth of civilisation there. Historians and Anthropologists believe that the population of Indus valley civilisation might have been of a uniform race initially, but it did not remain so for long and gradually there was a mixed racial concentration. It consisted of several races some of which were latecomers or came at the middle stage when development or growth of this civilisation was underway. Be that as it may, by the time of the decline, decay and final disappearance of the civilisation either due to a disastrous alteration of the course of Indus river causing destructive flooding of settlements and silting of fields or the general desiccation of the whole area or the adverse tectonic movements or combination of all the factors, it was assumed with evidence that there was a coexistence of less talented, socially and culturally inferior class as well as highly talented superior class in the valley.

During the Post-Harappan Period, however, Human cultures in India expanded in three different directions: One dominant section marched towards south into the Deccan where it contacted and even mixed with earlier Neolithic cultures. From the Deccan it advanced eastwards to Andhra and Bengal. A second section, another strong one, moved immediately towards east along the Narbada valley to the hills of central India, while a third vibrant section moved from north Rajasthan and the Punjab eastwards into the upper Gangetic valley and from there into the central Ganges region.

B.S. Guha[33] and other Physical anthropologists were of the opinion that during this period, or earlier, a brachycephalic race of the Alpino-Dinaric type with a short to medium stature, a round and broad face, and a long prominent nose immigrated into northern India. They believe that 'this race had its origin in south-west Siberia during prehistoric times from where it spread to eastern Europe and southern Arabia. It probably proceeded to Afghanistan and penetrated into India. It descended from the Pamirs through Afghanistan, Baluchistan and Sind, and spread along the west coast into Gujarat and Kanara; one branch crossed over to Bengal, and in a more southern route over the Deccan to Tamilnadu'. Thus, the aboriginal tribes of India are mainly survivals from the later prehistoric population groups. They do not form a uniform race in the Indian Peninsula. Since they had entered to this country from various corners and regions, they naturally belonged to and consequently formed different races and settled or choose to dwell in different parts of the country.

The tribal communities are found in different parts of the country in varying concentration. The states like Mizoram, Nagaland, Meghalaya and Arunachal Pradesh and two Union Territories namely Dadra and Nagar Haveli comprise the tribal predominant zones in which the concentration of tribal communities varies from 70 per cent to 95 per cent. All the tribal groups of the country do not make a homogeneous tribal society. The Santals of Gujarat and the Bhils of Rajasthan do not come within the same tribal category. Each tribal has its historical specificity.[34] Though the tribal communities are distributed in most of the states in India, there are a few concentration points of regional distribution. Broadly the tribals are concentrated in the following regions of India.[35]

The Abor, Garo, Khasi, Kudi, Mismi, Naga etc. tribes mostly belonging to the Mongolian racial stock are found in the North-eastern parts of the country. Tribes like the Lepcha and Rebha belonging to the same racial groups live in the Himalayan region. The Central India covering the states of Madhya Pradesh, part of Gujarat, Bihar, Orissa, and West Bengal is inhabited by a number of tribal communities. They include the Bhumij, Gond, Ho, Oraon, Santal, Munda and so on.

In the Western India region covering the states like Rajasthan, Maharashtra, Gujarat, Goa, Dadra and Nagar Haveli live a number of tribal communities, the most important of them being the Bhil. They racially belong to the Proto-Australoid group.

The states of Karnataka, Andhra Pradesh, Tamil Nadu and Kerala, in the Nilgir Hills and covering lines of the Ghats in South India live the Chenchu, Truli, Kadar, Kota, Kurumba, Toda etc., having Nagrito, Caucasoid, Proto-Australoid or mixed physical features.

The Island region covering Andaman and Nicobar, lakshadweep Islands has a number of small tribes like the Andamanese, Onge, Sentinilese etc. Let us now focus on the concentration and/or distribution of these tribes in various parts of India.

North India

Stephen Fuchs has given a detailed account of aboriginal tribes in different parts of India and their socio cultural linguistic features in his master piece "The aboriginal Tribes of India". North India particularly the Western part of it was mainly inhabited by three population groups, the Baluchis, the Brahuis and the Pathans. The Baluchis are divided into two large sections, the northern or Sulaiman Baluchis and the southern or Mkrani Baluchis. A large portion of the tribe was expelled from Baluchistan in a tribal dispute and settled in Sind. It is believed that members of these expelled clans joined with related tribes of the plain to give assistance to the Emperor Humayun when he tried to regain his dominion after his expulsion from India. After his successful return, the grateful emperor rewarded them with grants of land along the Indus from where they have gradually spread well up to the Chinab and Sutlej valleys. As a result of this migration, more Baluchis were found in Sind and the Punjab than in their native country, where they are outnumbered by the Brahuis. The Baluchis were divided into various tribes, each headed by a chief whose office was purely hereditary in a particular family. Among the populations of Baluchistan and upper Sind, the Brahuis are of special importance because their language contains undoubted traces of Dravidian character. It is considerably influenced by Sindhi and Baluchi, but the original Dravidian structure is still unmistakable. The Pathans (or Pakhtuns) tribes have been, since long ago, residents of the inhospitable hills of Baluchistan and north-western India. Pathans, as evidences suggest, were, extremely varied in origin. One such original tribe that has survived might be that of the Malchis, thin, ugly and of servile character. Their rugged and barren fields could support them only for three months of the year. But, at the same time, the Pathans, like all highlanders in the tribal stage, have a certain charm in their manly independence and in the practice of a few virtues in which they excel. The term Pathan, now a days, is commonly used to denote anyone speaking the Pakthun language, or Pushtu, and thus includes the Afghans, a foreign race which, however, has impressed its name upon a whole country. Many Pathans migrated to India for business and employment in the towns and taluks. They stay on permanently, but pay periodical visits to their northern homes. Earlier, they set up as itinerant hawkers of sundry goods or as moneylenders. Others, however, find employment with moneylenders (sowkars) to recover debts or collect rent from backward tenants.

In the tribes of the Himalayan and Sub-Himalayan regions,[36] there are also tribes which belong to the so-called Oriental race, such as the Dards, Chaks, Galawans, and others. They have a darker complexion, longer noses and broad or shorter to longer skulls. But in general, in the sub-Himalayan regions from Ladakh to Nepal, Sikkim and Bhutan, the population is of a Mongoloid type. They have a medium or tall stature, round head and face, high cheekbones from which the face rapidly narrows downwards, and a small retreating chin. Another tribe of probably similar origin are the Dums. But they claim descent from a Hindu king who became afraid of his numerous sons and scattered them all over Kashmir, giving them the job of village watchmen and police power. A tribe of similar racial type is that of the Galwans, who are either descendant of the Dums or of the Chaks. They are of a dark complexion. Originally they earned their livelihood by grazing horses, but in the course of time they developed criminal tendencies. The Chaupans is another Kashmiri race. Earlier, they were the shepherds of the villagers. In racial features they are not distinct from the peasants of the valleys, but they from a separate society, intermarrying only among themselves and occasionally with the Galawans. The Gaddis in Himachal Pradesh claim to be immigrants from the north Indian plains, of low Rajput stock. Gradually, they left Rajputana, fleeing before the Muslim invaders. They mostly inhabit the range which divides Chamba from Kangra. A few Gaddis have wandered down to the valley at the base of the range. Being semi-nomadic; the Gaddis spend half the year in search of fodder for their herds, and the other half they spend in their villages cultivating their meagre crops. Kanauras or Kinaras also called Kinners are another tribe in Himachal Pradesh. Generally they inhabit the frontier district of Kinnaur in the east of Himachal, near the Tibetan frontier. The Kinnaras are of mixed blood. Though originally from northern India, they have intermarried often with Tibetans and Gurkhas and thus acquired definite Mongoloid characteristics. Two classes in which they are divided, one is higher than the other. The Kinnaras rear sheep and goats for wool. They are pastoral people. But they also cultivate fields and keep gardens. The Pangwals in the valley of Pangi are another aboriginal tribe. They are divided into two main sections, a high class and a low class. Lahulis or Lahaulas are another tribal community in Himachal, beyond the Kulu valley towards the high hills. They, too are divided into two sections, an upper class and a lower class. Besides these tribes like Pangwals and Lahulis, there are also lesser tribes, such as the Jads, Khampas, Swanglas and Bhots (or Bhotias). The Jads and Khampas are originally inhabitants of Tibet. While the jads are mainly cultivators, the Khampas are pure nomads. However, both these tribes are Polvandrous and patrilineal. In Terai, on the southern slopes of the Himalayas, Tharus are another tribe. They were certainly aboriginals, but have completely abandoned their tribal culture, and are now considered a backward Hindu caste. They are the offspring of Rajput women who fled from Chitorgarh (Rajasthan) and sought refuge in these regions as they themselves claim. Lepchas or Rongs tribes are the original inhabitants of Sikkim who settled in Sikkim since the 13th century. They came from the Assam hills. Though some basic features of Tibetan Lamaism have overlaid their fundamental religious beliefs but they are primarily animists. In the Darjeeling area many of them have become Christians. The Lepchas resemble the Gurkhas in physical appearance. They are mainly farmers. Wherever possible they practise shifting cultivation and sow rice and maize. Plough cultivation is a lateral innovation among them. The Lepcha dialect belongs to the Tibeto-Himalayan section of the Tibeto-Chinese language group. Another tribe is the Bawarivas or Bauris tribe and their main centre is in West Bengal, Orissa and Rajasthan. They are also sporadically found in Punjab ,Uttar Pradesh and Andhra, where they are called Bavuri. They are basically a varied community. Both in their characteristics and physical appearance, the Bauris are distinctly separated from the agricultural castes, even in Punjab where they claim to have come long ago from Mewar and Ajmer. In several parts of their concentrations, the Bawariyas are subdivided into several sections most of which have taken to cultivation. They are indiscriminate in their diet but are not considered as untouchables by their neighbours. Another such tribe are the Bahelias who almost exclusively occupied in hunting and bird-catching. They are mainly found in Uttar Pradesh and West Bengal. In Bihar the Bahelias are also known under the name of Bhula. In the northern part alongside the Ganges valley, the Bahelias are often regarded as a sub-caste of the Pasis, and in the west they are claimed to be Aherias. However, all these tribes and castes in the Himalayan region are culturally and racially similar and it is not easy to keep them apart. Similar is the case of the Mahtams, a hunting caste in the Sutlej valley, now partly in Pakistan. Only a section of them still live as hunters, while most of them are settled cultivators and field labourers. They are very much industrious and law-abiding. In the sub-montane tract of the Punjab, there is another community of the same name but anthropologists believe that they have no genetic connection with the Mahtams in the Sutlej valley. This community is really a sub-caste of the Banjaras, and made its way from the east whereas the hunting Mahtmas reached the Sutlej valley coming from Rajasthan. Of course, this is not an isolated case. The Sahariyas of Bundelkhand and the neighbourhood are another of the vagrant castes. They go under various names, such as Sahariya, Sehariya, Sehria Saur, Sonr, Sor, Sosia. The Lodhas in West Bengal, Orissa and Bihar also claim descent from the Savaras. They speak a mixture of Bengali, Oriya and Mundari respectively. They are mainly nomadic food gatherers in the jungle tracts of these States. The Lodhas[37] are mostly known as a criminal tribe. However, social compulsions and economic necessities have brought them to this state. Though a few or a minor section of them has recently taken to agriculture, they are predominantly a food gathering community. The Turis of Bihar and West Bengal are a similar tribe. On physical grounds, Risley considered them 'to be a Hinduised offshoot of the Mundas. They still speak dialect derived from Mundari. The Dharkars of the southern Ganges valley were also once a forest tribe, but have settled in villages and employ Baiga priests or, at best, the Ojhas, degraded Brahmins or probably priests of non-Aryan origin. Into this group belong also the Rajwars and Musharas of Bihar and the east of Oudh. They are now labourers of low caste, but are of aboriginal descent. The Rajwars are the higher of the two, and employ degraded Brahmins for their ceremonies. They have retained a good deal of their tribal organisation but have settled down to cultivation and field service'.

A great deal of controversy has been generated about the Musahars. Their name is said to mean 'rat-eaters'. The Musahars are divided, like so many other similar tribes, into a settled and a nomadic section. Living in villages,the settled section does menial jobs and works in the fields, while the nomadic section have no settlements and haunts the jungles and collects forest produce which is sold in the villages. According to Stephen Fuchs, 'West of the habitat of the Mushars, in Bihar, Oudh and the districts of Uttar Pradesh lying south of the Jumma, are found the Bhars who, in their physical appearance, bear definite signs of their descent from a similar dark race. But they now hold a higher social rank than their neighbours. The Bagdis are another tribe of doubtlessly former aboriginal type which has settled in Rajasthan, Madhya Pradesh and West Bengal. The Bagdis speak the local dialects and profess a Hinduism with many elements of nature worship. In western Bengal and adjoining Bihar, along the Jumna and in Oudh resides another caste partly of settled and partly of nomadic habits. It is the Bediya caste. Many of the Bediyas are returned as belonging to the scheduled castes, while the rest is returned as a scheduled tribe. The caste is split into various functional sub-sections. Some of these sepcialise as acrobats and conjurers, others as hunters and fowlers, while quite a few earn their living as snake charmers. The more respectable members of the caste have settled down as cultivators. A similar vagrant tribe, found in the Decan and in the adjoioning southern tracts, is that of the Kaikadis. In Andhra and Kanara, they are known as Korwas or Korachas. They have many sub-divisions, each of which is again divided into four clans or goats. Each sub-division has its peculiar customs of dress, habits of living and ways of earning a living. The northernmost occupational caste of this type is that of the Bands or Bhagats, the minstrels of Kashmir. They combine the profession of singing and acting with that of begging. They are great wanderers and migrate as far as Punjab where they like to perform. A similar caste in Punjab is that of the Bahurupias, the 'caste of many disguises'. They are really a functional sub-division of the Mahtams, and specialise in the performance of dramas and plays of mainly a religious or mythological content. In the Ganges valley, on the other hand, the Bahurupias are regarded as a sub-caste of the Banjaras. They take brides from the Nats, another wandering tribe, but do not give their daughters in marriage to them. The Bhavaios of Gujarat are an acting caste performing comedies and dramas at weddings or other festivals before any village audience paying for it. The Gondhalis of Maharashtra are itinerant ballad singers, and dance a special set of figures in honour of a goddess at weddings and private entertainments. The Dafalis, for instance, and the Nagarchis of the Ganges valley are Muslims, with a sort of religious flavour about their performances. The Dholis of Rajasthan, like the Bajanias of Uttar Pradesh, are Hindu functional castes, recruited from the village menial and scavenging castes, wandering from village to village. The Turaihas of Uttar Pradesh blow horns; turhi being the name of the trumpet in their language. There are numerous castes of jugglers, tumblers, snake charmers, and the like, each with a different name, but all connected, at least in upper India, under the general term of Nat or Bazigar. The Nats, as a caste, are strongest in Madhya Pradesh, Uttar Pradesh, while the Bazigar are strongest in Punjab and Delhi.[38]

In upper India like Rajasthan, Uttar Pradesh there live the Kanjars. A section of them are still in the jungle or hunting stage, living on any fruits or roots which their women can collect. Other sections, are settled workers and have settled near the villages. They make their living by the manufacture of weavers' brushes, winnowing fans, baskets and the reed-mats (chattai) used for their own tents and the tilts of the peasants' carts during the rains. The Haburas are a small vagrant tribe. They live along the upper Ganges and Jumua, and claims descent from the Chauhan Rajputs. It is more likely, according to researchers that they are a sub-division of the Sansis. They resemble the parent tribe in the high status of the women and the propensity to thieving, but seem to be more Hinduised in their customs. The Bhantus are another well-known wandering tribe in India which, in the past, subsisted by organised robbery and thieving. Mostly, they are found in north and central India, though a small section of the tribe reside in the east. The Bhantus, also claim Rajput descent and consider Chitorgarh as their mother-city. The Waghris tribe mainly live in Gujurat though they are sporadically found in other parts of northern India. They claim kinship with the Sansis of the Punjab though they are more or less identical with the Baghris or Bagdis of central India.

Central India

Tribes of Central India constitute the largest part of the tribal population of India. They are spread out in loosely connected groups all over the central circle of the Indian peninsula, from parts of Gujurat across Madhya Pradesh, Bihar, Maharastra and Orissa to West Bengal. The Aboriginals of Central India are mostly concentrated in the adjoining corners of four States: Madhya Pradesh, Bihar, Orissa and Maharashtra. The Gonds and Bhils are some of the tribes whose numerical strength are very strong. They run into several million individuals in the aforesaid States. They are concentrated over a vast area and have developed a very high standard of culture. All other tribes in this belt are small in number counting just a few lakhs individuals. Their culture is very primitive and under developed. They are by nature, unsteady, shy, passive, self-retiring and submissive. There are a few main tribes numbering about a dozen whereas more than two hundred minor and less important tribes live alongside or are interspersed between the main tribes. These smaller tribes enjoy their protection and also being exploited by the main tribes. A majority of the Bhilala, Gond and Korku tribes, living in closer contact with the non-tribal farming castes, have gradually learned from them better methods of cultivation and as a result their economic conditions have improved substantially. Consequently distinct sections emerge since not all the members of a tribe can live up to the required standard of behaviour. Thus, the tribes of this category often split into two sections, a Hinduised 'upper' section and a tribal 'lower' section. Such divisions and dichotomy can be found, for instance, among the Gonds (Raj-Gonds and Jungli-Gonds), Korkus (Muasis and Paharias), Bhilalas (bara Bhilalas and Barelas), Raj-Banshis and many others. Examples of such tribes can be multiplied. The tribes of central India had no strong and viable tribal solidarity in the past. The Bhils and Gonds who are usually considered important tribes had no organisation comprising all the members of the tribe. They have never been unified, they rather live in small groups gathering only a small number of village communities in a specified area as a social unit. The Bhil tribe for example has been broken up and divided into many sections and sub-sections which are unconnected. They even bear different names and since they have partially mixed with non-tribal communities, they inherited some of their traditions as well as adopted their cultural traits. The Baigas are, it is believed, the most ancient survivors of the Aryan-speaking tribes, who still retain a tribal conscience. They practised, though sporadically, shifting cultivation of a primitive type, using only the hoe and abjuring the plough. The Kamars, a small tribe, are found in Chhattisgarh and are distant neighbours of the Baigas. J. Bell described them as wild hunters and foodgatherers, living in caves, they are today shifting cultivators and collectors of jungle produce. The Pardhans were mainly the minstrels, bards and servants of the Gonds. It is, however, doubtful if they are of Gond origin. At any rate, they speak a Hindi dialect. They are found mainly in Madhya Pradesh and Berar. A Similar tribe are the Ojhas living in the eastern tracts of the Gond area. They act as soothsayers and minstrels of the Gonds and Korkus from whom they receive their livelihood. Another tribe living in the habitat of the' Korkus and Bhils on both sides of the Narbada valley are the Nahals. In the Census of 1961, they appear as a sub-division of the Korkus. But they have a language of their own; at least remnants of it are still in existence. The Agarias reside on the Maikal range of the Mandla, Raipur and Bilaspur districts. They are aboriginal iron-smelters speaking an Aryan dialect. Their counterparts in Chota Nagpur are the Asuras whose iron-smelting occupation sets them apart from the Mundas and also the Dravida-speaking cultivators though they now speak Mundari. The Maler, now speaking a Dravidian language and living in the upper parts of the Rajmahal hills, have, like the juangs, originally no exogamous clans and observe only kinship exomgamy. Another such tribes are the Birjias found in the palamau district of Bihar. Some have now settled as cultivators in the valleys of the south. One of the most important tribes of this group is undoubtedly the Munda tribe. At present, the main stock of the Mundas is found in Bihar and Chhatisgarh and particularly in Chota Nagpur. The Hos also called Larka Kols, consider themselves the highest of the Munda tribes. 'Ho' is a Munda word meaning 'man'. Singhbhum district, a region of Chotanagpur, more fertile than other districts is their main habitat. The Kols from whom the early ethnographers of north-eastern central India coined the term 'Kolarian', by which they meant the Mundas as well as the Dravida speaking tribes, reside today for the most part in the Mirzapur district along the Ganges, in the Jabalpur and Mandla districts of Madhya Pradesh and in the Baghelkhand tracts of the Vindhyas.[39]Of equal or even higher rank are the Cheros probably because they are even more completely Hinduised than the Kharwars. They have the same tradition of having been expelled from a kingdom of their own in the south of Bihar. The Turis in Bihar and West Bengal, are engaged in the making of baskets, mats, brushes and other bamboo articles. They also do farm work. The Korkus are the most westernly of the Mundari-speaking tribes. They live in middle Madhya

Pradesh, mainly in the central parts of the Satpura Mountains, and are widely separated from the main block of linguistically related tribes. The largest and most widely-spread of the Dravida-speaking tribes of central India is that of the Gonds whose name comprises most probably a number of racially and culturally diverse communities. Some authorities trace the name 'Gond' to Konda, the Telugu word for 'hill', as in the case of the Khond or Kandh tribe. The Gonds certainly cover the hilly tracts of Orissa Westwards and northwards, with a strong concentration in the Satpura Mountains and its northern part.

Western India

Though from a purely geographical point of view western India includes Rajasthan and Gujurat in particular, here we also include the tribes of western Madhya Pradesh and Maharashtra since tribes in these parts are different from central India and more akin to the tribes of western India. The tribes of this western area appear to be racially and socio-culturally different from the tribes in central and north-eastern central India. Some of the western tribes, over a period of time, have migrated into central India and inter-mixed with, as well as influenced or been influenced by, the tribes of central India. The tribes of western India, according to fuchs, may belong rather to three different groups: (1) to a group of nomadic, mainly animal breeding culture, with a warlike tradition, possibly of inner-Asiatic origin, somehow closely related to the Rajputs and usually claiming descent from them. Minas fall under the category of scheduled tribes. (2) The second group is formed by the numerous tribes which go under the name of Bhils. Some of the Bhil sub-divisions have now become independent tribes. To the Bhil group belong the Barelas, Bhilalas, Dhnakas, Dublas, Gamits or Gamtas, Mankars, Mavchis, Pathias, Rathias, Tadvis, Talavias and Vasavas. The Girasias in Rajasthan are perhaps the northernmost Bhil group. (3) The third numerous population group of western India, now largely Hinduised and only partly tribal, bears the name of Kolis. This group, dvidied into many different tribes, is spread over Rajasthan, Gujurat, Maharashtra, Madhya Pradesh and even Punjab and Andhra Pradesh. Many communities still call themselves Kolis, though others go under a different name, such as Barias, Bhalias, Gedias, Chhodras, Khants, Kotwals, Naikdas, Patelias, Patanwadias, Takardas and Talabdas. The second main tribal group in western India is that of the Bhils.[40] It is a numerous race spread over western Madhya Pradesh, Rajasthan, eastern Gujurat and northern Maharashtra. E. von Eickstedt classifieds the Bhils as Gondids, with the Malids as a sub-section of the Veddids. B.S. Guha calls them Proto-Australoids, to which category he also assings the Veddids. The Bhilalas, who are originally recorded under the category of Bhils, are divided into two sections: the Bara Bhilalas (Great Bhilalas) and the Chhota Bhilalas (Small Bhilalas) or Barelas. The Bara Bhilalas are almost fully Hinduised, while the Barelas have retained many tribal features of the Bhils. The Dhankas are akin to the Bhils and Bhilalas. They reside in Gujurat and also in Maharashtra. They are found mainly in the Panchmahals, in Broach and in Baroda districts in Gujurat and in West Khandesh. The Pàtelias, who are Similar to the Dhankas in physical appearance, social habits and occupation, live in the same region as the Dhankas. The Tadvis and Pavadas, two Bhil sections which got separated from the main stock, reside mainly in the Satpuras of Khandesh. The Gamits or Gamtas, now claim themselves an independent tribe, but originally they were Bhils. They are found in north-western Maharashtra and south-eastern Gujurat. In the boarders of the three states Rajasthan, Madhya Pradesh and Gujurat, another important tribe in the area are the Naikdas. In the past, they were a revolutionary or rather turbulent and restless race, and the British had to suppress their revolts and raids on several occasions by force of arms. However, finally their warlike spirit was broken and they have not disturbed the peace now for quite a some time. Not very far from the settlements of the Naikdas, there is a small tribe of the same name, the Nayaks. They are different from the Kolis, although closely connected with the Dhodia tribe. They reside only in the south-eastern part of Gujurat. The Dhodias or Dhundias which literally mean 'hut-dwellers' in Gujurat, are probably of Koli origin, but settled in the plains, mainly in southern Bulsar district. The Koknas (or Koknis, Kuknas), are one of the dominant tribes of Gujurat. One third of them live in south-eastern Gujurat and two thirds in western Maharashtra. Their name would indicate that they came originally from the south, the Konkan. The Dublas another major tribe living in the same area, are the dependents and tenants of the land-owning castes. The Chodris are found mainly in the Surat district of Gujurat, have the tradition of a former home more in the north, in southern Rajasthan, from where they were evicted along with some Rajput clans by the Muslims. The Walis whose name means 'uplanders', are supposed to have come from the region above the Ghats. Some of the members of this tribe are still in the forest, in the north-eastern part of Thana district though majority of them are now resident along the coast

Eastern India

The Khasis and Syntengs (or Pnars), the Wars, Bhois or Lyngnams, tribes inhabit in the State of Meghalaya. Linguistically these tribes belong to the Austro-Asiatic or Mon-Khmer group. The Bodo group is now chiefly found along the northern bank of the Brahmaputra, from the western boundary of Assam to the Darrang district.[41] The Bodos are a sturdy independent, and remarkably clannish community of labourers. The Bodo group includes, first of all, the eastern sub-Himalyan tribes such as the Monpas, the Daflas, the Hrussos or Akas then the Miris, Galongs, Abors, Minyongs and Mishmis. South of the Brahmaputra are thr Rabhas, the Garos, the Lalungs, the Dimasas or Hill Kacharis, the Bodos or Plain Kacharis , who in Goalpara call themselves Mech. The Mikirs reside in the north-east of the north Cachar hills. The Tripuris who occupy the hills south of Silhet are also of Bodo stock. The Daflas in particular, live in the east kameng and the west of Subansiri. They call themselves Bangni, whichmeans 'man'. Since the time of Aurangzeb they had the reputation of being an independent and aggressive tribe.

Dalton[42] believed that the Miris, Galongs, Abors or Padmas, together with the Mishmis, Akas and Daflas, are all one common race, but they have their differences in language, economy, social organisation and religion. But some of their clans have settled in Assam for ages. The Abors or Padams live just north of Dibrugarh, west of the Dihang river. East of the Siang river, in the easternmost corner of Aurnachal Pradesh, is the home of the Mishmis. The Rabhas, the westernmost representatives of the Bodo group, in West Bengal and Assam, are related either to the Garos or the Kacharis. In fact, they are often said to be Hinduised Garos or Kacharis. The Eastern neighbours of the Rabhas are the Garos, who also belong to the Bodo group. They live in the westernmost part of Assam, south of the Brahmaputra. East of the Garos are found the Lalungs, previously residing on the northern slope of the Jaintia hills and gradually but slowly advanced eastwards. East of the Lalungs are the Hill Kacharis or Damasias, once the dominant people in the north Cachar hills (north-east of the Jaintia hills). They are a strong and vigorous race. The Mikirs, east of the Kacharis, inhabit mainly the hills named after them, but they have also spread to other parts of the country. They have mixed considerably with the Assamese of the plains. South of the Cachar hills, east of Tripura, is the habitat of the Kuki, Lushai and Chin tribes. From the similarlity of their dialects, it is clear that all three tribal groups belong to a common racial stock. The Lakhers (or Maras) inhabit the southernmost region of Mizoram. The Meithies, the inhabitants of Manipur State, belong to the Kuki tribes. Manipur was originally occupied by several different tribes, such as the Kumuls, Luangs, Moirangs and Meithesis. Of all these, the Meithesis became dominant and finally absorbed the other tribes. The Naga tribes[43] occupied mainly the eastern parts of Assam. The Nagas are divided into the Angami (including Kezhama), Ao, Sema, Lhota, Konyak, Chang, Rengma and Tungkhul Nagas. Down south, there is another group of tribes, the Chakmas of Tripura, and the Halam, Noatia and Mog tribes of the Arakan-Yoma hills. Orissa, however, is a major and dominant tribal state in eastern India and broadly, there are four distinct geophysical zones in which the tribes of Orissa have been distributed in uneven proportions. They are;

The Northern Plateau

Sundargarh, Mayurbhanj, Keonjhar, Bamra and Kuchinda area of Sambalpur, the interior plains of Balasore and Pallahara region of Dhenkanal districts come under the Northern Plateau. As many as 58 tribal groups totalling about 2 million people inhabit in this zone. The ITDAs, which are included in this zone, are Sundargarh, Panposh and Bonai, Baripada, Karanjia, Udala and Rairangpur, Keonjhar and Champua and Kuchinda. The Pallahara Paudi Bhuinya Development Project is also included in this zone.

The Central Tribal Land

This zone covers the whole of the Brahmani and the Mundari basins. There are as many as 45 tribal groups in this region. The population of two major tribes in this zone–the Gond and the Saora–constitute about one lakh each.

The Eastern Ghat Region

The Peninsular Plateaus are bordered on the east by the Eastern Ghats, a tectonic range out by many rivers into discontinuous blocks of mountains. Broadly it is divided into five sections.

The Northern Section starts from Nilgiri and stretches up to Boud border rising to a height of 2239 feet. The number of tribes inhabiting this zone comes to about 39. The Khond and the Sabar are most numerous. This zone includes the Nilgiri ITDA. The Central Section of the Eastern Ghats cover Boud, Baliguda, G. Udayagiri areas and the hills of this section are very high ranging in height from 1000 feet to 4000 feet. There are 29 tribal groups inhabiting this section. The Khond population constitutes a majority of the population. This zone can be called the Khond zone. It includes Phulbani and Baliguda ITDAs. The Rayagada Section comprises Parlakhemundi and Rayagada hill areas with an elevation of 1000 feet. These hill areas have been inhabited by as many as 43 tribal communities. The Khond and the Saora are the most numerous. This section includes Parlakhemundi, Rayagada and Gunupur ITDAs. The South-Eastern Section covers the areas of Koraput, Pottangi, Jeypore, Nowrangpur and Malkangiri. Many important and primitive tribes are found in this area. The Koya and the Bhuinya with relatively higher population live in the Malkangiri districts. The extinctive and primitive Bonda Paraja inhabit in this region. The Koraput, Nowrangpur and Malkangiri ITDAs come under this section. The South-Western Section comprises the Plain and the Dongar of Kalahandi district. The Dongar portion includes Lanjigarh and Thuamul-Rampur areas inhabited mostly by the Khonds who are very primitive. 46 tribal communities live in this section. This section includes Thuamul-Rampur ITDA.

Coastal Region

This region inhabits a total of 51 tribes. The Saora, Sabar, Santal, Khond, Bhumij, Kolha and the Munda are the numerous tribes.

South India

The tribes of South India, coming in contact with the inhabitants of other castes, have gradually lost their own language and speak Dravidian dialects. In South India some tribes, by virtue of their majority, are very dominant while there are also minority tribes who enjoy an inferiority status. Tribes like Kadar, Paliyar, Mala-pulayar, Hill Pandaram, Malasar or Malayor who are found in Coimbatore District of Tamil Nadu through racially not very akin have common customs.

Kerala is the home of the tribes like Nayar, Vishavar, Cheengannivedar, Cheruvedar, Manar, Badagas, Muduvar, Koragar, Irulur, Malapandaram, Malavedar, Bulla, Urali Kurumar, Malakarar, Vishavar, Kurichchar, Ulladar, Maratins, Kudiyas, Aranadar, Ulladans, Eravallens, Muthuwans.[44] Besides, Allar tribes are found in Palgahat District. Todas, scholagar, Irular, Kotas, Badagas, Jen Kurumbar tribes reside in Nilgiris. Chingather, Malayar tribes are the inhabitants of the connanore & Tellicherry Districts. Palliyar tribes are found in the States of Kerala, Tamilnadu and Karnataka mainly in the periyar hills. Katta Nayakar tribes have their base both in Kerala & Tamil Nadu. In Andhara Pradesh, Chenchus tribe inhabit the Nalamalas of kurnol districts. Koragar tribes are mainly found in Karnataka. Other tribes such as Uralis are found in the districts of Alleppey, Kottayam, Quilon and Trivandrum and Malavodans are inhabitants of Kottayam & Quilon districts of Kerala. Mannor are living in the Cardamon hills where as Karimpalar tribes are the inhabitants of cannanore and calicut districts and Malak Karans reside in Calicut district of Kerala. Kanikkar tribes are found in the southern states of kerala and tamilnadu. Malakudis or vishavans tribes mostly reside in the North Malabar in Kerala. They also live in the westernghats near the Mysore boarder. Malayalis live in the hills of salem, north & South Arcot and Tiruchirapalli districts of TamilNadu & cannanore district of Kerala. Adiyar, Malavettuvans, Mavilans tribe are mainly found in cannanore district of Kerala. Kalanadis tribes have their settlements in calicut district and Malakkuravas tribes in Travancore area. Kurumbas or the Kurumans tribe spread over a wide area of South India, but mainly found at wynaad in Kerala and Nilgiris in Tamil Nadu. Kurichchians are found mainly in north Malabar especially in the wynaad. Maratis tribes have been living in Keral and Mysore. Malapanickkar tribes have their base in calicut district and Mala Arayans tribes settle in the Kottayam & Ernakulam district of Kerala.

The oger, Paravar, Bagatas, Valar, and Arayar tribes are more or less pure fishermen. The Kavundar, Idayar, Todas and Lamanas are pastoral tribes in South India. Adiyar, Eravallar, Kalanadis, Kanikkar, Malasar, Mala Vedar, Mala Vettuvar, Malayariar, Malayar, Maratis, Thachanadar, and the kotas tribes are partly food gatherers and hunters, and partly field and plantation labourers. The Karimpalarm Kurichchiyar, Malayalar, Erukulas, Kalikadis, jungle Kurubas tribes are also partly shifting cultivators and party settled cultivators and others are or were in the past shifting cultivators. The Kudiyas, Kundu Vadiar, Mala Aryar, Mannar, Mavilar, Muthuvar, Palliyar, Pathiyar, Ulladar, Uridavan Gowdalu and Vishvar tribes are more advanced cultivators or farm labourers in the southern states of India.

Primitive and Backwardness are the characteristic features of the indigenous tribal population of the Andaman and Nicober Islands. They belong to the most backward and peculiar of all the primitive peoples of India. Years of seclusion and isolation have kept the islanders apart from any racial and cultural mixtures. Isolation has also played a stumbling block in preventing any stimulation towards cultural progress. They also did not feel any necessity for it on the islands because nature was always bountiful in providing for all the bodily needs of the small population.[45] Conversely, owing to their long isolation they are today one of the purest races of the world, with the least racial admixtures from outside world. They have a completely separate language and also speak a language of their own which so far linguists have not been able to connect with any known language group. Tribes of Andaman Islands have settled in different islands not properly connected with each other and due to their existence on various isolated islands, the Andamanese, in spite of their small number, have split into several tribes. These tribes are: the Chariar or Chari, Kora, Tabo or Bo, Yere, Kede, Bea, Balawa, Boigiyab, Juwai, Jarawa, Kol, Onge and Sentinelese. There are two distinct races in the Nicobar Islands;[46] Shom Pen, the very primitive and reserved tribe and the Nicobarese proper, a slightly advanced community. Due to their isolation and seclusion for centuries from outside socio-cultural influences and contacts until recent times they have developed a cultural identity of their own. They are completely different from the Andaman islanders both in physical appearances and racial qualities. Their social traits, ways of life, language, social organisation and economic pursuits, religious practices and the entire spectrum of their life style and living practices are diametrically different from other tribes of the country.

NOTES AND REFERENCES

1. G.C. Biswal (1985), "Tribal Development and Education, Some Issues", *VANYAJATI*, January, Vol. XXXII, No. 1, p. 14.
2. *Ibid.*
3. C. Parvathamma (1984), *Scheduled Castes and Tribes: A Socio-Economic Survey*, Asish Publishing House, New Delhi, pp. 4-5.
4. K.L. Bhowmick (1971), *Tribal India, A Profile of Indian Ethnology*, The World Press Pvt. Ltd., Calcutta, p. 1.

5. N.K. Behura (1990), "Tribal Societies in Orissa", in *Tribes of Orissa* (Ed.), H & T.W. Department, Government of Orissa, p.
6. Morris Desmond and Peter Marsh (1988), *Tribes*, Pyramid Books, London, p. 6.
7. Dr. Ghurye, "The Scheduled Tribes".
8. I.M. Lewis (1968), "Tribal Society", in *International Encyclopaedia of Social Sciences*, The Macmillan Co. and the Free Press, Vol. 16, p. 147.
9. Pathy (1976), *et al.*, "Tribal Studies in India: An Appraisal", *The Eastern Anthropologists.*
10. T.B. Naik (1968), "What is Tribe" Conflicting Definitions", in L.P. Vidyarthi (Ed.), *Applied Anthropology*, Allahabad, pp. 84-97.
11. Vimal Chandra (1968), *Handbook on Scheduled Castes and Scheduled Tribes*, Office of the Commissioner for Scheduled Castes and Scheduled Tribes, Government of India, New Delhi, pp. 27-28.
12. Stephen Fuchs (1973), *The Aboriginal Tribes in India*, The Macmillan Company of India Ltd., p. 25.
13. Beleille Andre, *The Definition of Tribe: Tribe, Caste and Religion*, Macmillan, India, p. 10.
14. F.G. Bailey (1960), *Tribe, Caste and Nation*, Oxford University Press, Bombay, pp. 263-266.
15. Suresh Chandra Rajora (1986), "Tribal Society and Its Differential Profile", *VANYAJATI*, Jan., Vol. XXXIV, No. 1, pp. 7-10.
16. Gail Om Vedt (1988), "Are 'Adivasis' Subaltern", *Economic and Political Weekly*, Sept. 24, Vol. XXIII, No. 39, p. 2001.
17. B.D. Sharma (1984), *Planning for Tribal Development*, Prachi Prakashan, New Delhi, p. V.
18. D.N. Majumdar and T.N. Madan (1980), *An Introduction to Social Anthropology*, Asia Publishing House, p. 241.
19. Guha, B.S. (1937), 'An Outline of Racial Ethnology of India', Calcutta, p. 130.
20. Von Eick Stedt, E. (1935), The Position of Mysore in India's Racial History, Mysore, p. 33.
21. Fuchs, Stephen (1973), The Aboriginal Tribes of India: Macmillan-India, p. 27.
22. *Ibid*, p. 28.

23. Guha, B.S. (1944), Racial Elements in the Population, London, p. 11.
24. Von Eick Stedt, E., *Op.cit*, p. 38.
25. Fuchs, S. *Op.cit.*
26. M.L. Patel (1992), "Directions of Tribal Development", *VANYAJATI*, Vol. XI, No. 2, April, p. 31.
27. Sub-Plan for Tribal Regions of Orissa, 1974-79 (Draft), p. 23.
28. *Ibid.*
29. N. Das, "A Plea for Revision of the List of Scheduled Tribes", Report of the Sixth Conference for Tribes and Tribal (Scheduled) Areas (otacamund; Bharatiya Adimajati Sevak Sangh, May 1960), p. 82.
30. Sub-Plan for Tribal Regions of Orissa, Government of Orissa, 1974-79.
31. *Ibid.*
32. N. Das, "A Plea for Revision of the List of Scheduled Tribes", *op.cit.*, p. 81 and Sub-Plan for Tribal Regions of Orissa, *op.cit.*, p. 24.
33. Guha, B. S. (1937), 'An Outline of Racial Ethnology of India' Calcutta, p. 134.
34. Suresh Chandra Rajora, "Tribal Society and Its Differential Profile", *VANYAJATI*, Vol. XXXIV, No. 1, p. 7.
35. Buddhadeb Choudhury (Ed.) (1982), 'Introduction' *Tribal Development in India, Problems and Prospects*, Inter India Publications, Delhi, p. XIX-XX.
36. P. K. Bhowmick (1986), "Reports on Scheduled Tribes: An Appraisal" in L.P. Vidyarthi (Ed.), *Tribal Development and Its Administration*, Concept Publishing House, New Delhi, p. 47.
37. Randhwa, M.S. (1970), The Kamaon Himalayas. Delhi.
38. Bhomick, P.K. (1963), The Lodhas of West Bengal, Calcutta.
39. Russel, R.V. and Hiralal (1916), The Tribes and Castes of the Central Princes of India, London.
40. Doshi, S.L. Bhils (1971), New Delhi.
41. Wood, R. (1953), The Hill Tribes of Assam, pp. 187-214.

42. Dalton, E.T. (1872), "Descriptive Ethnology of Bengal", Calcutta, p. 22.
43. Furer-Haimendorf, C. Von (1946), The Naked Nagas, Calcutta.
44. Luiz, A.A.D. (1962), Tribes of Kerala, New Delhi.
45. Dass, F.A.M. (1937), The Andaman Islands, Bengalore.
46. Mathur, K.K. (1967), Nicober Islands, New Delhi.

3 Economy and Economic Organisation

The economic organisation is a social action, involving the various combinations of human services. It is set in a social framework of relation between the persons expressed in different conceptual ways and with different emphases, as values, symbols, rules of product and patterns of behaviour.[1] The tribal economy is simple, non-structured and self-contained.[2] It is characterised as subsistence oriented. Subsistence economy is based mainly on collection, hunting or a combination of hunting and collection with shifting cultivation.[3] The tribes of India have variegated socio-economic spectrum.[4] At one extreme are the groups which had relatively a secluded and archaic mode of life while at the other extreme are the groups which are indistinguishable from the general agricultural communities. Short circuit in trade, associated with subsistence production tend to build isolated economies with very little economic interaction with each other.[5]

BASIC ECONOMIC ACTIVITIES

The basic economic activities of the tribals may be classified under seven major heads[6] such as; (1) Food gathering, (2) Pastoral, (3) Shifting hill cultivation, (4) Handicrafts, (5) Cultivation, (6) Trade and Commerce, (7) Labour. The tribes, however, can be broadly categorised according to their economic position into four categories. They are: Hunters and food gatherers, shifting cultivators including cattle rearers, settled cultivators and industrial workers.

HUNTERS AND FOOD GATHERERS

Normally, food gathering tribes like the Birhor, korwars and Hill Kharias in Chota Nagpur, the Kadar, Yanadis and Chenchus in south India and the Katkaris or Kathodis in Maharashtra and Gujarat preferred to live away from the habitats of other caste people, where their food gathering activity created less disturbance in the life of the settled population. Hence, they lived in predominantly tribal areas. Surprisingly, the food gathering tribes living in the plains among a cultivating rural population are economically not in the sound position. There is, in fact, no place for them in the rural areas. In the plains, the land has all been distributed among the farmers; its produce is closely guarded and there is nothing left for the primitive children of nature to live on. But in modern times, all the nomadic food gatherers of India are on the decline and dwindling in numbers. Since they require a large tract of uncultivated area to live on, the over populated and the fast growing population of India rarely afford to leave sufficient space for a food gathering economy.

The economy and economic conditions of the tribals in central India is rather unsatisfactory for reasons that are inherent in the traditional culture of the tribals. Encroachment of land of hungry and poor tribals and exploitation of tribals by the egregious moneylenders and land lords and above all their own weaknesses, such as extreme conservatism, undue improvidence, excessive love for drinking etc., add to their miseries. Even more deplorable is the lot of the nomadic hunters and food collectors whose hunting grounds are daily getting more restricted so that they eke out an increasingly precarious subsistence.

In south India, the economy of the nomadic tribes was entirely based on the accumulative method of gathering food and hunting. Tilling the soil, animal breeding or any handicrafts were originally unknown to them. The fertile jungle tracts yielded them plenty of nourishing food consisting of roots and tubers, fruits, vegetables, honey and other requirements. The primitive tribes, thus, enjoyed a healthy as well as diversified diet, the activities required to satisfy their day to day needs of sustenance and of clothing and shelter. It made their life many-sided and interesting. The primitive tribes were self-sufficient, healthy and carefree.

Hunting of wild animals and use of the products of nature, however, were the main means of sustenance of the food-gathering and hunting tribes. They seldom collected more than they needed for a day or two; the only thing they perhaps stored up was honey as a treasured luxury. But once the food supply was exhausted in one area they moved on to another one, but always in their own territory. By all means, trespassing was strictly forbidden. A very primitive foodgathering and hunting tribe in South India is that of the Palliyar in the States of Tamilnadu, Kerala and Karnataka. They prefer the higher altitudes of the mountains. They mostly collect jungle produce. They live principally by snaring and trapping wild animals and birds, and catching fish in the rivers. They do not have any personal property except the scanty clothing they wear, a cooking pot, a digging stick and a bill-hook or an axe and some few hunting materials. They do not even keep dogs. They depend largely on wild honey and on the sale of wax from its combs. To get the honey a man is usually let down over a cliff, by a rope of twisted creepers, to dislodge the beehives with his digging-stick.

Another such tribe, on the Nilgiris, is that of the Sholagar. Buchanan, in 1807, described them thus: 'They speak a bad or old dialect of Kannada, have scarcely any clothing, sleep round a fire on a few plantain leaves using the same to cover themselves. They live chiefly on summits of mountains which the tigers do not frequent. Their huts are most wretched bamboo bent and both ends stuck in to form an arch and covered with plantain leaves.'

In Kerala and Tamilnadu states, the Kattunayakar tribes believe that they are the progeny of a high-caste chief or the descendants of the ancient Pallavas who were defeated by the Cholas in the seventh century A.D. and had to flee into the forest. Whatever value these pretensions might have, they are mainly food-gatherers and hunters, while some are employed by the Forest Department as elephant mahouts and forest guards.

Another tribe of collectors of forest produce, who occasionally do agricultural labour and wood cutting on hire, are the Malasar or Malayar. They reside mainly in Coimbatore district of Tamilnadu while in the earlier Census Reports, a considerable number of them were found in Kerala. By nature, they are rather unsteady in their habits and desert a place or estate on the slightest excuse.

In south India, the food gathering and hunting tribes are: Allar, Aranadar, Chingathar, Irular, Kadar, Kader in the Wynaad, Karavashis or Hill Pulayar, Kattunayakar, Kochuvelar, Koragar, Kurmbar, Kuruvikkar, Kudubis, Chenchus, Advichinchar, Malakarrar, Mala Malasar, Mala Pandaram, Mala Panickkar, Mudugar or Muduvans, Nayadis, Urali Kurumar Uralis, Sholagar, Vettuvar, and others. The aborigines of the Andaman and Nicobar Islands who are divided into the various tribes such as Jarawas, Chariar or Chari, Kora Tabo or Bo, Yere, Kede, Bea, Balawa, Bojigiyah, Juwai, Kol, Onge and Sentilenese are also mere foodgatherers and hunters. They are numerically small in number. The Moger, Paravar, Bagatas, Valar, and Arayar are more or less pure fishermen. The Kavundar, Idayar, Todas and Lamanas are pastoral tribes. There are certain tribes who are partly foodgatherers and hunters and partly field and plantation labourers such as Adiyar, Eravallar, Kalanadis, Kanikkar, Malasar, Mala Vedar, Mala Vettuvar, Malayariar, Malayar, Maratis, Thachanadar, and partly the Kotas. The Karimapalarm Kurichchiyar, Malayalar, Erunkulas, Kaikadis, Jungle Kurubas and others were in the past shifting cultivators. The more advanced cultivators or farm labourers among the tribes of south India are Kudiyas, Kundu Vadiar, Mala Aryar, Mannar, Mavilar, Muthuvar, Palliyar, Pathiyar, Ulladar, Uridavan Gowdalu, and Vishvar.

The tribal groups who are at the stage of hunting and food gathering are very small in number, continue to live in their own little worlds,[7] struggling against the elements of nature, do not produce any food and depend upon nature's bounty for their maintenance. The best examples of such communities in eastern regions are the hill Kharia, the Mankirdia and the Birhor. They are found in the Similipal forest region of Orissa state. They lead the life in isolation without any trade relationship with their neighbouring communities. They have their own languages. Among them everything seems to belong to everybody and their society is almost of egalitarian type. The people do not know the use of pottery and preservation of food. Notwithstanding the fact that they lead a primitive lifestyle, their skills in respect of hunting and food gathering are highly developed. They have the expertise in locating beehives and collecting honey from them. In spite of the overwhelming impact of modern market structure, food-gathering economy still continues to influence the tribal life to a considerable extent. The great majority following them, however, do so only as the secondary or tertiary means of subsistence. The influence of stock raising on tribal economy is moderate. In comparison, institutionalised economic pursuits in general have made appreciable inroads.[8]

SHIFTING CULTIVATORS

Many tribes in south India, in central India, in Chota Nagpur and Bengal, on the slopes of the Himalayas, and in Assam practised, until fairly recent times, this slash-and-burn cultivation for which no plough or animals were required. The only implements required for this type of cultivation were the axe and the digging stick . The tibes which preferred shifting cultivation deliberately chose hilly and forested country for their habitats, and left the plains and broad river valleys to the plough cultivators. [9]

Shifting cultivation popularly known as *Podu,* a primitive form of agricultural practice is a part and parcel of the tribal way of life. It is the oldest method of agriculture in the world, practised by many primitive tribes inhabiting tropical and sub-tropical regions. It is surviving for the last 5000 years.[10] Shifting cultivation is a stage in the evolution of human culture and almost all the races have resorted to this practice in some stage or other.

Many tribal communities such as the Gonds, the Saora, the Kondh, the Bhuinya and the Juang of eastern India are still at the pre-agricultural stage of economy and primarily depend on shifting cultivation for their livelihood. This practice is popularly known as slash and burn cultivation or Podu cultivation.[11] In this method the trees and bushes grown in a hill slope are felled and cleared. When they are sufficiently dried, fire is set to them[12] and the ashes are spread all over the clearings. Seed of mixed crops are sown by broadcast and each of the crop is harvested one after another. A patch of land in the hill slope is cultivated for two to three years after which it is left fallow for a period of four to six years. Another plot of land in a nearby hill slope is selected for pursuing the same method of cultivation. Different types of minor millets, cereals and pulses are grown in the lands under shifting cultivation. This method of cultivation is mostly uneconomic in character. Seldom any investment is made for improvement of land and increase in production, and therefore, their basic requirements of life remain unmet.

DEPENDENT LABOURERS AND FOOD COLLECTORS

Many food-collecting tribes were gradually forced by the dwindling resources of the forests to surrender their freedom and to seek work in the plains. It made them utterly dependent on the land-owners. Such a tribe of low-paid agricultural labourers is that of the Adiyar who are mainly found in the Cannanore district of Kerala. The Eravallens also in Kerala, are in a similar situation. Originally a small forest tribe, they have now started to work as farm labourers. It is believed that they are related with the Kadar, but they are more steady and remain longer at one place. Their language is Tamil which would suggest that they are immigrants from Tamilnadu. There are many other such tribes in other different parts of the country who are only Dependent Labourers.

SETTLED CULTIVATORS, PEASANTS AND ARTISANS

When the productive system of the shifting cultivators failed, the economic activities of the neighbouring people attracted them. Human economic development was traced through evolution of hunting to pastoral and then to agriculture.[13] Thus, many tribal communities have eventually come within the ambit of present civilisation and are no longer self-content as the hunters and food gatherers happen to be. Consequently, some of the tribal communities have become a part of the caste system. There are many tribal communities who were formerly of tribal origin have turned into artisan castes. These tribal communities are in permanent economic relationship with other constituents of the local caste system. The tribal and the non-tribal communities living within the zone of cultural contact have developed inseparable symbiotic economic relationship with one another. However, the tribal settled cultivators continued to get low returns from agriculture. The poor agricultural performance of the tribals seems to revolve round their low asset position and in consequence inaccessibility to the input package. These evidences support Subbarao's hypothesis[14] that the institutional credit and input delivery system in the eastern states is strongly biased against small and tenanted farmers. The tribal cultivators have neither access to new technology, services, inputs and credits nor are they able to exploit the advantage of price rise of their products as they produce for their subsistence and not for the market. They, thus, continue to operate in subsistence agriculture.

INDUSTRIAL WORKERS

Industrial development in some of the tribal areas in the post-independent era brought about many changes. The development of road communication has increased their mobility. The tribal-folk come in contact with outsiders frequently on numerous occasions. In other situations, where they were displaced from their home and land, have turned into wage earners and destitutes. What they needed more than money was work. This was not available easily and the compensation that they received was often used to meet their day-to-day needs. Sizeable agglomeration of tribal population of different areas of the country has moved to mining, industrial and urban needs for earning a secured living through wage labour. During the past three decades, the process of industrial urbanisation in the tribal belt has been accelerated through the operation of mines and establishment of industries. Mostly people from advanced tribal communities have taken to this economic pursuit in order to relieve pressure from their limited land and other resources. In some instances industrialisation and mining operations have led to uprooting of tribal villages and the displaced tribals become industrial nomads. They lost their traditional occupation, agricultural land and other immovable assets.[15]

TRIBES OF HIGHER SOCIAL STATUS

Some tribes claim aristocratic origin, though now much reduced economically. They are the Kurumbas in the Nilgiris and their vicinity, or the Kurumans who are the Kurumbas but living on the western slopes of the mountains. The Kurumba section living in the plains is called Kuruba. It is assumed that after the downfall of the ancient Kurumba dynasties in the eighth century A.D., a part of the people escaped into the jungle where they have since remained after their defeat by the Cholas. Sometimes, it has also been suggested that their forefathers were the people who erected the domens and cairns found in great numbers in these regions.

The Kurichchians are another similar tribe, of good social standing,. They are found mainly in north Malabar, especially in the Wynaad. Their name may be Kanarese or Kuri-hill. The Kurichchians who claim Nayar descent are a community of relatively high social standing. Originally a hunting tribe, they also practise shifting cultivation for their sustenance. Many of them seek work in the plantations as labourers. More often than not, they are exploited by the local money lenders who used to take their whole paddy harvest as interest for outstanding debts. But the Kurichchians are excellent hunters; they use well trained dogs in the hunt. As Good bowmen, they shoot fish with bows and arrows. For hunting purposes, they also use the blow gun.

ECONOMY OF IMPORTANT TRIBES

The economy and economic pursuits of scheduled tribes of the country differ from region to region. In eastern regions of the country, Bagata tribes consider themselves to take the rank of 'soldiery and rather disdain the occupation of ryots (cultivators)'. Shifting cultivation is practised by the Baiga tribes. They live on wild fruits, roots and tubers and animal meat. They are darkish in complexion. They have no permanent homes as they move from place to place looking for fresh cultivable lands. The Baigas of the plains work as labourers. Binjar tribes were Formerly migratory in their habit and sold commodities in various places moving in large groups. History supports the fact that the Banjar were employed by the Hindu as well as Muslim kings to carry necessities for the soldiers to the war front. In course of time, they have migrated to different places in Orissa. The main occupation of the Bathudis is settled agriculture. Amount of land owned by most of the families is not sufficient to meet their requirements. There are landless Bathudis who solely depend on wage earning or petty business. Consequently, most of them work as part time labourers and do petty rice business. They grow paddy and other cash crops such as pulses, sugar, potato, groundnuts, etc. Hunting and fishing are no more practised as gainful economic pursuits.[16] The Bhottaras are also good agriculturists.[17] They know wet cultivation and do not practise shifting cultivation as a mode of their occupation. They work as wage earners when there is no work in the fields. A few of them also serve in firm and Government institutions. They produce all sorts of vegetables in their land. Paddy, sugarcane, pulses, tobacco are the main crops which they harvest. The sources of living of the Bhuiyans are food gathering, hunting and shifting cultivation.[18] They collect edible roots, fruits and worms (Kai) from the nearby streams. As agriculturists they practise shifting cultivation. Wet cultivation of rice and terracing the field are gradually adopted. The plain Bhuiyans are mostly settled agriculturists. Rice is their staple food and are considered superior to all other types. The Bhumiyas, in addition to agriculture work, prepare implements like *Kula* and *Duli*. From various kinds of fibres like jute, sabai and siali, they weave a large net for catching fish and *Kudarjal* for entrapping rabbit. From Siali leaves they prepare *Talari*, which is a country umbrella. They prepare other agricultural implements. Since the Bhumias are mainly agriculturists, they do not practise Podu (upland) cultivation. They grow grams, oilseeds, etc. The Bhumijs are agriculturists. Their main occupation is settled cultivation supplemented by wage earning, collection of jungle products and hunting. After harvest when they do not have openings for wage earning, the Bhumij men go to work in the mining quarries and in tea gardens of Assam. They stay there for a period of three to four months and come back when the agricultural operation is started for the next crop. They grow only one crop of paddy in a year. In addition to this they grow *rabi* crops such as oilseeds, pulses in their uplands and vegetables in the kitchen garden. As land holding is not sufficient for livelihood for most of the families, they work as part time labourer for the neighbouring cultivators when agricultural operation is in swing. Hunting as a gainful economic pursuit has been given up due to depletion of forest and restrictions imposed by the government.

The economy of Binjhals is based on agriculture. Majority of them are agriculturists. The landless Binjhals are labourers. Day labour is called *mulia* and those who work on annual contract basis are called *Halia* or *Goti*. Paddy is the major crop of Binjhals. They also grow pulses, summer and winter vegetables. The economic condition of the Binjhals is not as poor as that of the jungle tribes whose economy is based on hunting or crude type of agriculture. The Binjhals have adopted advanced type of agriculture.

Agriculture also constitutes to be the basic economy of the Binjhias. They are settled cultivators.[19] The Binjhias depend on the cultivation of Gurji, Paddy, Maize and Ragi, pulses like Kolath, Rahad and Mung, Biri, Gangei and oilseeds like Til and Rasi. They also grow vegetables like brinjal, tomato and chillies. The Birhors are one of the earliest nomadic tribes in India. As the very name implies, they are the people belonging to the forests. They not only belong to the forests but are in close association with the basic features of the forests and the connected environments from time immemorial.[20] The Birhors fall to the category of hunting and gathering group. Instead of being settled up in a particular place permanently, the Birhors wander from place to within a circumscribed area and, therefore, known as a nomadic tribe.[21] The Birhors are skilled monkey catchers. They use nets made of siali creepers for catching monkeys and consume the flesh of the monkeys. The skin is sold to the local scheduled caste people. Although the Birhors tap different sources for their livelihood, they run deficit in their food supply many a times. During scarce period, they eat mango kernels, which are preserved at home for use in difficult times. The staple food of the Birhors is rice. With the sale proceeds of ropes and forest produce, they buy their weekly requirements of rice and other things from the market. They also buy corn and minor millets in addition to cooked rice. They collect various types of green leaves and mushrooms, fruits such as 'Kendu', palm and mango from the forest for their consumption. While collecting barks from the forest, they dig out roots, fibres and collect honey, which supplements their principal cereal diet.[22] Bondas are mainly agriculturists. Gruel of ragi and rice are the chief food of the tribe. They collect wild vegetables, bamboo shoot, mushrooms, etc. They keep cattle, goats, pig and poultry. They drink enormous quantity of wine called salap, the juice of Sago palms. The Bondas are expert cultivators. The irrigated and terraced paddy fields on the high hills prove their skill in rice cultivation. They have their own hill cleanings where they practise Podu. According to customary practices these clearings become individual property and each household owns a number of sites on the hillsides, which are cultivated in rotation. In spite of their primitiveness and poverty, the Bondas enjoy a high degree of economic self-sufficiency. The geographic isolation has been a blessing in disguise as the Bondas are less exposed to exploitation by outsiders. Very rarely they borrow money from outsiders. The modern civilisation has not changed them very much. They maintain their primitive custom and tradition.[23]

Dals cultivate ragi and Kodua more than paddy and Gurji. Among the pulses, they grow are Kolath, Munga, Biri and oilseeds like Rasi and Til. Maize and Khed Jandre (millet type) are also grown. Vegetables like brinjal, tomato and chillies are grown in the kitchen gardens. Tobacco is cultivated by almost all. Apart from these, each Dal owns a number of Mahul trees. Mahul is collected and stored by each family on which they depend for their food. Mostly Mahul is exchanged for Ragi and Kondu with the contractors who bread liquor in the neighbourhood. The Kultas, Bhuitiyas and Marwaries also exploit by advancing loans before harvest. The Dals sell their products at a nominal rate as a precondition of getting loan.

The Desua Bhumij have taken to wage earning as the main source of income. Most of them are landless and only a few families have got land which is not sufficient to meet their requirements. Almost all of them work as labourers for the neighbouring cultivators. Children are employed to tend cattle. The depleted forest in the neighbouring area does not provide much scope for collecting green leaves, roots and fruits as in the past. With much difficulty, they can bring fuel and Sal leaves for sale. In leisure time, they manufacture bricks. During summer, a few Bhumij men go to work in the tea gardens of Assam or in Calcutta or in the Mining Quarries in Keonjhar district in orissa. Although rice is their staple food, they hardly get full meals throughout the year. They eat beef, pork, fowl, white ant, mouse, termites and other unclean food. Rice-beer and Mohua liquor are taken too. In olden days, the Dharuas were mostly agriculturists, though some of them were employed in military service maintained by the native Rajas. In course of time a great change has taken place in their economic life. Now, besides being agriculturists, they are found in different wage-earning jobs. The Hill Didayi practice shifting cultivation whereas the plain people have adopted settled agriculture. Both the groups cultivate ragi and susan extensively, which is their staple food. The Didayis of the plains do not have sufficient virgin forest for practising shifting cultivation. They depend on paddy and ragi. The hill and plain Didayis collect a variety of roots and fruits during the entire year to supplement their food. The Didayis are voraciously addicted to juice or salap which is available in abundance in the forests. Thus, the hill Didayis live on subsistence level whereas the plain Didayis are economically better off having scope for wet cultivation as well as for raising various types of cash crops like oilseeds and pulses. In case of Gadaba tribe the main source of their livelihood is cultivation. Since cultivation provides food and work to the members of his family, an Ollar Gadaba considers it more stable, dependable and regular than any other occupation.[24] The Gadabas practise both shifting and wet cultivation. Those who live in plain adopt some amount of shifting cultivation in a localised area. Each family divides its holding for shifting cultivation in two parts and cultivates a part, when the other remains barren. The places are alternated once in every three years. The chief agricultural products are paddy, ragi, suan, maize, several types of grams, etc. Their staple food is ragi. Rice is only a supplementary food. Since their production is insufficient, they resort to food collection in the jungles. Mango Kernel, edible roots, etc. support them for two months in a year.

Gonds are tillers of the soil. Their main occupation is agriculture supplemented by the collection of jungle products, hunting and shifting cultivation (only among the primitive Gonds of Koraput). They grow rice, millet, maize, mustard and a few varieties of pulses. They also grow tobacco and vegetables. The Hinduised Gonds have developed a commercial sense and do petty business in the local markets. The Hos are purely agricultural people. The people of this community are engaged in agricultural operations during rainy season. The womenfolk take part in all agricultural pursuits except ploughing. The Hos use cows and oxen as drawing animals. They do not take the milk of the cows. Buffalos are also preferred to plough land. Paddy, maize, and ragi are the main crops they cultivate in the hill slopes. Besides these, they grow vegetables like brinjals, gourds, etc. in their kitchen gardens. Hunting and collection of edible roots and tubers are a part and parcel of their economy.The main occupation of holva tribe is agriculture. They cultivate the land as owner and on share basis. Many of them remain as labourers with the people who own land. Shifting cultivation is almost given up. The main produces are paddy, suan, ragi, maize, pulses and different types of gram. Sugarcane and tobacco are also cultivated. They collect jungle products. They take resort to hunting as leisure activity. Fishing is also practised occasionally. A few have accepted jobs in Government and under different firms. They have started sending their boys and girls to the schools for education. They are economically, educationally and socially better off than other tribals. The Jatapus are mainly agriculturists but the poorer sections earn their bread by wage earning or being employed as labourers.

Primarily the Juangs are agricultural people. They practise two types of cultivation: Jhum or shifting cultivation and wetland cultivation.[25] In most areas of the Orissa state, the Juangs have switched over to Toila land cultivation in the highlands and wetland cultivation in low lands. The studies show that the Juangs have given up shifting cultivation long ago and its place has been taken up by permanent cultivation. In addition to agriculture, food gathering occupies a prominent place in Juang economy. They collect roots and tubers, green leaves, mushrooms from the jungles to supplement their diet. Moreover, they collect minor forest products like honey, wood, leaves and sell them in the villages and towns and earn money for their subsistence. Very few people among the Juangs possess good cultivable land. The rest of the population are landless and earn their livelihood by earning daily wages and selling fuel and other minor forest products in the market. The point, however, remains that when fast changes are taking place in the Juang community, their old network of relationship in economic activities and marital and religious ceremonies remains and is being strengthened wherever it is being weakened.[26] The ethnic unity is strengthened by social solidarity movement which is being launched by the progressive section of this community and it is this unity which gives the Juangs an assurance of security. Kawar tribes have given up their traditional occupation of military service and they are now cultivators and labourers.[27] Routias weave ropes and make sleeping cots, but the other Kawars consider such work to be degrading. Hunting in the forest is carried out at times. Collection of edible roots and forest product supplement their food and economy. Kharia tribe is broadly divided into three divisions, viz.-the Pahari or hill Kharia or Erenga Kharia, the Dhelki Kharia and Dudh Kharia. Besides, there are a few more divisions such as Munda Kharia, Oraon Kharia, Berga Kharia and Setera Kharia; but these are minor sections. The three divisions represent the three grades of primitive culture. The hill Kharia depends mainly on food gathering.[28] They collect honey, skin, cotton, lac, the edible herbs and tubers and other minor forest products. The Dhelki Kharias have adopted settled plough cultivation. The traditional occupation of Kharias was to carry Dholis or Palanquin. At present they are mostly agriculturists. Besides agriculture, they depend greatly on daily wages. A large number of Kharias used to go to tea gardens of Assam in the past. But now most of the Kharias are employed as farm servants. Some educated Kharias have been employed in different types of government services. But hill Kharias still remain backward. *The Kandha life and culture are based on the* forest economy. The self-sufficiency that they enjoy is mainly due to their living in the midst of forests. Their life revolves round the forest from where they produce food and shelter.[29] The chief occupation of the Kondha people is agriculture. The hill Kondhas practice shifting cultivation or Podu and Desia Kondhas have learnt ploughing from non-tribals. They depend upon nature. The most important crop they raise is turmeric. But due to primitive method of cultivation, it is less profitable. The Kondhas on the hills practise shifting cultivation. In the summer months, before the outbreak of monsoon, the Kondhas who live on the hills cut woods and set fire on them. When woods are turned into ashes they leave it till the onset of rain. The site is ploughed and maize or paddy seeds are sown. They harvest paddy or maize in the months of October/November. The particular piece of land is cultivated continuously for one or two years. Now a days, the Kondhas are experiencing change and transformation. The Kondhas formerly possessed little property. A new cloth or a brass plate was rare. Today in most of the houses one can see brass utensils. They have acquired considerable wealth in terms of silver and brass ornaments. They have now abundance of food and a liberal supply of raiment. Cultivation is extended and they grow large quantity of cotton, oilseeds and turmeric for export. Barter economy widely prevalent among the Kondha society is now replaced by money economy.[30] This inevitable replacement of the barter economy by money economy was a great economic change, which facilitated easier communication between the tribals and the people of the plains. Indebtedness is one of the occurrences in the life of Kondhas. The Panos (non-tribal Harijans) who live nearby and other rapacious and unscrupulous traders exploit them through money lending. Paternal debts are repaid by their successors. Another type of exploitation is selling them ornaments, agricultural implements, clothes at high rates by the non-tribals. The Kisans are both industrious and intelligent. Most of them possess land. They work hard in their fields. Even the wealthy Kisans do not hesitate to work in the fields along with the labourers.[31] The Kisans are efficient earth workers. Some of them have acquired the skill of carpentry and bricklaying. Most of the poor cultivators and all the landless people depend greatly on daily wages or serve as *Goti* or *Halia* under rich cultivators. Besides, they also supplement their resources by way of food gathering and collect Mahulchar, Kendu and other green leaves and tubers. Educationally they are still backward. After independence, the situation has improved and a good number of Kisan youths are now entering into schools and colleges. A few educated Kisans now serve in different government jobs and in factories. The Kolhas were subsisting on hunting and gleaning in the past. Their gradual contact with the Hindus led them to practice cultivation and to adopt plain-land wet agriculture. Their long contact with the Mahato community enabled them to learn the techniques of agriculture in a more sophisticated way. Most of them depend on agriculture either as cultivators or as agricultural labourers. But the main source does not prove adequate to sustain them throughout the year and they are, therefore, allured by the remunerative daily wages. They prefer to be engaged as daily labourers in industrial areas. This sort of employment opportunity and eventual cash earning exposed them to the evils of an urban industrial culture. Agriculture has become an occupation of the old and disabled. Whatever landed property is possessed goes into the clutches of moneylenders. Paddy is produced in the lowland. During summer 'Dhipa' land are used for growing vegetables, blackgram, redgram, and many other local varieties.

Malhars are a nomadic tribe whose main occupation is collection of honey. The Kolis are a class of weavers. They are two separate tribes who bear apparently no regional or ethnic affinity. However, under what circumstances both these tribes have been clubbed together is a matter for more detailed enquiry. Madras Census Report of 1901 mentions Kolis as a fisherman and boatman caste of Bombay who were found in South Canara. It is also stated that a low class Bengal weavers called Koli migrated to Orissa and were found in Ganjam district. Some Kolis, however, claim that the members of the tribe were once in numerical preponderance near and around Ichhapuram of Andhra Pradesh and were living in close association with the Telugu-speaking people. They were in primitive state. Some were weavers and some of them were rearing goats and poultry. Subsequently they migrated to different regions of Orissa. The Malhars are a semi-nomadic community. The traditional occupation of the Malhars is collection of forest products. In the absence of land and plough, they do not practise cultivation. They also work as daily labourers to supplement their income from forest collection. After the denudation of forest, their economic condition has gone down. Due to their poor economic condition and traditional occupation of forest collection, the Malhars have not developed like the Kolis. They have remained backward as before.

The Pedda-Kondalu tribes depend mainly on agriculture, both shifting and wetland cultivation. Some of the Chinna-Kondalu people hold low-rung government jobs. A few of them work as labourers in the nearby villages. The Konda-Doras are not only consumers but also are producers. The Pedda-Kondalu grow and harvest paddy, millets and other crops. Majority of this group own acres of paddy land and are very rich. They sell their surpluses to the nearby villagers. With the impact of industrialisation and establishment of new townships around the areas inhabited by the Konda-Doras, they have changed a lot. Changes in the economic, religious, political and social aspects are noteworthy. Due to the establishment of Factories, many Konda-Doras have established shops and have got employment in the new towns and factories around Koraput, their original home. Digging tanks, making road and earthwork is the traditional profession Kora tribes. In course of time, they had adopted the making of catchu as their procedure. Having cut down a tree, they strip off the bark. The inner wood is cut into pieces and the pieces are boiled with sufficient water for 4 days. A black paste is obtained. The water is let out and the residue is dried under the sun in the form of cakes. It is consumed with betel leaves. The adoption of this profession depends on the availability of catchu plants. Most of them have now given up this profession and have taken up agriculture. Today they are first-rate agriculturists and labourers.[32] They produce paddy, pulses and different kinds of oil seeds from their field. Hunting in the forest is carried out at times. Fishing is rarely practised. Collection of edible roots and forest products supplement their food and economy. The Kotias are also an agricultural tribe. Most of the people who have landed property are settled agriculturists. Those who do not have land take to agricultural labour and wage earning. Catching of fish is one of their subsidiary occupations as they like fish very much. Fish trap and nets of various types are found in their houses. Dried fish is preserved for use in future. The Koyas were primarily shifting cultivators. But now a days they have taken up settled cultivation. As the yield of paddy does not suffice for a family to pull on for the whole year, the Koyas resort to other types of food quest i.e., collection of roots and fruits from jungle and growing of minor crops like Suan, Maize and Pulse. The Mahul trees abound in the Koya areas. During the months of March and April, large quantities of Mahul are collected, dried and stored for future use. The Koyas own large herds of cows and bullocks. Towards the interior regions one will be surprised to see a family possessing three or four hundred heads of cattle. The Koyas seldom milk their cows. The calves will die if the cows are milked, they believe.

The Kulis are like Kuli weavers by occupation. They are known by their title as Mehar. The sole occupation of the Kulis is weaving. Agriculture is a subsidiary occupation for a small fraction of people. Less than one per cent of the Kulis own lands and in no case the holding is more than two acres. Both the sexes participate in this. A couple can weave 20 to 25 pieces of clothes per month ably under ideal conditions. The limit does not exceed twelve pieces as they face problems of capital and market. The Lodha tribes are economically backward.[33] Most of them are in a pre-agricultural stage of economy. Their occupational pattern varies according to local environment. The Lodhas living in the forest area stick to their age-old pursuits like hunting, food gathering, collection of minor forest produces, tassar cultivation, etc. They also work under forest department and forest contractors in plantation programmes and timber operations. Apart from collection of edible fruits, roots and tubers for their own consumption, they collect Kendu leaves to roll bidi, sal and siali leaves to make leaf cups and plates, sabai grass to make ropes, tassar cocoons, honey, lac, resin, sal seeds, mohua, firewood, etc. They sell the forest products to earn their livelihood. They hunt with bow and arrow and use different kinds of traps and snares to catch animals. With rapid deforestation and prohibitory forest laws, they have been deprived of their forest-based subsistence. The Lodhas living in plains mainly thrive on wage earning as agricultural labourers and construction workers. They also earn and supplement their livelihood from a variety of occupations like petty trades, rearing of livestock, carpentry, weaving, mat-making and rope-making. They also earn by selling the hide of the reptiles which are in great demand for making musical instruments, shoes and fashionable articles.

The primary occupation of the Mahalis is basket-making. A few who have sufficient land have got agriculture as their main economic pursuit,[34] but for the rest it is a subsidiary source of income. All families know basket making. They do not grow bamboo, but purchase it from the locality. They exchange their baskets to the neighbouring population for cash or food grains. Boys above eight or nine years of age are required to earn by tending cattle. Girls of this age group are trained in the craft of basket-making, collection of jungle products such as fruits, green leaves, roots and tubers to supplement their diet.

The main occupation of the Matya community is settled agriculture. Most of them cultivate their own land. They produce maize, paddy, suan, pulses and tobacco. They cultivate various types of vegetables. Forest products are collected and fishing is resorted to at times. Some of them have taken up jobs. They are expert in each work and are employed in it by the contractors. They take paddy for a part of the year. They manage with edible roots of the forest, mango kernel, maize flour and suan, etc. for 4 to 6 months in a year. Liquor of various types like rice beer, salapa, mohua liquor, date palm juice are their favourite drinks. The traditional occupation of the Mirdha tribe is earthwork. They are, therefore, known as Koda. The term Mirdha means head coolie. Previously they used to serve as earth workers not individually on the basis of daily wages but worked in groups on contract basis. The headman of such groups is called Mirdha. Thus, the so called Kodas have adopted the honourable terms Mirdha instead of derogatory term Koda, which means earth working labourers. The omanatya tribes are good agriculturists and practise wet cultivation. Shifting cultivation is not practised. Sugarcane, paddy, tobacco, ragi, several varieties of pulses, oilseeds are their major crops. Vegetables like brinjal, onion, potato, etc. are cultivated. Fishing is usually carried out. Hunting is practised as a leisure time activity. A few of them have joined government service. Most of them own some amount of land. In the social scale, they enjoy higher status. They do not touch the untouchables like Dom, etc. They do not take food from

Bhottaras, Bhumias. They are gradually taking interest in education. Agriculture continues to be the main source of livelihood of Oraon tribe. Many of them have acquired proficiency in several rural crafts such as carpentry, tile, brick and rope-making. Women still weave mats of wild date palm and make broomsticks from wild grass. Whenever there is leisure and opportunity, they work for wages. It is not uncommon to find educated Oraons serving in offices, schools and factories. Their principal crop is paddy, which is grown once in a year. They also grow millets, maize and several varieties of pulses in their uplands. Hunting, fishing and collection of jungle products have ceased to be profitable sources of livelihood. Depletion of forests and pre-occupation with the expanded settled cultivation have forced them to give up hunting. The main occupation of Parenga tribe is agriculture. They practise both shifting cultivation and wet cultivation, but they depend mostly on shifting cultivation. Collection of forest products like edible roots, fruits is often resorted to. Fishing is practised. Hunting is made at times. They are mostly exploited for their illiteracy. Interests at a very high rate are realised from them by the moneylenders and businessmen at the time of recovery. They are duped by the traders of cloth and salt.The Parajas are primarily cultivators, but the poorer sections are mostly landless labourers. They are not considered to be impure and some Paraja boys allow their hair to grow long and to form a bunch on the head. Educationally the Parojas fall far behind like many other tribes. They have remained socio-economically backward as compared to the general population. The main occupation of Pentiya tribe is settled agriculture and they do not practise shifting cultivation. As major crops, they harvest paddy, ragi, niger, pulses and different kinds of gram. They grow vegetables. Fishing is often practised. Hunting is resorted to as leisure time activity. Collection of edible roots and other forest products play important role in their food quest. They live upon rice. In the months of scarcity they take ragi, mango kernel, sweet potato to supplement their diet. They do not eat beef, pork, but they take meat and mutton, etc. Agriculture is their main occupation of Rajaur tribes. But their economic condition is like those of the landless labourer. They do not eat beef, pork, and other unclean food. They take fowl and alcoholic drinks and the leavings of the higher castes.

On the other hand, the Santal people, in addition to agriculture, go for fishing as a supplementary occupation. They rear goats, pigs and fowl which are butchered on festive occasions. Of late, there has been horizontal mobility in their occupation. Traditionally they were engaged as small and marginal farmers and agricultural labourers. The scope for occupational mobility was provided with the emergence of mining and industrial units in and outside the districts. A good number of them are now found in Jamshedpur in Bihar and the neighbouring districts of orissa. They work as unskilled workers in the industries. With the spread of education among them, some Santal people have taken up government jobs. Both the men and women participate equally in their day-to-day economic activities. They harvest a single crop from their land. Therefore, agriculture does not prove to be profitable for them. Nor does it provide them adequate livelihood. They are, therefore, forced to depend on the forest products and wage earning for a living. The weekly market called *hat* plays an important role in Santal economy. They mostly depend on their *hat* for buying their daily requirements and selling their agricultural and forest products. Of late, the LAMPS and TDCC centres were established in the Santal area to provide articles of daily consumption at reasonable rates. The main source of livelihood for the Saora tribes is shifting cultivation. Whenever any valley of the hills are available they practise wet cultivation in terraced fields where two crops of paddy can be grown in a year. The Saora terraces reveal their magnificent workmanship. They grow several varieties of millets, varieties of pulses, oilseeds, turmeric and ginger is the clearing (bagad) on the slopes of hills by axe cultivation. Paddy is mainly grown in wetland. Tamarind and Karanja plants are plenty in the area. During summer they collect and sell them. Sometimes oil is extracted from Karanja seeds for their use. They grow sago-palm and collect Mahua flower for wine. It is said that Saoras generally grow comparatively more than many of the neighbouring tribes. But they lead miserable life due to chronic indebtedness. A large chunk of their expenditure is to meet the expenses of innumerable feasts, festivals and treatment of diseases. The main item of Saora food consists of gruels of rice, millet or pulses added with edible leaves. The Saoras sell some of their products in the local weekly markets. The local Doms and Kumtis who are the agents of the big merchants from the plains buy their items. The transactions which take place between the Saora seller and the Dom and Kumti buyers are mere exploitation.[35] But, the chief means of Sahara economy is cutting and supplying fuel in the neighbouring villages. They collect herbal plants and roots from the forest to sell to the local *Kaviraj* (medicine man). The Saharas also cultivate paddy fields of the neighbouring villages and work as labourer in the nearby towns. These simple tribal-folk remain as a prey to the Sahukars (local merchant) for their continuous poverty. The Dombs (a Scheduled Caste) also take advantage of their simplicity. However, impact of industrialisation, development of science and technology has brought changes in the social, political and economic organisation of these people. Most of the Sounti tribes are landless, they work mostly as contract labourers, day labourer and agricultural labourer for the local cultivators who require the extraneous labour. Those who have land do cultivation themselves.[36] But in most cases, amount of land is not sufficient to meet the cost of their living. So some of them work as labourers and some do petty business such as buying rice at a cheaper rate from one locality and selling at a higher price in another place. Hunting and collection of jungle products have been given up due to depletion of forests. Their staple food is rice, which is taken throughout the year in whatever quantity it may be available. From rice flour, cakes are prepared and taken especially on holidays. Non-vegetarian food is much more relished, but they are handicapped by their low income.

ECONOMIC ORGANISATIONS

Agriculture and allied sectors constitute the major economic organisations of schedule tribes. The economy and economic organisations of tribals mainly centre round the activities such as: Agriculture, Horticulture, Sericulture, Animal Husbandry, Fishery, Forest etc.

AGRICULTURE

Various human activities are dependent on land which is our basic natural resource. The Indian economy as a whole is agro-based. It is little wonder than that the whole life of the tribals is centred round agriculture. Agriculture, therefore, deserved and rightfully accorded highest priority in the country's development. It should be developed at a rate necessary to support the development of the other sectors of the economy. The mainstay of tribal economy was and still is agriculture, which existed usually in a rudimentary form and provides a subsistence level of economy. Agriculture is the means of livelihood for a majority of tribal population. But many of them practise shifting cultivation which is unproductive as well as non remunerative. That apart, fertility of the soil is destroyed and the forest products which sustain the tribal people are perished. It results denudation of the hill slopes and make it barren. Moreover, there is acute soil erosion due to destruction of the valuable forests which ultimately leads to drying up the water sources below the hills. Hence, slash-and-burn cultivation or shifting cultivation or Podu or Jhum is harmful and primitive. Besides it's economic non viability and wasteful practice by a sizeable section of tribal people, has a negative impact on the vast forest area. A majority of the tribal workers are engaged in cultivation and a substantial section are agricultural labourers. But the productivity of agriculture continues to be low. The main constraints of agricultural development in these areas are uncertain and Irregular monsoon rains, meagre irrigation facilities, traditional inefficient cultivation practices, inadequate input supply position, unsatisfactory marketing arrangements and extreme poverty of the tribal farmers. These are the factors which contribute to low level of agricultural development.

From a stagnant agriculture, the planned approach to agricultural development has enabled to achieve some positive results on the production front, especially on the production of food grains. Though some advance has been made in the field of agriculture, there is yet a large gap to be bridged up. The strategies in agriculture development in the context of tribal economy adopted during the Plan periods mainly focused: (a)To gear up the credit institutions for providing adequate institutional finance to the farmers and to enable them to avail the subsidy component provided under various scheme, (b) To saturate all the irrigated areas with high yielding crops and adopt multiple cropping pattern, (c) To take up oil seed cultivation in an extensive scale, (d) To adopt timely plant protection measures among the tribal cultivators, (e) To organise demonstration over the lands of the tribal farmers to acquaint them with better agricultural practices, (f) To adopt mixed cropping practices to ensure minimum substantive production under erratic weather conditions, (g) To ensure adequate marketing facilities for the surplus agricultural produce of the tribals, (h) To substitute less remunerative paddy crops by relatively more remunerative drought tolerant non-paddy crops like pulses, oil seeds and millets, (i) To provide adequate irrigation facility through construction of more dug wells, energisation of dug wells and construction of irrigation projects, (j) To popularise use of chemical fertilisers among tribals to increase crop productivity, (k) To use quality certified seeds of improved variety, increase in the productivity of different crops through adoption of improved cultivation practices and motivate the tribal farmers to adopt the technology for higher production.

In view of the agricultural character of tribal population, it is necessary to observe their pattern of land ownership. Among the cultivating land owning Scheduled Tribe households, a large percentage of land owners own less than 2 hectares of land among the total cultivators.[37] There is an increasing trend of deterioration in the land ownership pattern among tribal households. Several studies made in this context revealed this trend.[38] Not only the pattern of land ownership is extremely unfavourable to vast majority of tribal households, but average per capita holding also shows a declining trend.

For development of Agriculture in tribal areas certain positive steps were initiated. For monitoring the agricultural programmes and motivating the farmers to adopt the improved technology for higher production, the extension system has been reorganised. As per the present set up, a village agricultural worker (VAW) is in-charge of some villages, having more than 500 farming families. There are VAW Circles in the tribal sub-plan area in which VAWs and Agricultural Overseers are working for the economic growth of the tribal farmers. The departmental seed sale centres have been increased from one at each block headquarters to two or more in the block area for easy availability of the seeds. Incentives have been provided to the Secretaries of the Primary Societies and VAWs to boost up the off-take of chemical fertilisers. Agricultural education has been provided to the students in secondary/high schools. Adaptive research stations located one in each district continues to evolve suitable varieties and agronomic practices for the area. Seed multiplication particularly of the varieties suitable to the area will continue in the department farms located in the sub-plan area. For tribal culture whether it be agriculture, horticulture or silviculture, application of manure and fertiliser would be desirable to obtain higher yields. Hence, the farmers are educated for production of quality manure out of rural wastes and forest litters and their larger use for raising the productivity of their land. Soil testing is key for economic and efficient fertiliser use. Therefore, soil-testing laboratories have been established in each district barring minor aberrations. Incentives have been provided to farmers for free distribution of fertiliser for improved high yielding varieties. Krushi Vigyan Kendras have been established in tribal sub-plan areas. The principal goal of the scheme is to impart training in the latest technology relevant to a specific agro-ecological and socio-economic condition to practising farmers.

Over and above the general schemes which apply to tribal areas, special schemes have been designed to cater their needs under tribal sub-plan with an attempt to mitigate the disadvantages faced by tribal farmers and make them conscious about their role for agriculture production. Large farmers have relatively greater access to the credit and subsidy for agriculture development than marginal and small farmers. This also corroborates the findings of many other studies conducted, which indicate that farm size and credit flow have a close but positive relationship.[39] However, funds have been provided for the purchase of debentures from Cooperative Land Development Banks with a view to giving loans to the tribal agriculturists for land shaping, land development, horticultural and purchase of agricultural implements for agricultural purposes.

Tribals because of their tradition, orientation and closed group norms have not been able to introduce many new crops, new implements, new fertilisers and other new areas in agriculture. The experiments to introduce vegetable crops, cash crops, fruits and new fruit crops are likely to yield good results.

HORTICULTURE

Horticulture constitutes an important component of the development strategy of the scheduled tribes. It not only ensures better returns than traditional agriculture, it also generates more employment. The development of horticulture creates conditions for the growth of ancillary and tertiary sector industries. Horticulture is essentially a 'Podu' prevention programme in the context of tribal development. The tribals are probably the pioneer horticulturists and their love for and knowledge about fruit trees is indeed impressive. They have special attachment to fruit bearing trees and will not normally fell them. This attitude of tribals towards fruit trees is being taken advantage of and horticultural plantations are undertaken for discouraging the practice of shifting cultivation. Further, the agro-climatic condition of the tribal areas is suitable for horticultural development. The main thrust of horticultural development programmes in the tribal areas has been laid on creation of conditions favourable to extensive fruit tree plantations especially on deforested lands. The *in situ* method of fruit plantation was introduced during the Fifth Plan period in the tribal sub-plan areas. This method of plantation was found suitable for unirrigated high lands, undulating lands, hill slopes, *podu* ravaged lands and other lands, not suitable for annual cropping. By and large, this method has become popular among the tribals.

In tribal areas, soil erosion is a serious problem owing to undulating topography, shifting cultivation practised by the tribals besides improper land use programmes. As such, to prevent soil erosion different approved soil conservation measures like land reclamation, land development including field bunding, contour bunding, terracing of agricultural land, construction of water harvesting structures, farm ponds, gully control measures, development of pasture lands, plantation of economic tree crops like fruit and fuel species, sisal, coffee, cashew, sabai and bamboo etc. are taken up in the land of tribals in a government land in the sub-plan areas. Hill tribes have their indigenous methods of soil conservation and land development which though, neither technically sound nor effective in preventing soil erosion. Water management, catchment area and wasteland management approaches are applicable to hill areas. Catchment area approach is to study the ecology, geo-physical property etc. Watershed approach is mainly to study geo-hydrological position. Forest can catch and hold rainwater. Degree of conservation of rainwater is dependent upon soil. In order to increase agricultural productivity, comprehensive and diversified land use programme on watershed basis was considered necessary. Therefore, during the Five-Year Plans it was programmed to carry out different soil conservation measures in an intensive manner in the tribal sub-plan areas.

FOREST

Forest plays a vital role in the economy of tribals. Forest is an inalienable and integral part in the life and culture of tribal people. Scheduled Tribes are, therefore, called Vanya Jati (forest caste) Giri Jan (men of hills) etc. The tribal people have lived for hundreds of years in the forest areas and have an ineradicable conviction that forest is theirs. By tradition and necessity, tribal people and forest dwellers, forests have shaped their life and economy. A study in Bihar reveals that while the forest dwelling tribes like the Birhor and the Maler depend on the forest to the extent of 90 per cent, the agricultural tribes like the Munda and the Oraon depend on it to the extent of 45 per cent. Forest caters to the basic needs of the tribals by providing food, fodder, fuel for domestic purpose and timber for construction of dwelling units, agricultural implements and other saleable minor forest products. Hence, forest management practices have an important bearing on the economy of tribal people. Development of forestry ensures agricultural progress while maintaining the ecological balance. As the forests are a part of the tribal economy, any forest policy with less stress on tribal development will be lopsided. On the contrary, any plan for tribal development should give priority to exploitation of forest for the benefit of the tribals. There must be interlinkage between tribal development and forest policy. The main objectives of the forestry planning have been to develop forests without destruction. Therefore, following strategies were adopted for development of forest for sustaining tribal economy. (i) Improving the environment by protecting forests meant for long-term vegetative cover and also undertaking massive afforestation on such land where the forest coverage is degraded, (ii) Affording strict protection to wildlife and its habitat, (iii) Undertaking a massive programme of social forestry, farm forestry and village fuel wood plantation to meet the over-growing rural fuel energy needs, (iv) Linking forestry regeneration programme to individual tribal families to ensure regular income to them, consistent with ecological requirement, (v) Increasing the productivity of forest products so as to achieve self-sufficiency in meeting economic, industrial and housing needs, (vi) Generation of employment and rural development with the focus on the preservation of the existing forests through intensified protection measures and with the people's participation, (vii) Increasing the forest cover through afforestation, wasteland development and restocking the degraded forests.

FISHERY

Tribal fishermen are mostly agricultural labourers, who undertake fishing as an off-season occupation. Fishing provides them with a supplemented avocation. In some tribal areas, fishery development has great potential in existing reservoirs, tanks and ponds. Emphasis was laid in the plans to improve the socio-economic conditions of the fishermen in tribal areas by enabling them to acquire country boats and nets at subsidised rates and fishing in inland waters and to take up pisciculture in the tank. Priority was given for production of quality spawn. To encourage the tribal people in pisciculture, subsidy in shape of inputs was given for water area. The main objectives of pisciculture development in tribal areas during the different Plans were to: (i) Make tribals aware of the modern methods of pisciculture and its nutritive value, (ii) To help them to supplement their earnings through self-employment, (iii) Improve the nutrition standard of the tribals through intake of cheap animal protein like fish. To achieve these objectives in the sub-plan area the following steps have been taken: (a) Fishery extension officers have been posted in blocks of the tribal sub-plan area for dissemination of inland pisciculture technology, (b) Institutional finance for operation of the fishery schemes has been made available, (c) Training facilities in pisciculture are provided to tribal people, (d) For supply of fry and fingerlings in tribal areas, the departmental fish farms are being remodelled to produce the required number of fry and fingerlings, (e) Assistance is being provided to the traditional inland fishermen by way of subsidy for acquiring country boats and nets for fishing in rivers and reservoirs. Reclamation subsidy and input subsidy are given to tribals for development of pisciculture under FFDA, (f) Fishermen cooperative societies, which are in moribund condition are being reactivated and new ones have been organised in the sub-plan areas for the improvement of the socio-economic condition of the tribal fishermen, (g) The reservoirs in tribal areas are being developed by way of stocking fingerlings and giving them on long-term lease to fishermen cooperative societies of tribal areas for fishing.

In addition to normal state plan schemes, some schemes were implemented with special central assistance to help the tribal people to augment tank fisheries. Initially, much headway could not be made because most of the tribal people were landless. It was not possible to settle fishing right of the government on Panchayat tanks in their favour. Subsequently, the Gram Panchayat Act was amended. It allowed lease of G.P. tanks for 10 years with the beneficiaries. It is, therefore, felt that a lot of possibility is there to introduce tank fisheries amongst the tribal people.

Basing upon the status and need of the individual tribal in the sub-plan area, subsidy was provided in the first year to different categories of tribal beneficiaries to renovate a tank and take up pisciculture therein.

ANIMAL HUSBANDRY

Livestock rearing is practised as complementary to crop production and has traditionally been an important secondary source of livelihood in tribal sub-plan areas. This is one of the oldest occupations that man has adopted. Tribal economy is predominantly agriculture-based. Livestock occupies a position second to land in the tribal areas. Though the tribals practising shifting cultivation do not use animals in their farming operations, they rear animals and birds to meet their requirements of domestic consumption, community entertainments and for animal sacrifices resorted to propitiate Gods. For many years to come, livestock will continue to be a source of supplementary income to all the tribals belonging to different occupational group.

Keeping in view the inclination of the tribals for small animals like goat, sheep, pig and poultry, efforts have been made to implement programmes of development of small animals in the tribal areas. On the basis of the suggestions of the Planning Commission, the strategy under animal husbandry and dairy development sector were devised. Appropriate schemes were prepared for rehabilitation of a large number of poor families through animal husbandry programme and reciprocating mixed farming. Emphasis was laid on multiplication and supply of small animals and on extensive programme for popularising artificial insemination to upgrade the breeds. In accordance with the recommendations of the Working Groups on tribal development, special programmes for development of animal resource and dairy development were prepared during different Plan periods.

SERICULTURE

Sericulture industry is an age-old predominant culture practised by almost all the tribal people of hill areas. Its historical perspective has been to satisfy man's quest for clothing with concurrent assurance of self-sustainment and self-dependence. Most of the schemes for the development of sericulture implemented in tribal areas provide employment to tribal people by way of rearing various types of silkworms, reeling and spinning yarn and cultivation of feeding plants. State Governments provide technical and organisational support including training facilities, financial assistance, etc. mostly to tribal people for the development of sericulture. Tassar silkworms rearing is an important economic activity of of Scheduled Tribe families. Emphasis has been laid for expansion of mulberry sericulture in hilly areas where agro-climatic condition are quite conducive and tribals and other agriculturists have shown interest for such profession. ERI silkworm rearing, as a subsidiary income generation programme, has also been given importance. During the plan periods state governments have, therefore, laid considerable emphasis on the sericulture industry in tribal dominated areas in their states.

HANDLOOMS

Because of greater employment potential of the handlooms sector, steps are taken to develop handloom units in tribal areas. The programme consists mainly in bringing tribal weavers under organised sector by promoting cooperative societies. This is for the modernisation of looms, training of tribal weavers, supply of raw materials and provision of marketing assistance. Cooperative societies are bringing within their fold many tribal weavers and training facilities have been provided to such weavers.

Tassar silkworm rearing is a traditional occupation of tribals in many tribal areas. During the Plan periods cooperativisation of tribal tassar rearers, supply of disease-free Tassar silkworm eggs to the rearers, plantation of host plants for increasing tassar silkworm, rearing area, marketing of tassar cocoon as well as facilities for development of reeling and spinning of tassar cocoons were given due support. Attention was also given to the development of technological base under inter-state tassar development programmes.

Most of the tribal sub-plan areas of the Country provide congenial condition for Mulberry culture. In order to help the tribals in this culture, supply of mulberry cuttings, silkworm eggs and training the farmers are being planned by the State Governments. Mulberry demonstration farms and seed supply stations have been established in the tribal areas. Tribals are being assisted to take up mulberry cultivation in their own land and they are being assisted for plantation of mulberry, supply of rearing equipment, construction of rearing houses etc. Mulberry rearers-cum-reelers cooperative societies are formed where the tribal growers are its members.

Tribal people have also fascination for ERI silkworm rearing. Tribal families have been assisted with supply of ERI silkworm eggs and training facilities providing them subsidiary income. The ERI seed cocoon production centres in tribal areas aim at popularising ERI silkworm rearing by tribals to supplement their income.

NOTES AND REFERENCES

1. D.P. Biswas (1985), "Nature of Economic Organisation Between the Two Villages in West Bengal", *Vanyajati*, October, p. 11.
2. B.D. Sharma (1978), *Tribal Development, The Concept and the Frame*, p. 89.
3. N.K. Behura, "Tribal Societies in Orissa", in *Tribes of Orissa* (Ed.), H & T.W. Department, Government of Orissa, pp. 12-13.

4. P.K. Bhowmick, "Rregional Strategy For the Development of the Tribal Communities", in *Tribal Problems of Today and Tomorrow*, p.
5. D. Naik and S.C. Patnaik (1987), "An Approach to the Rural Development Through Rural Markets with Special Reference to the Bonded Trade of Turmeric in Orissa", Paper presented in the Post World Economic Congress Seminar, Utkal University, Bhubaneswar, 6th and 7th March.
6. N. Das (1960), "A Plea for Revision of the List of Scheduled Tribes", Report of the Sixth Conference for Tribes and Tribal (Scheduled) Areas (Ootacamund: Bharatiya Adimmajati Sevak Sangh, May, p. 81.
7. B.D. Sharma, *Tribal Development, the Concept and the Frame, op. cit.*, p. 2.
8. Karl Polanyi (1957), "The Economy as Instituted Process" in Karl Polyani *et al.*, (Eds.), *Trade and Market in Early Empires*, The Free Press, Glencoe.
9. Fuchs, Stephen (1973), The Aboriginal Tribes of India, Macmillan India, pp. 47-48.
10. D.P. Tripathy, "Shifting Cultivation in Orissa", p. 8.
11. M.K. Mohanty (1990), *Tribal Society Programmes, Planning and Economic Change*, Chugh Publications, Allahabad, p. 84.
12. L.M. Srikant (1956), "The Integration of Aboriginal Population of India", *International Labour Review*, Vol. LXXIII, No. 3, March, p. 256.
13. D.P. Biswas, *op. cit.*, p. 11.
14. K. Subbarao (1984), "Price and Non-Price Policies in the Design of Rural Development Strategy for the Eastern States", in K. Prasad and S.C. Patnaik (Eds.), *Rural Development Strategies for Weaker Sections*, p. 50.
15. N.K. Behura, *op. cit.*, p. 15.
16. H. S. Mishra, "Binjhals", in *Ibid.*, p. 74.
17. N. Prasad (1963), *Land and People of Tribal Birhor*, Tribal Welfare Research Institute, Ranchi, 1964; S.P. Malhotra, "Kinship Organisations of Birhors", *Bulletin of the Bihar Tribal Research Institute*, Vol. V, No. 2.
18. B. Chakrabarty (1988), "Relationship Between Ecology and Economy-A Study of the Birhors", *Bulletin of the Cultural Research*

Institute, Vol. 12, No. 1 & 2, 1976; W.H.P. Driver, "Birhors", *Journal of Asiatic Society*, Vol. 57.

19. S. Bose, "Carrying Capacity of Land Under Shifting Cultivation", Monograph Series, The Asiatic Society, Calcutta, Vol. XII, pp. 88-102.
20. N. Patnaik (1964), "Caste in Formation Among the Juang of Orissa", *Man in India*, Vol. 44, No. 1, January-March.
21. *Tribes of Orissa, op. cit.*, p. 134.
22. U.C. Mohanty, "An Analysis of the Improved Economic Life of the Tribals of Orissa and the Way Towards Integration", in B.C. Ray, *Tribes of Orissa*, pp. 125-126.
23. G.B. Sahoo, "Kora", in *Tribes of Orissa*, p. 168.
24. B.B. Mohanty, "Sounti", in *Tribes of Orissa*, p. 263.
25. S. Bose, "Carrying Capacity of Land Under Shifting Cultivation", Monograph Series, The Asiatic Society, Calcutta, Vol. XII, pp. 88-102.
26. N. Patnaik (1964), "Caste in Formation Among the Juang of Orissa", *Man in India*, Vol. 44,No. 1, January-March.
27. *Tribes of Orissa, op. cit.*, p. 134.
28. Harimohan (1961), "Socio-Economic Organisation and Religion Among the Hill Kharia of Dalbhum", *Bulletin of the Bihar Tribal Research Institute*,Vol. 3, No. 1, pp. 180-212.
29. N. Patnaik (1972), *Tribes and Their Development: A Study of Two Tribal* Development *Blocks of Orissa*, NIRD, Hyderabad, p. 108.
30. F.G. Bailey (1957), *Caste and Economic Frontier: A Village in Highland Orissa*, p. 301.
31. U.C. Mohanty, "An Analysis of the Improved Economic Life of the Tribals of Orissa and the Way Towards Integration", in B.C. Ray, *Tribes of Orissa*, pp. 125-126.
32. G.B. Sahoo, "Kora", in *Tribes of Orissa*, p. 168.
33. S.C. Mohanty, "Lodha", in *Ibid.*, p. 191.
34. K.C. Mahali (1986), "Mahali, The Aboriginal Tribe-An Introductory", *Vanyajati*, Vol. XXXIV, No. 4, October, p. 4.
35. U.C. Mohanty, "An Analysis of the Improved Economic Life of the Tribals of Orissa and the Way Towards Integration", in B.C. Ray, *Ibid.*, pp. 126-127.

36. B.B. Mohanty, "Sounti", in *Tribes of Orissa*, p. 263.
37. *Report on* Agricultural *Census of Orissa, 1970-71.*
38. Government of Orissa, *Economic Survey of Orissa*, Vol. I, 1954-55, pp. 130-131; Government of Orissa, *Living Condition of Scheduled Tribes, Scheduled Castes and Other Backward Classes in Orissa*, 1963, pp. 76-79.
39. C.H. Hanumantha Rao, "Farm Size and Credit Policy", *Economic and* Political *Weekly*, 28 December 1970; V.G. Rao and P. Vatam, *Agricultural Finance by Commercial Banks*, Asish, New Delhi, 1980.

4 Social System and Political Structure

The scheduled tribes of India have varied Social Systems and elaborate Political Structure. Their socio-Political organisation, religious and cultural factors have a direct bearing on their economic development. Tribals living in isolation develop their own customs and socio-economic institutions which are the results of hundreds of years of gradual adaptation of their environment[1]. Among the nomadic food gathering tribes, the social structure is based mainly on the natural family. Usually several such families, united by ties of kinship, form a local group. They live together, hunt and collect together and share out among themselves what they have gathered. They have obligations towards each other in want, sickness and old age. Social life, however, is not entirely restricted to the local group wherever it exists. The local groups meet occasionally to celebrate feasts, for the agreement of marriages and other important matters.[2]

The Scheduled tribes have well organised and systematic social structure. The social organisation of the tribes which practise a primitive form of cultivation is more developed. The nuclear family of the food gatherers expands frequently in to a joint family, the sons remaining after marriage with their father and helping him in the field work while the women look after the house and the children, and also help in the field work. Since members of one group now settle in more compact villages and stay permanently together, the local group develops in to a village community. Descendants of one ancestral village regard each other as relatives. They have a strong community system. The village community, consisting of members of one tribe, arranges, witnesses and supervises wedding and funeral feasts. It settles marriage disputes and declares a divorce. It discusses property disputes, settles quarrels and chastises those who offend tribal law. It excommunicates, punishes or fines the culprits besides dealing with outside communities and disputes.

Totemism in its various forms can be found in wide areas of the Indian peninsula. It is absent only in the north of India and in its southernmost corner. It is not at all restricted to tribal communities. It is strongest in central India from where it probably spread out in to Bihar, Maharastra, Orissa, Andhra and Kerala. In the East and North- east of India other objects of various kinds, like ocean, gun, corals, cakes, garden, island, magic, darkness, white and red colours, etc. prevail as totems. Totemism is found patrilineal as well as in matrilineal societies. Totem membership is inherited in the paternal line in Chota Nagpur, in the Deccan and in the south east of India. Totem membership is inherited matrilinealy in Assam among the Garos and Khasis, perhaps also among the Lalungs and Kacharis. In south-west India, in south Kanara, the Tulugu speaking castes, like the Billavas, Devadigas and Madivalas, and Kanarese-speaking castes of North Kanara inherit both totem membership and property patrilineally.[3] Some tribes of eastern and central India have adopted, or retained the totemistic - clan system, with clan exogamy and clan taboos, whereas the nomadic tribes in south India, in particular those in Kerala, have adopted the matrilineal system partly or fully. This has resulted in a breakdown of the family system and laid to practical promiscuity in some tribes. Divorce is frequent and premarital and extra-marital sex relations are at least tolerated. These tribes, too, live in small local groups, with a permanent or temporary headman, whose authority depends more on his personal character and ability than on his office.

Social status is an important factor for establishing the mental equilibrium of the individual as well as of a whole community. Social prestige is a powerful stimulant for human ambition and drive. This axiom holds good also for the aborigines of central India. In the past they have been living apart and keeping to themselves. But gradually they are coming into ever-closer contact with the non-tribal population of India, which is predominantly Hindu. The aborigines are thus necessarily drawn into the still all-compelling Hindu caste system. The tribes of central India react differently to this social adjustment. Some tribes, like the Bhils and Gonds, Bhilalas and Minas, have decided to adopt Hinduism and aspire to the social rank of Kshatriyas (Rajputs). They therefore, observe the social rules and taboos of the high-caste Hindus with anxious correctness and avoid any lapse that could create the slightest suspicion of unorthodoxy.[4]

The money lenders and contractors, however, contrived to create new artificial needs in the tribals. They introduced and encouraged the tribals, through free gifts, to become addicted to alcohol, opium and tobacco; they insisted that to be respectable and civilised the tribals had to dress properly; they appealed to the vanity of the tribals, and sold them ornaments and other luxuries. All this required money for which the tribals had to work. And wherever the tribes refused to be tempted, labourers from outside were brought in who not only deprived the tribals of their livelihood and depleted the forests, but also played havoc with the tribal sex mores and social safeguards. This practically resulted in a breakdown of tribal morality and social structure; particularly effective in this destructive process was probably the introduction of matriarchal social elements, accompanied by polyandry and the visit marriage custom prevalent among some of the Hindu castes of south India. Today, many of the hill tribes have adopted elements of this matriarchal system, and in some tribes, it has led to practical promiscuity in sex behaviour and a breakdown of family life. The vices of civilisation have thus been introduced as welcome helpmates in the drive for increased production. They certainly have been very destructive towards the economic, social and moral structures of the south Indian hill tribes. Unfortunately, the accompanying benefits of civilisation, better and more effective tools and implements, medicine, education and industrial enterprises, have not been made equally available to the tribals. The contact of the tribes in south India with modern civilisation has been largely detrimental to them.[5]

SUB-TRIBE AND CLANS

Most of the tribes are divided into a number of sub-tribes, which are further divided into clans. The large tribal groups such as the Kondh, the Saora, the Gond and the Santal spread over wide areas in the eastern part of the country have many subdivisions among them. The Kondhs and Saoras have 20 to 25 sub-tribes respectively. These sub-tribes with a sizeable population function as independent tribes. Among the Kondhs, there are Kutiya Kondh, the Dasia Kondh and the Dongria Kondh who not only function as separate entities but also are culturally distinct. Similar is the case among the Lanjia Saoras and the Saoras. Cultural differences are very much pronounced among them. The small tribal communities like the Bondas and the Birhors, the divisions are small in number. The Bondas are divided into the plain Bonda and the Hill Bonda. Both of them are not only distinctive sections but also are conflicting groups. Similarly, the Birhors are divided into two groups namely the Jagi, the settled groups and Othul, the nomadic group. Both these groups have distinctive economic life, social organisation and ritual cycle.

The next bigger unit in the social system is the sib or clan which is the pivot of all socio-economic activities. The number of clans and tribe varies from tribe to tribe. The clan organisation is prominent among the Kondh, the Gadaba, the Paraja, the Juang and the Santal. Among the Juangs, as many as 24 clans have been recorded. Among the Kondhs, different sections have different clan names. In most of the tribal communities the clans seem to have totemic origin named after grains, trees and animals. The members of a clan believe to have descended from a common ancestor, observe certain totemic taboos and show a high degree of reverence towards the totem.[6] The clan organisation which is unique to all the tribal communities is conspicuous by its absence among the

Saoras. In their case the main exogamous unit is the extended family called Birinda, descended from a common ancestor. A remarkable feature among the Saoras is that a woman belongs to her father's Birinda even after her marriage. Among the other tribal groups, the woman after marriage belongs to the clan of her husband. Kinship is treated as the basic organisation principle among the tribes. Among them there are both consanguineal and affinal kin groups. They use both classificatory and descriptive terms in their terms of address. The descriptive terminology refers to the application of a particular term of address for each relationship. Another distinguishing feature of the kinship system is the presence of joking and avoidance relationships.

HOUSE, FAMILY AND FOOD

In the social organisation family is the universal social unit. It is a social group characterised by common residence, economic cooperation and reproduction.[7] Among the tribes, simple or nuclear family consisting of married couple and their unmarried offspring is the usual form and it is found in preponderance over all other types. Joint or extended families are rarely met with. A boy after marriage establishes a neo-local residence. The family is patrilineal, patrilocal and patripotestal.

Tribals generally lead a communal life. The happiness and miseries of life are shared by the whole community. Individuality in the true sense of the term is rather submerged in the communal life of the tribals. Men and women occupy equal rights in the social and economic fields. Women are often the bread earners for the family.[8] There is, however, a marked difference in the House, Family and Food of different Indian tribes. Bagata tribes are primarily a fishing community. Some of them are hill cultivators in the agency tracts of Vizagapatam. They are considered as an offshoot of Kapus caste. The head of a single village is called a Padal, the Padal being the name of an exogamous sept of the Kapus. Banjaris are a small tribe mainly found in the districts of Kalahandi, Koraput and Sambalpur.[9] Russel and Hiralal describe the tribe as having migrated from Rajputana and its surrounding places. They also deduce from the word Bangara, which is a derivation from the Sanskrit word Banijya Kara, a merchant. Bathudis are said to be a branch of Bhuiyan tribe. According to Russel, the 'Bathurias' form an inferior subsection of the Bhuiyans and are looked down upon because of having taken food from other low caste. Most of the families possess more than one living room, built around a rectangular courtyard. Houses are built either in a linear or in a scattered fashion. Most of them own Kachha houses with mud walls and straw thatched or local tile thatched roof. Sometimes, walls are made of wooden planks planted up right and plastered with mud. Rice is their staple food. Some green leaves or vegetables constitute side items. They prepare cakes from rice flour. Alcoholic drinks such as Mohua liquor and rice beer are generally avoided. At present, they have a status of a clean caste in the caste hierarchy of the Hindu society. The Bhottaras are one of the efficient agricultural communities of Orissa. It is believed that they are immigrants from Bastar district in Madhya Pradesh. They speak a regional languages. Nuclear families are more in number than the extended ones among them. They live in heterogeneous villages along with other neighbours like Omanatya, Dom, Rona, etc. The village is a unit from socio-political point of view. The term Bhuiyan is derived from the Sanskrit word 'Bhumi', meaning land. They consider themselves as the children and the owners of the land and hence are known as Bhuiyans. The Bhuiyans have no other tribal language of their own and they speak regional languages. Birhors are nomadic tribes. Birhor means people (Hor) of the forest (Bir). They are dark skinned, short-statured, longheaded, wavy-haired and broad-nosed people. There are two types of Birhors, the Uthuls i.e., nomadic and the Jagi i.e., settled Birhors. These nomadic or mobile Birhors move from one place to another in different groups in a specified area within the state. The primary occupation of the Birhors is preparing ropes from the bark of siali creepers. In addition to this, the Birhors make small baskets (Tupa) out of the siali barks. Chenchu is an important South Indian tribe. Their population is small.

They are semi-nomadic food gathering tribes. They live exclusively under tree in small conical or oblong huts. Their huts are haphazardly scattered and reconnected by a network of footpaths. Dharuas or Dharua Gonds are one of the oldest tribes. According to Risley, "They are one of the several steps of the Gonds and are otherwise known as Naiks"[10]. He is of the opinion that the Dharus are the ordinary Gonds, who in most of the district form an endogamous group. According to Russel, the word Dharua may be derived from "Dhur" (dust); that is the common people and they are inferior to Raj Gonda.The Gadabas are one of the early settlers of this country and trace their origin to the time of *Ramayan*. It is said that their original home was Godavari from where they have derived their name Gadaba. They have their own language known as Gutab or Gadaba language. A few of them living near the towns and working as labourers in firms. The Gadabas are not a migratory folk. They live permanently in villages situated on inaccessible mountain areas.[11] During the pre and post-independence periods, various writers like Col. E.T. Dalton and Sir H. Risley have described socio-cultural life and values of the Ho, Kol-Lohara, Kolha and Larka-Kol. Most often, these terms have been used to denote a single group of people inhabiting different areas. The name Munda seems to have been given to these people by their ancient Hindu neighbours. The Munda called themselves Horoko (men) and their tribe Horo (mankind). The appellation 'Kol' generally used for Munda, Mundari, and other Kelarian tribes is now strongly resented by them simply because it is regarded as derogatory. The term Munda is liked by them as in their own language it signifies the well-to-do secular village headman. This tribe inhabit the mining and industrial belt of Bihar-Orissa border and is exposed to the force of industrialisation right from the beginning of the century. The Kolhas constitute a sizeable section of the total tribal population in eastern part and scattered throughout the area. They live along with their Kolarian tribes like Santal, Munda, Ho, etc. The Khonds are a well-known tribe found in different eastern region and the Konda-Doras are a section of this major tribe and are found in different parts of this region. The major concentration of this tribe is in the district of Koraput of Orissa. Means of livelihood between both the groups are different. According to Risley, Kora is a Dravidian caste. Probably they are an offshoot of the Munda tribe. They are good earth workers and cultivators. It is said that they owe their name 'Khaira' from their occupation of making catchu (Khair). The Koyas constitute the principal tribe of this group. The Koya villages are situated on patches of clearings in the midst of forests. Approach to the villages are by narrow footpaths diverging from the *kachha* road. The language spoken by the Koyas belong to the Gondi dialect of the Dravidian group with mixed Oriya and Telugu words. This dialect also differs among the two groups of the north and the south. Madia tribe forms a part of the Koya tribe. In 1908, the Imperial Gazetteer of India wrote, "The Maria Gonds are almost a separate race"[12] and by this it fulfils the significant separation between the Maria and the Gonds. Grigson coined the name Hill-Maria and Bison-Horn-Maria and he stressed himself "whatever the derivation of the word Maria and the Muria, they are not Gondi words. It has been suggested that Muria is formed from a word meaning root, the term meaning 'aboriginal' and that Maria means merely "Man of Woods".[13] The Oraons tribes concentrate mainly in the boarder districts of Orissa and Bihar. They have their own language, which has been classed as a Dravidian language. But they know Hindi. The Paraja are otherwise called Paroja, Porja or Parja. The name Paraja appears to be derived from the Sanskrit term Praja, a subject. Carmichael has stated that by far the greater number of these Parajas are akin to the Kandhas of the Ganjam malias. Russell and Hiralal, on the other hand, hold the view that Parajas are akin to the Gonda and not Kandhas. Their tradition traces their original home to Bastar. The term Paraja is so broad a term that it includes in a very loose sense of the term, a number of other communities. At times the Bondas and Gadabas also refer themselves to be Bonda Parojas and Gadaba Parojas respectively.

The Savaras or Sauras constitute a major tribe in the state of Orissa. They are one of the oldest tribes of the world.[14] They live in the Eastern Ghat region. The great majority of Sauras have lost their own language and now speak local languages. A Saura is an uncultivated language and has no recognised standard. It varies considerably not only between villages but also between individuals. The Bhumij, writes Risley, are nothing more than a branch of the Mundas who have spread to eastward and migrated with the Hindus and thus for the most part severed their connections with the parent tribe. In some areas, Munda is another name for Bhumij. The tribe has got its aboriginal tongue and they speak Bhumij at home. Rice is their staple food and is taken throughout the year. They take rice beer and Mohua liquor like the neighbouring tribes.A Bhumij house is rectangular in size. Ordinarily verandahs are built in the front. The houses with mud walls have generally straw or wild grass thatched roof. Most of them own more than one room with opening to the courtyard. As regards dress and ornament, they follow their Hindu neighbours. The Bhunjias eat pork, but abstain from beef and the flesh of the monkeys. Rice is their staple food. Rice is the staple food of the Binjhals. Generally they take food twice a day. Their meal consists of rice, vegetables and occasionally meat or fish. Rice beer is the important drink of the Binjhals. On the high hills to the northwest of the river Machkund lives the wildest, rudest and possibly the most interesting tribe known as 'Bonda' or naked people. The scanty dress of Bonda women and homicide tendency of Bonda males have made them most fascinating and thus, they stand in sharp contrast from other tribes. Bonda tribes are extremely aggressive. Age-old isolation, poverty, intoxication and fear of sorcery are the chief reasons of their aggressiveness.Their house and food habits still display their primitiveness. The Desi or Desua Bhumij are also known as Sing Bhumia. Bhumij constitute a section of the Bhumij tribe of Munda origin. They have totally forgotten their aboriginal language and have adopted local languages as their mother tongue. Rice is the staple food of Bhumij tribes but they hardly get full meals throughout the year. They eat beef, pork, fowl, white ant, mouse, termites and other unclean food. Rice-beer and Mohua liquor are taken too.The Didayi are a primitive hill tribe inhabiting the 4,000 feet plateau of the Eastern Ghat range. They are described as a wild tribe by V. Elwin (1950) and as the stratum of primitive semi-nomadic shifting cultivators by C. Harmendor (1995). Didayi tribes are divided into two groups i.e., the hill and the plain Didayi. The people living the hilltops have social ties with the plains people who, to a considerable extent, have been influenced by the Telugu-speaking people living close to them. The houses in hill as well as plain villages lie scattered all over and no regular street is found. The houses are built in an individualistic manner and the villagers do not share a common roof like the Kandhas. The staple food of Gonds is rice, gruel of millet and maize. The Hinduised Gonds abstain from eating beef, pork and other unclean foods and drinking of rice-beer or wine. But among the primitive Gonds, every householder breeds a large number of goats, pigs, and poultry for meat. They drink rice beer and alcoholic drinks. The Hinduised Gonds who claim themselves to be Kshatriya, have styled themselves as Hindus by copying many Hindu customs and practices.[15] The Gonds are honest and trustworthy people. If a Gond dies without clearing his debt, his son would not rest till he repays his father's debt. The Hos form a major tribe among this group. The word 'Ho' has probably been derived from the word Horo, which in their language means man. The little known tribe, Kisan, remained obscured on account of its Hindi appellation, which means cultivator. The tribe seems to be an offshoot of the great Oraon tribe, which belongs to the Dravidian groups. But at present they take pride in declaring themselves as a separate tribe and calling themselves as Kisan. Rice is also the staple food of HO tribes. The females collect the roots, tubers, green leaves, mushrooms from the jungle. The Hos go for wage earning to earn their livelihood. They prefer to wage in terms of kind rather than wage in money terms. Every Ho village is a social as well as a political unit. The headman is the supreme controller of the village. They are gradually developing in all aspects of life and are coming forward to associate themselves with the national endeavour for progress and prosperity. The Holvas are an agricultural community. They trace their caste name from the term 'holo' means a plough.[16] They claim Bastar district in Madhya Pradesh to be their original home from where they have migrated to other parts. They speak local dialect with outsiders but their own dialect is peculiar to them. Holva family is nuclear. Extended and joint families are seen to a certain extent. The village acts as a socio-political unit for all practical purposes.Among the aboriginal tribes, the Juangs form a major group. The Juangs were considered 'most developed' by the Scheduled Areas and Scheduled Tribes Commission of 1961 and were specified as 'backward' by the study team on tribal development programme in 1969. The family of Juang tribes, which is the basic unit of the social organisation, is mostly of nuclear type. There are few joint families in the Juang society. The Kondhas are the seventh largest tribal group in India and they are twice the size of the better-known Naga people of Assam.[17] The tribe is divided into different subdivisions according to different localities. It has separate names in separate regions. Mainly the Kondhas are divided into three subdivisions: (1) Desia Kondhas wholive in plain area along with other non-tribals. (2) Dangaria Kondha live on highland hills. The name of Dangar means highland. (3) Kutia Kondhas are found in Phulbani district.[18] The Kisans do not reside in any compact area of their own, but live in multi-caste and multi-tribal villages. They have their own Tola or ward at the end of the village.The social status of the Kolis is higher than the other tribal communities. They speak Oriya with Telugu accent. Weaving is the main occupation of the Kolis. They do not prefer agriculture as an occupation. The tribe is very much acculturated. Many of them are highly educated and some of them have become doctors and engineers. In the social status hierarchy, they occupy a higher status among the scheduled communities.

The jungle and hilly terrains of Chhotnagpur Plateau running across Bengal-Orissa-Bihar border is the homeland of the Lodhas. Instances of organised highway robbery, murder, theft, burglary, committed by the Lodha gangs mostly in West Bengal-Orissa border areas have made terror. The problem of Lodha criminality is of psycho-emotional nature. Attempts have been made to socio-economically rehabilitate them in rehabilitation colonies. The Mankidia is a nomadic tribe scattered in the forests.[19] They had migrated from Chhotnagpur of Bihar long ago. The Mankidis carry on rope-making from the fibres of Siali creepers. They catch monkeys and birds and gather roots and tubers from the forest. They visit weekly market places to sell their ropes. They have formed into several bands called Tandia. Each band consists of 10-12 families belonging to different lineage groups. Each household of a Tanda sets up its hut called Kumbha made of twigs and sal leaves. Each Tanda has a bachelor's dormitory called 'Dangua-Kumbha' and spinster's dormitory called 'Gitishikumbha' where young boys and girls above 10 years of age spend nights. Each Tanda has a headman called 'Dehuri' who is supposed to be elected by divine power and assisted by a messenger called 'Naya'. Dehuri serves as a religious headman. The band-life, continuous migration from place to place within the district, hunting, monkey catching and food gathering are the cultural landmark of the Mankidia society. Matya family is nuclear and is the main social unit. The sons get separated as soon as they are married and live in separate hamlet. Village is the next larger unit. The secular headman is known as Nack, the religious head is Pujari, the village attendant is Barik and the attendant of the visitors is Challan. The villagers join together in hunting and festivals of the village. The Omanatyas or the Amanatyas are one of the agricultural communities. It is said that their ancestor was a minister (Amatyan) of Sri Ram. After Ram had gone to heaven there was no one to take care of them and hence they took to agriculture. They have the different titles given by the king such as Pradhani, Pujari, etc. They have no other tribal language of their own. The Omanatyas live in heterogeneous villages with other communities like *Bhottada, Rana Dom, Paik,* etc. Nuclear families are the chief social units. There are extended and joint families but the number is very few. The Parenga tribe has been treated by Thurston as a subdivision of Gadaba as they have some similarities with Gadabas. But Bell has dealt it as a distinct principal tribe of Munda group. There are certain similarities among the Parengas and the

Gadabas. The village is a socio-economic unit. The festivals are observed in the village communally, they go to hunt together. All the births and deaths are communal affairs where all the villagers participate. The Pentia villages are mixed ones. They live on plains. Agricultural lands and forests surround their villages. Fowl is their favourite food. However, they occupy a high social position. The Santal tribes were nomadic in the past. They wandered in search of agricultural land. Now they have permanent settlements. The Santal village consisting of a number of households is surrounded by agricultural fields. An average Santal village has 50 to 100 households. Consequent upon their interaction with the non-tribal people, there has been a change in the dress habit of Santal people. The Santal women do not use the traditional ornaments like the brass bangles, anklets, armlets, coral beads, etc. But tattooing remains to be a common practice. *Handia*, a kind of rice beer, is their favourite traditional drink. Not only do they treat their friends and relatives with *Handia*, but they also offer this to their ancestral spirits on ceremonial occasions. Malaria fever, influenza, scabies, itches, etc. are the common diseases found among them. But the Malaria Eradication Programme of the government has helped to eradicate Malaria to a great extent. The Sabars or Saharas or Sa-A-ars are a section of the great tribe of Saora. The Sabars and the Saharas are separate branches of the same tribe, though sometimes a line of distinction is drawn between them. Generally the village or ward (*Sahi*) inhabited by the Saora tribes is located and situated at the outskirts of the clean-caste village or near forests. The name Sounti is derived from the word 'Sounta' meaning 'gathered in'. The Sounties reported to have a separate identity only in the 16th century. The Sounti tribes are considered ritually clean having some functions connected with the ruler of the state in the past. In their ceremonial customs and manners they follow the Brahminical system and employ Brahman, Barber and Washerman. It is not easy, however, to find exclusive Sounti villages. They mostly live in the midst of Hindus and other tribes such as Bhumij, Gonds, Kharia, etc. In such villages they occupy a separate ward.

Marriage

Marriage is an important institution in the social organisation. It has an important bearing in the social life through which alliance between two clans is established. This expansion of the network of relationships is central to the establishment of most tribal units.[20]

Tribes, generally, observe local group exogamy. The members of a local group have to select their marriage partners from outside groups. The marriage bond is loose, divorce is frequent and chastity is not strictly maintained by the women and girls. This is, however, not the custom among the tribes living in the forest, but more among the tribes living in the plains among the rural population.

In eastern India in communities with a matrilineal social structure, the clan solidarity may prove stronger. This seems to be the case in Assam among the Khasis and Garos. A village is usually occupied by a single clan, with matrilineal descent, and a female clan head, who is generally the head of the oldest and highest family in the village. The management of the clan need not always be exercised by a woman; often it is her brother who acts in her name. Thus the male element reasserts itself. The kinship ties may be so strong that neither husband nor wife are prepared to separate from their kinship group. Consequently, a man does not live with his wife, but visits her only at times fixed by convention. This is called a 'visit-marriage'. In the past this custom was found among some Naga tribes (in Manipur) and also among the Khasis.[21]

In case of tribes of Central India, though most of the tribal marriages are monogamous, polygyny is prohibited by no tribe. On the contrary, it is regarded as a symbol of wealth and increases a man's social prestige. Polyandry is normally not found among the tribes of central India, though it is sporadically reported in old sources relating to some primitive tribes. There is, however, some sort of fraternal polyandry in existence, because sex relations of a woman with her husband's younger brothers are easily condoned, among some central Indian tribes, though this is not publicly admitted. But it is generally observed that no tribe of central India permits or even tolerates other forms of extra-marital sex relations. Adultery warrants severe punishment.

Among the primitive tribes of southern India, no uniform family pattern can be discovered. Most of the tribes have been strongly influenced by their neighbours who are more advanced in culture. Parents are generally anxious to have their children married as early as possible. By an early marriage, the eventuality of scandals is removed, young couples are supposed to fend for themselves and to be thus, no longer a burden to their parents, and aging elders like to see grandchildren growing up.

In South India, Marriage by purchase is the most popular form among the Scheduled tribes. The bride-price has to be paid either to the father or the maternal uncle of the bride. Some groups permit the payment of the bride-price in instalments. Sometimes presents given to the bride or her parents before or at the wedding are considered equivalent to a bride-price. Some tribes, like the Kadar, demand a dowry, which means that the father of the bride has to pay it. Among the Aranadar and Allar, for instance, the payment of the bride-price is repeated annually. The Kalanadis and Vishavar, however, do not demand any bride-price or dowry. The payment of a bride-price can be avoided by an exchange of sisters. The Uralis of Kerala, for instance, always demand a girl in exchange; a boy who cannot give a sister or cousin in exchange has no chance of getting married, while on the other hand a boy with several sisters can marry as many wives as he has sisters. The Uralis do not accept payment of money as a substitute for a girl. Such an exchange of sisters is usual also among the Vishavar, Mala-Vedar, Mala-Pandaram, Irular, Kurichchar, Ulladar, Maratis, Kudiyas and other tribes. In choosing their mates, many tribes in south India have a preference for their cross-cousins; this is the established rule among the Hill Pandaram, Kannikar, Kundu Vadiyar, Kurichchiayar, Kalandis, Nayadis, vishavar and Muduvar; it is also found among the Veddas. It is always the marriage between the children of a brother and a sister, cross-cousin marriage is further preferred by the Ulladar (with the daughter of a boy's maternal uncle), the Kuruvar (who allow marriage oly with the daughter of the maternal uncle), the Mala Arayar (who allow marriage also with the daughter of a father's sister), the Mala Vedar, Mala Pulayar, Palliyar, Mannar and Kadar. The Mulla Kurumar, however, prohibit cross-cousin marriages, as do also the Eravallar, Adiyar, Kattunayakar and Maratis. They prefer a wife from an unrelated family. Among the Mala Kuruvar, Mala Panickkar and Ulladar marriage with the paternal aunt's daughter is prohibited. It appears that tribes which possess landed property favour cross-cousin marriages; they strengthen the family ties and prevent the loss of a field. Some of the tribes also practise levirate, that is, the younger brother marries the wife of his deceased elder brother. This custom is found among the Veddas, Ulladar, Kannikar, Kadar, Mannar and Mala Pulayar. Among the latter, the elder brother may even marry the widow of his younger brother; the same is permitted among the Palliyar. Levirate is prohibited among the Adiyar, Muduvar and Mala Vedar. No uniformity exists with regard to the numerical pattern of marriage. Some tribes, like the Kadar, Vishavar and Nayadis, practise compulsory monogamy, at least so long as the marriage lasts. Another wife can only be taken after the first one has been divorced. Other tribes permit polygyny, or polyandry, or both. Generally, when an excessive number of women is found in a settlement, polygyny is practised; but it is also practised if the fact of having several wives helps a man to live in greater comfort and to acquire greater wealth. This may be the case when remunerative employment can be found in estates and plantations. Polygynous marriages are permitted by the Muduvar who give a superior rank to the first wife. It is in practice among the Adiyar, Aranadar, Chingathar, Vishavar, Uralis, Malakuruvar and Mala Pulayar, and prevalent among the Ulladar and Mala Vedar.[22]

Among the tribes of eastern regions, mostly adult marriage is in vogue. Among most of the the tribes, barring a few exceptions, the boy is always elder than his marrying partner. Although monogamous marriages are held ideal, polygamous marriages in the form of polygamy are found among some tribal groups. For example, among the Saora, many well-to-do persons have got more than one wife. It is a sign of prestige and prosperity on the part of a Saora to have more than one wife. It also implies expansion of hill cultivation and greater accumulation of food grains. The practice of polygamy is also prevalent among other tribal groups. Pre and extra-marital sex relationships are not unseen. Pre-marital sexual chastity is not rigidly insisted upon in a number of tribes.[23] Before marriage love affairs and even intimate relationship are permitted and widely practised among the Bondas, Koyas, Gadabas and Saora tribes. Post-marital laxity is found among the Hos and Oraons during important festivals.[24]

There are rules and regulations which govern the marriage in tribal society. Some of the tribal groups observe clan exogamy while others observe village exogamy. Marriage within the clan is prohibited among the tribes of Orissa. Marriages within the same village is not generally approved.[25] Further, the status of both the parties are given due consideration before finalising the marriage proposal. Payment of bride price forms an integral part. The amount of bride price differs from tribe to tribe. It may be in the form of either cash or kind or both.

Marriage by negotiation, capture, elopement, etc. are the important ways of acquiring mates. Besides levirate, surrogate and cross-cousin marriages are preferred to. Probationary marriages, marriage by trial and intrusion marriage are found in limited areas.[26] Divorce, remarriage of the widow and widower on reasonable grounds are permitted. However, each tribal marriage is accompanied by a lot of feasting and dancing. These are done at the bridegroom's house at his cost. In a note to the Bagata tribes, Mr. C. Hayavadana Rao writes, "the Bagatas are divided into a number of exogamous septs or *intiperulu*". Girls are married either before or after attaining puberty. Cross-cousin marriage is almost obligatory.[27] The system is called 'menarikam'. Bride price is known as "Voli". The bride price is in the form of jewellery by the groom's parents. Among Banjara tribes, as described by Hiralal and Russel, the two parties of a marriage meet at a particular place where bride price is fixed. The groom goes to the bride's house to stay for few days after the negotiation. Widow marriage is prevalent. When a man dies, the widow is taken either by the elder or younger brother of the deceased. Marriage among the Bathudi is an expensive affair when compared with their economic condition. Previously there were marriages by capture and marriages by service. But now these are rarely practised. Widow remarriage is allowed. Divorce with the approval of the village council is prevalent. The most significant and elaborate event in the life of the Bhottaras is their marriage ceremony. They follow both adult and infant marriage systems. Widow remarriage is permitted. Marriage by arrangement and by capture are recognised in the society. The former seems to be honoured and widely prevalent. Polygyny is adopted if the wife is found to be barren. The Bhuiyan tribes adopt both child and adult marriage. Marriage among them is endogamous so far as the main divisions are concerned, but exogamous so far as *Kutumbs* are concerned. Widow marriage is prevalent in their society. Arranged and forced marriages are the practises among the bhumia tribes. Arranged marriages are fixed by the parents of the boy and girl. When the boy is incapable of paying any bride price, he forcibly takes the girl to his house. Bride price in the shape of a fowl and rice is paid. The bhumij tribes practice both child and adult marriage and thus, there is no fixed age for marriage. The most common type of acquiring a bride is through negotiation and by payment of bride rice. Divorce is allowed and divorced women can remarry. The exogamous division of the Bhunjia tribes are derived from those of the Gonds. The Choukathias marry off their daughters before puberty. The marriage takes place in the bridegroom's village. The function is conducted by a priest known as Dinwari. Widow marriage and divorce are permitted; but a husband would often try to avoid it. Among the Binjhals exogamy is the general rule. Marriage is allowed between a boy and a girl having blood relationship. The girls marry after they attain puberty. Child marriage is not followed. The selection of spouses in case of Bonda tribes is left completely to the individual choices. Once such selection is made, the consent of parents are subsequently obtained and marriage rite is performed. Widow marriage is permitted in the Bonda society. The Bonda domestic life is affected by two usual factors. The first is that the wife is often older than the husband. Older girls prefer to marry younger boys who would earn for them when they grow old. Secondly, the husbands are found at times intriguity with younger brother's wife.Arranged marriage is the most commonly prevalent form of marriage among the Dals. In choosing a bride, father's sister's daughter and mother's brother's daughter are preferred to. A person can marry the 'Kanya' or wife of a person belonging to his own clan if the person dies. Arranged marriage is the general rule of Desua Bhumij. But there are also marriages by capture and marriage by intrusion prevalent among them. Marriage is an important social obligation of Dharua tribes. There is no prescribed age for the marriage for both the sexes except that they should marry as early as possible. However, the practice of both child and adult marriages are found among the Dharuas. The widows and widowers are allowed to marry again without any function.

Generally, three forms of marriages are prevalent in the Didayi society. They are *Bihay* or marriage by negotiation, *Gube* or marriage by capture and *Posiamundi* in which the girl forcibly enters the groom's house and enters into sexual relationship with him. Marriage by negotiation is very elaborate and expensive and is generally avoided. Preference is given to cross cousin marriage. Marriage takes place after the attainment of puberty among Gadaba tribes. The usual age of marriage is 19 to 21 years for boys and 15 to 18 years for girls. The cross-cousin marriage is usually preferred to. The marriage of a widow is permitted. Polygyny is also in vogue.

For gond tribes, Marriage is strictly forbidden within the same clan and brother-clans. Cross-cousin marriage, marriage by service and regular marriages arranged by the parents are commonly practised.

Among the Hos, there are various ways of acquiring a mate. The principal among them are *Andi, Diku Andi, Oportipi,*

Rajikhusi and *Anadar*. In the first two types of marriages, ceremony plays an important role. Andi is their traditional form whereas *Diku Andi* is borrowed from the Hindus. Marriage by capture is known as *Oportipi*. The *Rajikhusi* type of marriage is done by mutual consent without any ceremony or bride price whereas *Anadar* is marriage by intrusion. In case of Holva tribes, Girls are usually married off at the age of 10 or 12 before they attain puberty. In case they fail to arrange a bridegroom, they perform the pseudo marriage with a Mahua tree. They adopt two forms of wedding known as 'Small and Large'. The former being held at the bridegroom's place with less expenditure and is much cheaper than the latter which is held at bride's place. Marriage is arranged through a mediator called Mahalia. The small wedding is more popular among the Holvas. The widow and divorced woman can remarry by the simple procedure of marking vermilion on her head. Jatapu Marriages are performed generally after the marrying partners become adults; but child marriage is not completely absent. Various forms of marriage like marriage by arrangement, by capture, by service, by mutual consent, and by selection and negotiation from 'Dhangda Bass' are prevalent among the Jatapus. Remarriages are approved by the society. Divorce is permitted and divorcees are allowed to remarry. Marriage within the same sept is not allowed for the Kawaras. They practise adult marriage. A man can marry his wife's younger sister but marriage with wife's elder sister is prohibited. Marriage by negotiation is common among Kawars. The proposal for a match always comes from the boy's father. The boy's party have to pay the bride price known as 'Sule'. Widow remarriage is permitted except in the Tanwar sub-caste. The younger brother of the deceased has the right to keep her. If the widow intends to marry, she looses her right to property. Neither it involves any ceremony nor does any bride price is paid. Polygamy is permitted, but is not common. Divorce is permitted for serious disagreements or bad conduct on the part of the wife.

Kora tribes adopt both infant and adult marriage. The Hindu marriage ritual has been developed. Polygamy is permitted. The widow is allowed to marry again. The husband can divorce the wife but not vice-versa. Kuli girls are generally married between the age of 5 and 12 years and if a girl is unmarried till puberty, she is married to a bow and arrow tied to a post made up 'Mohua' wood. Divorce is allowed in case of incompatibility of temper or if the wife is unfaithful or is barren. For Mahali tribes, Marriage is arranged by the parents in most cases. Marriage by service and marriage by capture are not uncommon. Widow remarriage is allowed and the younger brothers can marry the deceased brother's wife. Divorce is permitted.Cross-cousin marriage is the rule of Matya tribes. In case of refusal, the male is entitled for compensation from the boy who marries her. Bride price is paid. The four forms of marriage such as *Jhiamaga* (arranged), marriage by elopement, captured marriage and marriage by service are adopted. The widow and divorced women are allowed to remarry. Marriage is of great importance in the life cycle of a Mirdha. Marriage by negotiation is the common occurrence. Divorce is socially approved and divorced women can remarry. At times, the Omanatyas take recourse to marriage by elopement and marriage by service as is the case with Bhottaras. But Cross-cousin marriage is the general rule. The instances are very rare. Polygamy is allowed. The younger brother marries the wife of the deceased elder brother. Widow and divorced women can marry again. The Oraon tribe is emphatically and rigidly endogamous. A person marrying from any lower or higher caste would be outcasted and at no cost he or she would be readmitted into the tribe. A bride belonging to one's mother's totemic group is given the first preference in marriage. Marriage among them is monogamous though polygamy is practised in certain cases. In case of Paraja tribes, Marriage is strictly prohibited by the members of the same clan. Cross-cousin marriage is the general rule. Marriage is performed after the boy attains 18 years of age and the girl is above 15 years. Marriage by arrangement is the common form of marriage but a few cases of marriages other than arranged marriages like love marriage, marriage by capture, marriage of the widows and the divorced women are seen.

The Pentiya tribes adopt adult marriage though the occurrence of child marriage is not rare. Cross-cousin marriage is preferred to. The widows can marry again. The younger brother may keep the wife of the deceased elder brother. Polygamy is permitted. The Rajuar tribes practise both adult and infant marriage. Polygamy is allowed. Widow remarriage in the Sarga form is prevalent. Divorce is allowed on reasonable grounds such as adultery, incompatibility of temper, etc. Lanjia marriage is not an elaborate affair. The most common form of marriage among them is arranged marriage. They have also marriage by capture and by service. Marriage by arrangement is the regular type of marriage prevalent among the Saharas. Love marriages are also not infrequent among them. A widow is at liberty to remarry. Marriage amongst the Sounti tribes is mostly adult and there is no bar for child marriage. Bride price is paid by the groom before marriage. Polygamy is permitted and widow remarriage is allowed.

Youth Dormitory

The youth dormitory is a social organisation among some tribes. It discharges certain responsibilities to the community. Sometimes guests are accommodated here. People, young and old, meet here for recreation.[28] In Eastern India, this institution functions among many tribal communities in some form or other. It is variously called by different tribal groups. The Juangs call it *Majang* and *Darbar*, the Kondhs call it *Dindaghar*, the Bhuinyas call it *Dhangarabsa* and among the Bondas, it goes by the name *Ingersin*. It is chiefly used by the boys and some times by the girls to seek one another's company in singing, dancing and lovemaking. Secrecy is maintained as regards to the happenings inside the dormitory This happens particularly in view of the fact that amorous affairs are freely carried on inside the dormitories, although sexual relationship is not generally permitted within the walls. The significance of the dormitories lies in the training that they provide to the members. The scope of the training imparted at dormitories is much broader than that provided in the school. Training in dormitories cause no tension because both play and recreation go hand in hand with training. This brings about a harmonious parent-child relationship.[29] The Oraon bachelors in a village spend nights in a dormitory, participate in ceremonial hunts, helps in the villagers on marriage occasions and other festivals, look after the comforts of the guests who are accommodated in the bachelor's house and so on.[30]

Women's Position in Tribal Society

Although the tribal society is patriarchal and marriage is polygynous, women enjoy a high status and women have their distinct position. Women being an economic asset are not treated as chattels. In the economic activities, they work more than men. They do the household work, rear children and prepare food. The men, therefore, are mostly dependent on them for their livelihood.

Women in food gatherer hunter appropriation and in extensive system of agriculture (slash and burn), do the major portion of the labour and provide a major part of the maintenance for the family. The rise of lineage means that there is a differential access to production of resources. Women's labour is crucial in realising the possibilities of differential accumulation.[31] Male domination increases in these tribes as we move away from some reliance on food gathering to a fully settled agriculture. Male domination is stronger among the Santhals who depend on agriculture for livelihood. But, for all these tribes, the right of a woman to her earnings still holds.[32]

POLITICAL STRUCTURE

The Scheduled tribes had a strong, well organised and a neatly structured political system. Their Political Organisation, it is believed, developed even before the formation of coordinated social structure of other communities. But the political organisation of the aboriginal tribes in India which comprised of a wide range of forms was much disturbed and virtually superseded by the modern Indian Government. The early and primitive tribes had literally no political structure. Among the nomadic food gatherers and hunters, and also many of the vagrant tribes and castes, the disciplinary and juridical matters of the groups are managed by the heads of the family. They have usually no chiefs or head of groups.

The Political Structure of Primitive cultivators is inextricably blended with their land tenure system. Feudalism in India developed during the rule of the Maurya and Gupta dynasties. The rights of land became divided among the chiefs of state, the village communities and the individual cultivators. The monarchy had gone independent on the eve of the Muslim invasion. They largely disowned the village communities and usurped proprietary rights over all the land. The new tenant cultivators were scarcely aware of this change as long as land was freely available. Where the new ownership was enforced they could always retreat into the virgin forest, clear some land and prepare new fields. But feudalism spread even into the heart of the tribal communities when prominent clan, village, and district headmen of the Mundas, Gonds and Korkus, the Bhils and other tribes turned themselves into chiefs or rajas, adopted the royal style, usurped all the land of the community over which they ruled and gave parts of the lands to Brhamin priests and court officials. Their tribal subjects, thus, are reduced to mere tenants in their own habitat.

During the British Regime, the British Tenancy Acts took away all the communally-owned land which remained with the tribals and gave, sold or auctioned it off to land lords. The fallout was that even those tribals who had till then retained their lands, were reduced to tenants. They were at the sheer mercy of landlords who more often gave their land to more efficient Hindu farmers for cultivation in order to get a better return. Increasing scarcity of arable land and oppressive exploitation were the consequences. This ultimately led to severe tribal unrest and occasionally in armed revolts. The Hos, Santals, Mundas, Maler and Kols repeatedly revolted against their oppressors and suppressers.

In western India as well as northern India, before independence, the jagirdari system of land tenure was in force. The jagirdar behaved as if he were the owner of the land and exercised control over his tenants. He fixed the rent for the land, much in excess over the amount he paid to the

Government. Usually, he also usurped the right of turning out tenants and taking others who promised to pay more rent. This resulted in rack-renting as lands were let out to the highest bidder. The tenants, in addition, had to do forced labour and to render other services also. Moreover, they had no security of tenure. Due to this suppressive nature of the jagirdars, tribal discontent in western India was high and sometimes exploded into bloody revolts. The Bhils, Naikdas and Kolis often revolted when exploitation became unbearable. After Independence, the jagirdari system was abrogated in 1952, with a subsequent amendment in 1954.

The scenario was different in eastern India. The tribal land belonged either to the village or clan community. Village leaders or clan elders played a key role. Field plots were distributed to the families by the clan or village elders. Plots under cultivation were either inherited from generation to generation, or redistributed at certain time-intervals. But the outside usurpers or land grabbers created havoc everywhere. There was that slow but inexorable advance of the land-hungry Assamese or Bengali peasants population which greedily appropriated every available field-plot. The tribals were no match to the peasants of the plains in efficiency of farming or in holding on to the land and they could not resist the dominant force.

Barring a few small communities in South India, the majority of the tribals were either food gatherers or shifting cultivators. They had no land as during the 'settlement transactions', most of the tribal land was appropriated by cultivators and by large estates, tea gardens, coffee and rubber plantations which were started at that time. The tribals were allowed to live on their old hunting and collecting grounds as before as long as land was plentiful. With the increase in Population, the labourers and farmers from the plains were introduced and invaded the hills and jungles and they settled down to farm gradually.

The primitive cultivator has a governing body. It is usually the council of elders of the village community. Normally it is called panch or panchayat. There are no chiefs but only headmen. These headmen are only ceremonial and do not have much power over their subjects. Mainly, a democratic tribal council controls matters concerning the welfare of the tribal group and especially racial and ritual purity. It consists of the headmen of a number of village councils which may meet and decide matters of great importance.

The tribes in north-eastern central India, however, of much greater numerical strength. They are more conscious of their importance and have a more elaborate political organisation. They have a system of federation as well as a confederation structure. Not only do they have village councils and more influential headmen, with other village officials in support, but often well established headmen over a number of villages, a sort of confederacy of village communities. Their annual meeting is often initiated by a ceremonial hunt and other ceremonies. In the past, these headmen occasionally assumed princely powers and became rajas, often with disastrous consequences to their tribal subjects.

Democratic tribal councils also exist side by side with the institution of chiefs in the eastern regions of India, Assam, Orissa and the adjoining regions. These chiefs are either elected or inheriting their position. There is also a more pronounced hierarchy within certain tribes, with ruling families, commoners, and even slaves. Judicial cases of some of the tribes are settled by open-air assemblies. They also decide over the tribal policy and execute administration. The individual members are bound to attend these assemblies which in their parlance are darbar. Sanction of these assemblies is mandatory without which the chiefs cannot dispose over land or forest, cannot impose taxes nor promulgate new laws.

After independence, scenario changed drastically. Increasing pressure of the administrative control of the Indian Government threatened the traditional political organisation of the tribal communities in India, permitted to function until recent times by an ineffective or indulgent Government during the pre-British and even throughout the British times. The leaders of the National Congress Party viewed the traditional panchayat system as beneficial for better governance and sponsored it and tried into the administrative system of India.

But, their experiment did not yield expected result. Their political system protected by the Indian Government often acts as a parallel governing body, working side by side and often against the traditional panchayat system which is still in vogue. The result is that this has caused in the decay and often complete breakdown of the traditional as well as the newly introduced panchayat raj systems of Government.

Sensing gradual disempowerment, the Indian tribals have in some areas started active movements for a certain degree of political autonomy and self-rule or even for complete independence. Such movements however, were not found in south India where the tribals are more scattered and were often completely demoralised and without any influence. In ChotaNagpur where the tribals were especially strong and vigorous, live in great concentration and were numerically very strong, where they also had a tradition of self-rule in the past and even boast of rulers and princes of their own, the Jharkhand Movement was born and found a powerful leader in an educated Munda, Jaipal Singh. Even after his downfall and death, the Jharkhand Movement did not die out though it faced strong opposition from the non-tribal classes of the area as well as from the Congress party. The carriers of the Jharkhand Movement aspire at an autonomous state within the Indian Union in which the tribals would rule themselves.

The demand for political freedom was also aired by the tribes of Nagaland. In Nagaland, it was especially the Mizos who pressed for autonomy and even complete independence. Various attempts had been made to achieve political independence, sometimes even with the assistance of foreign neighbouring countries who had an interest in existence of small buffer states between themselves and India. The leaders of these independence movements were partly Christians, since the Christians in these areas formed the most educated groups and consequently more fervently desired self-rule and political independence. The aborigines of central India had in the past no strong tribal unity and solidarity. Some of the important tribes like the Bhils and Gonds had not and never had an organisation comprising all the members of the tribe.

They rather lived in small groups gathering only a small number of village communities in a certain area as a social unit. The Bhil tribe in particular was broken up into many unconnected sub-sections which even had different names and partly mixed with non-tribal communities. Thus, the splintered groups of different tribes could not translate their desires for political freedom in to action.

This absence of tribal solidarity was certainly one of the main reasons why the tribals of central India, in spite of their numerical strength in certain districts, were politically so powerless. Some other factors were doubtlessly their general poverty and backwardness, their high rate of illiteracy, their sheer indifference and non-inclination to greater political issues and to affairs beyond their immediate concern and need.

Unfortunately, even those few tribal representatives who have succeeded in getting themselves elected to the legislative assemblies and to parliament are often either alienated from tribal culture and have adopted a strongly non-tribal outlook and mode of living (graduates, landlords, local chiefs), or they are so inarticulate and inexperienced in their new and strange surroundings that they cannot play an effective part in political life. No wonder that such representatives are hardly able, or scarcely try, to defend the interests of their tribal compatriots on the political platform.[33]

Till recent times, however, some degree of tribal consciousness and the existence of a tribal leadership could be found only in Chota Nagpur. It was there till formation of a separate Jharkhand State. But the tribal leaders in these areas had raised to demand for a separate state with the ardent intention that they would be left to themselves, could rule and govern themselves and be rid forever of any interference by non-tribals. The underlying motives for this demand was a nostalgic desire for a return to a happy past, aversion to outsiders exploiting them and interfering with their traditional way of living, and above all a desire for working out their own fate.

The Khasis and Syntengs in eastern India, closely allied to one another, are divided into four clans: the royal, priestly, minister and plebeian clans. The chiefs are always taken from the royal or priestly clan; clanship is inherited in the female line.

Every Ho village in eastern india is a social as well as a political unit. The headman is the supreme controller of the village. They are gradually developing in all aspects of life and are coming forward to associate themselves with the national endeavour for progress and prosperity.

A systematic and definite order of precedence is there in public and state affairs among the clans, but no social barrier exists with regard to intermarriage. One of the redeeming features is that their social position is indicated less by the shape and material of the house but by the pattern and colours of the clothes worn. However, the chiefs' houses are usually larger. The post of chief is hereditary and not through nomination or election. The dignity of a chief is inherited by the eldest son of the eldest sister, after his death by his eldest brother or by the maternal grand-nephew. If male heirs are absent, the eldest sister (or eldest sister's daughter) has the right to succession. The queen, in turn, is then succeeded by her eldest son or another male relative. Politically, the Khasi area was in the past divided into twenty five Khasi states which were independent. Though headed by a chief who is called 'siem', administration was on democratic lines. A Khasi chief was only a ceremonial post. He had no powers over land or forests. He had no authority to impose taxes or promulgate new laws or any policy without the Darbar's consent. Such a Darbar was an open-door assembly in which all the male adults of the state took part. Attendance was compulsory.

The plitical organisation of the Bodo tribal group is in the process of steady dissolution. The communities living in the hills only are still able to retain their old tribal customs and laws, while in the valleys, the Bodos are in the habit of replacing them for Hindu customs, rules and regulations. Discipline of tribals with regard to clan laws has considerably weakened. The Garos, one of the Bodo tribes, are much sub-divided. They have four main clans, each of which has numerous exogamous sections. Their political structure is democratic. Heads of families play a vital role in decision making process and political affairs. In fact the Garos have no chiefs. The headman is only a nominal head. Important affairs are decided by village councils consisting of elders or heads of families, including the headmen.

There is three tier administrative structure in case of Mikir tribes. In their threefold village administration, the lowest office is filled by the Achom Asar, usually an old, influential man well versed in Mikir customs. He is appointed by a Habe, the next higher authority, the headman of a village whose jurisdiction does not go beyond the limits of the village. But he settles all disputes within his village. The Habe is, in turn, appointed by a Pinpo who is selected from the clan to which his predecessor belonged. Over all the Pinpos is the Karbi Recho, a Mikir king. Hajong tribe is a small Bodo tribe, akin to the Garos. A part of the tribe has descended from the the Garo hills into the Surma valley. This descent into the valley resulted in the formation of two sections, one, the upper, remaining true to its tribal ways of life, while the lower valley section became Hinduised and abandoned even its tribal dialect for a corrupt form of Bengali. Of the Bodo tribes on the southern slopes of the Himalayas, the Abors have a chief and a council in every village. All affairs of the community are discussed in the village hall called morang. Even the type of daily work is discussed first in the morang and a resolution must be passed before work can begin. The village boys act as messengers and run through the village lanes making the council decisions known to everyone.

The headmen of Akas tribes are chosen by the people. The villages of the Akas are governed by councils presided over by headmen. But the two largest villages have influential ranis (queens) descended from the old ruling family. The Akas are a warlike community, and in addition to their general title which is not used by them and the meaning of which is unknown, they have two sub-divisions, each of which is known to the Assamese by a title implying 'plunder'. The Galong community is ruled by a village council presided over by a headman who acquired his position by wealth and personal influence. In the past the Galongs were a warlike race, blood-revenge and plunder being the purposes of their raids. The Daflas, another Bodo tribe, live in small unstable viallges which are loose aggregations of long-houses and in the past were constantly involved in feuds, murders, kidnappings and the theft of cattle. They still are a happy-go-lucky, swashbuckling people, occasionally infringing on their hard-working agrarian neighbours, the Apa Tanis.

Naga villages present a different picture. The political organisation of the Naga tribes is marked by great diversity. Some of the Naga tribes are subject to chiefs who rule almost autocratically, while other tribes form democratic village communities in which the headman has only a nominal authority. On the whole it can be stated that the Naga tribes are organised on democratic lines; only two tribes, the Konyaks and the Semas, having autocratic chiefs. Bachelors' halls of Naga tribes are the real centres of social and political life and most of the Naga tribes have bachelors' halls though less so among the Angami and Sema Nagas. Usually each clan has its own morung, as these youth dormitories are called in Assamese. It acts as a Socio-cultural ahd political centre of the tribes. The unmarried men sleep there, and strangers are accommodated in it. All public affairs of the clan are transacted in morung.

In the northern district, the Konyaks are subject to a chief who is sacrosanct and tabooed, and rules often several villages with much authority. He is regarded as the repository of tribal fortune, virtue, or its life-principle. In some villages he is , or was, so heavily tabooed that he was not permitted to touch the ground, and on a journey had to be carried, and leaves and branches were spread wherever he sat down. He never tries to enjoy powers and position. His very sanctity prevented him from exercising his powers.

The Angamis of Naga tribes reside in unusually large villages some containing as many as 800 houses. The villages are set upon hills, and carefully stockaded and guarded against eventual attacks. The primary unit of the tribe is not, however, the village, but a sub-division of the population thus concentrated, called khel or tepfu, which is exogamous. It is said that the word is derived from a single ancestor. Faction fights between these bodies are frequent and used to be bloody. Sometimes, outside help was called in to take part. The Ao Nagas live in villages which are independent democratic units. These villages are only nominally governed by a headman. The constitution of an Ao village community is intricate; it consists of elders representing various clans and kinship groups governing for fixed, though fluctuating, periods. Entrance into the Ao dormitory was given to the boys periodically every three years, while those age grades that were allowed to leave the morung and to marry entered the lowest grades of the village council. A regular custom among them was the enslavement of members of the neighbouring tribes, now more or less suppressed. The victims were treated well, except when paid over as fine or ransom to another village, when they were usually sacrificed.

The post of headman or chief is a hereditary in case of Sema Nagas. He is endowed with considerable authority and privileges. But he can retain his ruling power only if he is able to persuade his younger brothers and sons to leave the native village and settle with their retainers elsewhere. It is believed that if they remain in the village they can claim share in his authority, which of course soon reduces his political power considerably. The Sema Nagas have no morung. The front part of the chief's house is usually the meeting place where public affairs are discussed. The Kuki-chin group in the Kachar hills, on the other hand , with the exception of the Rangkos are all organised under the rule of hereditary chiefs. They are very clannish, and evince great solidarity with their chiefs and fellow clansmen. The Rangkos has a system to elect a headman for each village and allow him to manage its affairs. The Lushais, of the same race as the Thados or Kukis, live in villages headed by entirely independent chiefs. They have certain duties towards their fellow villagers, and in return, receive a certain share of each man's crops. At times, Thado chief exercise enormous powers and become autocrat. The only remedy against a too despotic headman is flight and change of one's allegiance to another village headman.

In south India, the tribes love to lead a secluded life. They mostly live in small groups dispersed in jungles or in the outskirts of the villages of the cultivators. Usually they live a life of their own and try to avoid interference from outsiders, be they government officials, police, social workers, or junior or senior officers of the block including block development officers or even people of other castes. They simply want to remain aloof and pursue their own way of life what they learnt from their parents and forefathers .Of them, a few ambitious or educated people want to get on in life and to improve their status both socially and economically. They have long since separated and have been assimilated in the main villages of the plains. They think themselves civilised and superior and look down upon their fellow tribesman.

Some of the nomadic tribes have no such institution as a headman of a settlement or a group. Only heads of each families manage their problems. The heads of the single families simply come together and settle the affairs of the group whenever problems arise and decisions have to be taken. Other tribes, however, have the institution of headmen. He may be elected as such and can be deposed when they become unable to carry out their duties or for some reason or other loses the authority or respect of the community, which so far they have enjoyed. In other tribes, the office of a headman is hereditary and often connected with a certain family or clan. In more developed tribes, the headman may even be assisted by other office bearers to whom specific duties are assigned. Their offices are also hereditary. In Kerala, the Allar and Aranadar have no headmen. Affairs of the community are discussed at a gathering of elders whose decision is normally binding. Those who disagree with the decisions, he has to simply leave the group and join another one. While social disputes and even cases of marital infidelity, etc; are usually settled amicably, sometimes serious quarrels may result over the just distribution of a kill in a hunt and a compromising and mutually agreed formula is devised by the elders of the group.

The Chingather of Cannanore district, too, do not seem to have headman. But they have a priest who performs multifarious functions of the clan. He accomplishes the ceremonies at their spirit dance. This priest may play the role of a headman as well. Members of a family are supposed to obey the senior male member. The same is true of the Erâvallar. The institution of a headman that existed in their early society has practically disappeared. In their settlements, it is now the much respected priest who performs the duties of a headman as well in addition to his normal functions. Among the Kadar, too, the hereditary institution of the headman (muppan) has ceased to exist. The Kochuvelar, too, have priests who act occasionally as headmen. The Koragar do not seem to have headmen. Headman is conspicuous in its absence among the Mala Vedar, a very primitive tribe of hunters and food gatherers. Even among other food gathering tribes, where he exists, he had not much to say except to preside over some ceremonies at a birth or marriage.

In case of the Mala Vettuvar tribes, the office of the headman is not hereditary for he is usually appointed by the landlord for whom the group works. The headman was enjoying certain rights and privileges, but at present he only receives little attention and commands and only slight obedience. The Malayadiyar do not seem to have headmen in their settlements. The Mathas do have a headman in their settlement but he is seldom obeyed or treated with respect. The only privilege he enjoys is an invitation to a wedding or a funeral feast. Among the Kurumar tribes, only some groups have a headman. Their social problems are usually discussed and decided at a tribal meeting consisting of elders. The headman presides over it if he is present. Among the Kannikar, the headman was in the past an important and influential person entitled to the contributions of the community of which he was the head. But in present times his status has declined considerably. The Karavar tribes respect and obey their headman and his wife. He has an assistant and an executive officer. His office is hereditary. In the past, the community had to cultivate his fields and maintain him but today no contributions are made.

The headman is often also the priest of the community. The Kattunayakar, too, respect and obey their headman; nothing can happen in a settlement without his approval. In the past he had civil and criminal jurisdiction over his community. He is often the priest and shaman of the settlement and acts as their oracle. He commands a respectable position in their clan. Among the Kudiyar, the headman is still an important person though not as much as in the past. He is at the same time their priest who performs the weddings and funerals and other ceremonies. Disputes are settled by a council of four or five elders. Among the Kundu Vedar, the headman plays the same role. Among the Malakarar, the headman is still an important person. The community makes small contributions to him. He is being constantly informed about everything that happens in the settlement. Often he is also the priest. His office is hereditary and is inherited by his nephew. Among the Mala Kuruvar the headman is so important that a member of the settlement who disobeys him is outcasted. The Mala Kuruvar, have even a council of headmen. But in a settlement, decisions are taken in a meeting of elders over which the headman presides. The Mala Malasar have, as a headman, a person with outstanding abilities and skill, courage, and bravery. Besides, knowledge of the forest and a talent for hunting are the requisite qualities of a headman. He must be present at all important functions in the settlement. The headman of the Mala Pandarams and his wife are treated with respect. His office is hereditary. Thus, the political organisation of tribes in South India and procedure of management of their clan affairs is very strong, systematic and well coordinated.

Recent Initiatives

Recently, some perceptible changes have been taking place in the political arena in tribal areas. Tribal Advisory Councils have been constituted in some areas to look into such matters pertaining to the welfare and advancement of the Tribal communities. Certain tribal areas have been designated as autonomous Districts and Autonomous Regions and also District Councils, Autonomous Councils and Regional

Councils have been constituted for administration of the Scheduled Areas.

In a move towards political empowerment of scheduled tribes, there are some constitutional provisions for reservation of seats for the Scheduled Tribes; in the House of People under Article 330, in the Legislative Assemblies of the states under Article 332 and in every Panchayats under Article 243D. Besides, to ensure effective participation of the tribals in the process of decision making, planning and execution, there is extension of the 73rd and 74th Amendments of the Constitution to the Scheduled Areas through the Provisions of the Panchayats (Extension to the Scheduled Areas) Act. All these efforts and initiatives have a definite and positive impact towards making the Scheduled Tribes politically sensitive and conscious.

NOTES AND REFERENCES

1. R.R. Prasad (1989), *Bhotia Tribals of India, Dynamics of Economic Transformation*, Gian Publishing House, New Delhi, p. 7.
2. Sarkar, S.S. (1954), The Aboriginal races of India, Calcutta.
3. Ferreira, J.V. (1965), Totemism in India; Oxford University Press, Bombay.
4. Fuchs, Stephen (1973), The Aboriginal tribes of India, Macmillan India, p. 142.
5. Fuchs, Stephen; *ibid*, p. 245.
6. Totemism refers to that social organisation of tribe, which is associated with a form of supernaturalism consisting of certain typical attitudes towards species of animals or plants or classes of natural objects.
7. K.K. Verma (1977), *Culture, Economy and Population*, National Publishing House, New Delhi, p. 92.
8. S.C. Patnaik and S. Patel (1982), "Impact of Modernisation of Tribals, Economic Dualism and Path of Change (A Case Study of Malkangiri Subdivision of Koraput District", Paper presented in the Seminar on Prospects of Economic Development of Koraput District held in October, (Mimeo), pp. 6-7.
9. *Tribes of Orissa*, (Ed.) H.&T.W. Department, Government of Orissa, p. 264.

10. P.K. Mohapatra,"Dhanua", in *Tribes of Orissa,* p. 95.
11. J.P. *Rout,* "Godaba", in *Tribes of Orissa,* p. 103.
12. *The Imperial Gazetteer of India,* Vol. X, 1908, p. 153.
13. M.V. Grigson (1938), *The Maria Gonds of Bastar,* Bombay, p. 42.
14. N.P. Mohapatro, "A Study of the Social and Health Conditions of Saora Tribe in Orissa", in B.C. Ray (ed.), *Tribes of Orissa, op. cit.,* p. 84.
15. S.S. Shashi, *Our Tribal Children,* p. 6.
16. S. Routray, "Holva", in *Tribes of Orissa,* p. 119.
17. B.C. Ray (1989), *Tribes of Orissa, The Changing Socio-Economic Profile,* Gian Publishing House, New Delhi, p. XII.
18. P.S. Das, "Kondha", in *Tribes of Orissa,* p. 138.
19. L.K. Mohapatro and N.C. Das, *Tribes: Problems of Today and Tomorrow,* p. 9.
20. Desmond Morris and Peter Marsh (1988), *Tribes,* Pyramid Books, London, p. 101.
21. Fuchs, Stephen (1973), The Aboriginal tribes of India, Macmillan India, pp.55-56.
22. (i) Aiyappan, A. (1955), 'The Tribes of South and South-east India' in, the Adivasis, the Government of India, Delhi.

    (ii) Fuchs, Stephen (1973), The Aboriginal Tribes of India, Macmillan India, pp. 250-251
23. P.C. Mohapatra, *Economic Development of Tribal India,* p. 68.
24. *Ibid.,* p. 69.
25. Nilamani Senapati and N.K. Sahu, in *Tribes of Orissa,* Government of Orissa, Bhubaneswar, pp. 129-130.
26. D.N. Majumdar and T.N. Madan, *An Introduction to Social Anthropology,* Asia Publishing House, 1980, pp. 86-91.
27. A.C. Sahoo, "Bagata", in *Tribes of Orissa,* Government of Orissa, Bhubaneswar, p. 34.
28. (i) P.C. Mohapatra, *op. cit.,* p. 66

    (ii) B.B. Jena, *op. cit.,* p. 243.

29 D.N. Majumdar and T.N. Madan (1980), *An Introduction to Social Anthropology, Asia Publishing House,* p. 139.

30. P.S. Das, in *Tribes of Orissa*, Government of Orissa, Bhubaneswar, pp. 107-108.
31. D.N. Majumdar (1988), "Significance of Women's Position in Tribal Society", *Economic and Political Weekly*, Vol. XXIII, No. 26, June 25, p. 1311
32. *Ibid.*, p. 1312.
33. Fuchs, Stephen (1973), The Aboriginal tribes of India, Macmillan India, p. 144.

5 TRIBAL CULTURE

Culture can be used to convey various meanings. It stands for beliefs, ideas, customs, law, morals, art and other capabilities and skills acquired by men and women as a member of the society. A person's culture is what he has in totality of his life and interests.[1] The tribal people express and display their cultural identity and distinctiveness in their social organisations through their languages, rituals, festivals and through their dress, ornaments, art and craft.

RITUALS AND FESTIVALS

The traditions and taboos, beliefs and behaviour of scheduled tribes are reflected in their Rituals and Festivals. The amazing conglomeration of traditions, beliefs, sorrows and philosophies that together constitute and vitalise the religion of the tribes has descended from antiquity and has been preserved unimpaired to the present day. Every facet of their life covering activities round the year is intimately connected with religion. It is these aspects of their culture that gives meaning and depth to their lives and solidarity to their social structure.[2]

The tribes believe that their life and work are controlled by supernatural beings whose abode is around them in hills, forests, rivers and houses. It is very difficult to standardise the Gods and spirits as their composition continually changes when old ones are forgotten with the introduction of new ones. Their Gods differ from one another in composition, function, character and nature. Some are benevolent, some are neutral and some are malevolent. The malevolent spirits and Gods are cared more than their benevolent counterparts as they can bring misery.

Manipulation of environment being the main concern of the tribals, all the ritual acts are directed towards stimulating natural processes. Illness or misfortune is attributed to displeasure and malicious act of the Gods or ancestors. The sacrifice of different kinds of life-stock, accompanied by all the rites and ceremonials of fetishism is considered appropriate appeasement. Moreover, their extremely superstitious nature prohibits the undertaking of any enterprise unless the Gods are first interrogated and the omens, after being carefully considered, are adjudged to be propitious.

The ceremonies and festivals of the tribes can be classified into two groups, that is, those related to the individual families and those that relate to the village as a whole. The ceremonies and rites relating to birth of a child, marriage, death are observed family-wise whereas those relating to various agricultural cycle, eating of new fruits, hunting, etc. are observed by the village community. Some of the important festivals observed by the tribal communities include Guar Ceremony of the Saora, *Gotar* of the Gadaba, *Push Punei* of the Juang, *Kedu* of the Kondh, *Karam* festival of the Oraon and *Chaitparab* of the Bonda and *Magha Parab* of the Santal. With the advent of time, traces of borrowing from Hindu pantheon and religious ceremonies are noticed among these tribes. They have started worshipping Siva, Parbati and Lord Jagannath. Hindu festivals like *Raja, Laxmipuja, Dasahara* and *Gumha* are also becoming popular among them day by day. Among the tribes, there are religious functionaries who cater to their ritual as well as spiritual needs. The hierarchy of priests among the Saoras may be divided into three categories. The *Buyya* is a priest who presides at agricultural festivals and offers sacrifices that especially characterise their occasion. The *Kuden* combines the functions of priest, prophet and medicine man. The sacerdotal head among the Juang is called *Nagam* or *Buita, Pujari* or *Sisa* among the Bonda and *Jani* among the Kondh. The post of these officials are mostly ascribed but not achieved.

Taking the case of other tribes, the Bhuiyans perform public feasts and festivals all the year round so as to ensure safety and prosperity in their seasonal occupations. They are very fond of dance and music. The bhumia tribes are divided into totemistic units or clans. In their community, the clan organisation is a simple one. In every village *Naik* is the accepted leader. He is ordinarily the richest man possessing land and cattle in opulence. *Bhat Naik* is second in the hierarchy. Both these offices are ordinarily hereditary. The Bhunjias, in spite of their strict observance of many rites for virtual parity, they rank lower in status than the Gonds. They have their own method of curing and they hardly go to Government dispensary for medicine. The most popular method of curing disease is by branding the skin with a hot iron. The festivals observed by the Binjhia tribes are Hindu festivals. They are *Rath Jatra, Gamha Purnima, Dashara, Holi* and *Dipavali*. The calanderical year of the Birhor centres round three seasons i.e., rainy season, winter season and summer season. Their movement from place to place is more frequent in summer than in other seasons.[3] The frequent change of settlements is primarily responsible for search of livelihood. Some groups of Birhors change their place of abode frequently that indicates the extent of availability of forest products in different areas. Moreover, the destruction of the forest by some other tribal communities who practice shifting cultivation and by non-tribal people who gather fuel wood from the forest make it difficult for the Birhors to earn their livelihood. The Bonda tribes concentrate on or near the high hills, named after the tribe as Bonda hills. Though few in number, the tribe has successfully retained the distinctive features of its culture, chiefly on account of its geographical isolation and more perhaps due to its stubborn and independent spirit. The Bondas call themselves 'Remo' and speak a very difficult Austro-Asiatic language belonging to Mundari group. The Bonda houses are individual huts with some enclosure either in its front or around it. The walls are of mud mixed with straw or these are plastered bamboo. The roof is supported by a number of wooden pillars and is thatched with grass. The modern civilisation has not changed them very much. They maintain their primitive custom and tradition.[4] The Bhumij tribes celebrate every festival and the marriage ceremonies with dance and music. Girls in a row dance while the boys play on changu. The acculturated Gonds live in villages inhabited by other castes and tribes. They especially live along with Kondh, Bhuyan and Gour. The primitive Gonds live in homogeneous villages. The Juangs principally observe festivals like *Amba Nuakhia, Dhana Nuakhia* and *Magha Parab.* They give high priority to music and dancing.[5] The Kolhas have the specialisation in crafts too. Some families in the village have the reputation of being competent brewers and they are approached to brew liquor at the time of feasts and festivals. Basket-making and rope-making from Bobai grass is a skill possessed by everybody. Mahali festivals are mostly communal in nature. Every festival is marked by communal dancing and music. They have separate dance and song for separate occasions. Both males and females dance. Their priest is called *Naga*. The Parenga tribes are fond of dance and music. The important dances are Dhemesha Nach, Gotar Nach and Ghumura Nach.

DANCE, SONG AND MUSIC

Songs are sung alone or in company, when grazing the cattle, doing fieldwork, on long journeys or in the evenings and especially at dances. Songs differ according to the seasons. They run the whole range of human emotions; they sing not only of the eternal beauty of nature, but of all human relations, of love and hatred, praise and mockery, reverence and bitter sarcasm. Many songs deal with religion, the praise of Gods and the Goddesses, they may be prayers and invocations. Songs accompany wedding and funeral ceremonies. Occasionally, they describe in ballad form important events in the history of the tribe, or the life of heroes. Women sing when rocking the cradle to Lull their babies into sleep, or when they are grinding the grain early in the morning; sometimes in gatherings of women and of course during the dance. The melodies of the tribals are usually very simple and have no wide range of tunes in complicated keys. They please, and often intoxicate, singers and audience more through incessant repetition than through the variety of melodies.[3]

The Scheduled Tribes posses a wide range of instruments and materials for the purpose of their music. They have various instruments to produce their simple music. They, very often manufacture their musical instruments themselves, out of primitive materials ready at hand. Their primary instrument is the drum. They usually have a great variety of drums. The most important basis for their singing and dancing is rhythm. Accomplished drummers are much sought after and often invited for meetings and dances. The flute is also the main instrument and second in importance. It is played in certain seasons, often by boys herding cattle and goats. Many tribals make a variety of wind instruments out of the dried shells of gourds. With strings of gut or other materials string instruments are fabricated of bamboo or wood. These instruments are usually used in accompaniment to songs along with the drum which is their main instrument.

The tribals normally dance in a group. They have a great number of dances, which are danced only in certain seasons. A special feature of tribal singing and dancing is that of their social character. Tribals hardly ever sing and dance singly. They sing and dance for their own pleasure in jolly company and good fellowship, not for the entertainment of an audience. Men have their own dances, as have also the women, but certain dances are in mixed company, a row of men facing a row of women, with the musicians standing and playing between the two rows which advance and retreat. The most famous dance in eastern central India is the Karma dance with a branch of the sacred tree kept in an upright position in the centre of the dancers. But the tribals have also mimic dances in which they imitate certain animals, the peacock, or the tiger, for instance. For some dances they put on masks, or ride hobby-horses, or dress up as Hindu mendicant monks, as officials, policemen or Europeans. Most of the dances, danced communally, follow a simple pattern. They please and intoxicate the tribal people mainly through the incessant repetition of certain simple rhythms and tunes in harmony with corresponding dance steps and body movements. The tribal dancers can carry on for hours and often throughout the night.[7]

Mixed dancing and the generous consumption of alcoholic drinks during the dance are, however, viewed with strong disapproval by puritanical Hindus and Hinduised tribal leaders. For this reason, communal dancing among the tribals is gradually being abandoned. With the decay of tribal dancing, the other arts, too suffer. No one bothers any more to prepare the elaborate dancing costumes or to fabricate the musical instruments used in the dance; the songs inspired by the rhythms of the drum and the melody of the instruments remain uncomposed, and the tribal life becomes dull and drab, lacking the excitement of the senses caused by this artistic combination of sound, rhythm and movement. Besides, commercialisation of tribal dance is also another reason for decay and abandonment of their traditional dances. The style and structure of dances change gradually and now a days it has a tinge and flavour of modernity.

The tribes, despite poverty and preoccupation with the continual battle for survival, have retained the rich and varied heritage of colourful dance and music[8] which forms an integral part of their festivals and rituals. Among them, the dance and music is developed and maintained by themselves in tradition without aid and intervention of any professional dancer or teacher. Among the tribals, dance and music constitute a way of life. The performance of these only gives expression to their inner feelings, mode of self-expression, their joys and sorrows, natural affections and passions and appreciation of beauty in nature and in human beings.

Although the pattern of dance and music prevalent among them vary from tribe to tribe, there are certain features common to all. Tribal dances have some accompaniments by means of which the rhythm is maintained. This consists of clapping of hands or beating of drums or an orchestra of different instruments. Every dance is accompanied by a song, which is sung by the performance. Both men and women, young and old dance and invariably sing. The male members usually provide the accompanying orchestra or music. Tribal dance is characterised not only by its originality and spontaneity but also for its wide range of movements. Many parts of the body such as head, back, arms, feet, fingers etc. are brought into play. Some of the tribal groups put on colourful dancing costume during their performance.

Like dance, the songs sung by different tribal groups differ from one tribe to the other. Among the tribes everyone is a musician and poet. When happily inspired they can coin a song instantly and sing it. The songs contain humours jokes, romance, satires, criticisms, acquisitions and anger. On the occasion of Pujas and observance of festivals, songs sung are different. These songs describe the history of Gods, the process of creation and some epic stories.

The tribals have songs for every occasion and music for all the sentiments. Almost all the tribal men and women are born composers. They do not care much for the art of style or diction. They simply render these feelings and emotions into age-old musical tunes of nursery songs, marriage songs, ritual and seasonal festival songs, funeral chants and songs of hunting expedition. Their stories are equally fascinating for their wit, humour, satire and pathos. The tribal folk literature is a dependable source of information for reconstructing tribal cultural history as well as for providing the ethnographic picture of a tribe.

LANGUAGE AND LITERATURE

The languages clearly form a part of their cultural heritage. The language of each community is an expression of its cultural traditions and all the customary functions are carried out in the ancestral language terms. There was a general misconception that tribal communities did not possess languages but dialects. With extensive study of tribal languages, linguistics have come to the conclusion that tribals do possess languages. Tribal languages contain the same features, which other languages possess.

More often than not, it is found that a large portion of the Indian tribal population, however, has given up the original language and today speaks the dialects of the neighbouring peoples possessing a superior culture and also a more developed speech form. Interestingly, these tribes may have retained in their newly adopted language certain syntactic and phonetic peculiarities of their old idioms, even a number of words. Generally, the Austric languages are divided into the Austronesian and Austro-Asiatic Language Groups. The letter group includes the Munda languages in central and eastern India, Nicobarese, the Mon-Khmer languages of Assam (Khasi), Burma (Mon or Talaing, Paloung and Wa), Indo-China (Khmer or Combaodian, some lesser known dialects like Stieng and Bahnar, possibly Cham of Vietnam and the Sakai dialects of Malaya). In India the Munda or Kol tribes in central and eastern India speak Austric languages, as also the Khasis in Assam and the Nicobarese islanders.[9]

The Munda tribes themselves have, however, preserved their original languages. Always, they have, at least in their core, formed a fairly compact racial and cultural group. This is the main factor why the superior cultures around them had never such an overpowering influence on the Munda tribes that they could destroy their tribal, racial and cultural identity. Tribes living mostly in the northern and north-eastern border regions of India and in Assam are the second large group of aboriginal tribes that speaks its own original languages. These tribes speak Sino-Tibetan languages. The Sino-Tibetan language group is sub-divided into two main groups: (1) the Tibeto-Burman and (2) the Thai-Chinese groups. Another language group of this type is also found in north Assam. It includes the idioms spoken by the Akas, Abor-Miris, Daflas and Mishmis. But most important is the Assam-Burmese group which is again divided into two sub-sections: the Bodo-Naga group and the Burmese-Kuki-Chin-Kachin-Lolo group. From among the Burmese-Kuki-Chin-Kachin-Lolo group only the Kuki and Chin idioms are spoken in India. Meithei or Manipuri, the state language of the Manipur State is the most advanced language of this group. Lushai too is a Kuki language. The aborigines of the Andaman Islands speak another isolated and exclusive language. It is an idiom of equally unknown affinities. The Andamanese language is divided into several dialects which are closely related to each other. The tribal population in most part of the country speak languages which are not indigenous to them; they are largely either Indo-Aryan or Dravidian type. The Indo-Aryan languages are all derived from Sanskrit. The Aryans spoke Sanskrit language at the time of their arrival in India. The tribals of northern India speak either Austric, Sino-Tibetan or Indo-Aryan languages whereas all tribal groups of southern India have replaced their original idioms by the regional Dravidian languages. Dravidian is the second important language family in India. In central and eastern India, several rather primitive Dravidian dialects are spoken by aboriginal tribes such as Gondi (in Madhya Pradesh, Andhra and Tamilnadu), Kandh or Kui, Praji and Ollari (in Orissa), Kurkuhi or Oraon (in Bihar and Orissa), and Malto in the Rajhamal hills (Bihar). Thus, it may lead to the fact that the tribal languages wherever they still exist are on a steady decline and are perhaps in the process of final extinction. Many have attempted for their revival. But all these efforts have so far not met with much success. This degradation and decline of the tribal languages has set in a long time ago. Indo-Aryan and Dravidian languages widely accepted and subsequently adopted by a large part of the tribal population of India is testimony of this process of gradual decline. Many reasons can be ascribed to this development. A major factor responsible for this is that the tribals were detribalised and assimilated by superior Dravidian or Aryan immigrants who either forcibly occupied their habitats or subjugated them in course of time. Another possible reason is that the tribals themselves sought contact with the new-comers who had an advanced culture. Since tribals had no words for the new goods and commodities which they encountered in their daily lives, they used the words of the new comers and gradually they completely adopted the new languages, especially if they became economically dependant on the immigrants. It is a widely accepted fact that the tribal languages are generally deficient in abstract terms and also lack the richness of expression found in other languages.

In recent times, school education is the most effective reason for the tribals adopting the superior languages. Generally, Education is imparted through the medium of the regional language. More so, even elementary education, barring a few aberrations is rarely given for tribal children in their own language. The most inevitable fallout is that the children become more fluent in the regional language than in their own and increasingly neglect the latter. Very often it happens that educated tribals feel ashamed of their tribal language and refuse to speak it. Men of the community start the usual process of changing from the tribal language to the regional one. They are more exposed to contact with the outside world, and for this reason find it necessary and profitable to learn the regional language. The women of the community may continue to speak the tribal language for a longer time. But slowly they also acquire some fluency in the use of the regional language, especially in the villages with a mixed population. Once the women begin to speak the regional language, the fate of the tribal language is sealed.

The tribes of Eastern India, particularly Orissa, are ethno-linguistically classifiable into three groups: Munda (Austric), Dravidian and Indo-Aryan.[10]Each group has its intercommunity language affinities. The language of each group has a common source, common ancestry and cultural heritage. On the other hand, above the group level or inter-group level they share certain basic features in their verbal behaviour regardless of their own linguistic ethnicity. The most fundamental characteristics of human verbal behaviour are preserved in their language in vocabulary, sound symbolism, grammatical structures or any other aspects. Thus, Santali and Saora of the same Munda family and Bonda, Paraja and Desia of Munda, Dravidian and Indo-Aryan families show certain remarkable common features in nature and structure of tribal language.
The demolinguistic picture of the tribal language and dialects of Orissa is like this. The Bhumij, Birhor, Bonda, Didayi, Gadaba, Ho, Juang, Kharia, Korku, Koda, Mundari, Perenga, Santali, Saora fall under the Munda category. The Gondi, Konda, Kui, Kuvi-Kondh, Kisan, Koya, Kolami, Naiki, Oraon,

Ollar (Gadaba), Parji, Pengo come under the Dravidian type. Bathudi, Bhatri, Bhumia, Bhuiyan, Desia, Halbi, Jharia, Kurmali, Sadri Sounti belong to the Indo-Aryan group.

The tribal languages are mostly spoken languages. with no script of their own. Their speeches, which have a value for the philologist were reduced to writing only in the Nineteenth century by Christian missionaries. Santalis and Mundari have folk tales and songs which are quite distinctive. Very good collections have been made by the Scandinavian missionaries as well as by the Indian scholars.[11] Khasi and Santali have been recognised by the University of Calcutta as 'Minor vernaculars'. However, writing systems or scripts have been invented in recent past for four languages, namely, Santali, Saora, Ho and Kui.

The tribal languages have a rich oral literacy tradition comprising folk literature in the forms of myths, tales, songs, proverbs, riddles, invocations, etc. However, some written literatures have been created and published in 'OL CHIKI' script of Santali and Soran Sompen script of Saora as there are printing presses, and some literature in a few languages have been translated in Oriya and Roman script. But the bulk of folk literature in the tribal languages exist in oral tradition and in these stories and songs are enshrined the philosophy of the tribal folks and the ethos of the tribal personality.

ART AND CRAFT

The tribal culture is varied so is their art and craft. It is through this endeavour their cultural self-image and aesthetic sensibility are visualised. The artistic skill of the tribal people is not only manifested in their dance and music but also in their dress and ornaments, wall-paintings, wood carvings and decorations etc.

In comparison to other primitive tribes in Africa, America and in the Pacific, even Australia, the Indian tribes appear to be less talented in the fine arts. Anthropologists believe that this is so for several reasons: one reason is that certain materials were prohibited for the tribals due to the Hindu prejudice with regard to certain occupations using 'unclean' materials. Thus, work in iron and bronze, in clay (pottery), even weaving and basketry work were carried out by 'impure' and often 'untouchable' occupational castes. The tribals who wanted to attain and keep the status of a respectable caste were thus not allowed to use these materials and could not acquire the necessary skills for the production of works of art. Moreover, the members of the higher Hindu castes have, in modern times, convinced the tribals of the inferiority of the latter's art products, and consequently most tribals have given up the production of articles of their own creation and replaced them by the products of the traditional artisan castes whose work is indeed superior in the quality of the materials (gold, silver, etc.) and in the perfection of the technical execution of the objects, but vastly inferior in originality of conception. The real superiority of tribal art has only been recognised in modern times since originality of conception and the apposite expression of an idea are more highly valued than the quality of the material and technical perfection.[12]

Most of the tribes are fond of body painting and decoration. Tattooing is a widely practised art in the decoration of the body, though in present times it is often carried out by semi-aboriginal professional tattooers, usually women. This often differs for each tribe though they have their traditional methods. Many tribal women of eastern and central parts of the Country are often tattooed all over the body, but for each tribe the patterns are different and varied. For decorative purposes, the tribals use various materials, perishable ones like flowers, leaves and feathers, but also more durable seeds, beads and shells, or ornaments of bamboo, wood and metal. Some tribal women swear hairpins of horn, bone, wood or metal; also head bands for the hair and various other ornaments; likewise ornaments for the ear, nose, neck, and for the arms and legs. In all regions of the Country, the dress, especially of tribal women, formerly often consisting of leaves or bark cloth, is now usually of cotton cloth. The colour combination of the cloth is often traditional and differs with every tribe. Though weaving is now usually done by professional weavers and the tribals buy their weaving apparel in the weekly markets. The weavers of localities pay due attention to the choices of the tribes and produce the cloth in the desired colour and quality. The tribes of central India often use cowrie shells for further decoration of their dress. A special artistic head dress is worn by the Bison-horn Maria Gonds of Bastar. Their turbans are decorated with bison-horns and peacock feathers. These turbans are worn at their dances and this gives a majestic look. Gonds, Khonds and many of the tribes of central India often possess tobacco cases which are decorated with elaborate carvings, usually of geometrical patterns and this is a part of their status in the community.

Decorations of a more secular nature are usually found on doors and house walls. The youth dormitories especially are often decorated with carvings and paintings. The figures of men and animals are often highly stylised, often in silhouette or in simple geometrical outlines. A common method of symbolisation is the production of a part for the whole: thus for a woman the breasts or the vulva are depicted, for a bird its wings, for a fish its bones, and so on. Totemic emblems are found especially among the Oraons of Chota Nagpur.[13]

The beautiful wall-paintings and floral designs of the Santals are the icons of the Saoras. They depict geometric designs and stylistic figures of plants and animals and are the best example of tribal art. The multi-coloured designs and figures of living beings decorated on the walls of *Mandaghar* in Juang society are arts of high order. Similar wall-paintings and decorations noticed among the Mundari group of tribals are attractive. Some of the tribal communities like the Bonda and the Gadaba have their own looms to weave their clothes. These hand-spun textiles of coloured yarn are examples of best artistic skill. Embroidery prepared on scarfs among the Dongria Kondh women is a reflection of their artistic skill. The tribal women in general and the Bonda, the Gadaba and the Dongria Kondh women in particular are very fond of using ornaments. The Bonda women who are considered most primitive, look majestic when they wear head bands made of grass, necklaces of coloured beads and girdles made of brass on their bodies. All these are expressions of their artistic quality and aesthetic sense. The tribal people prepare handicraft items for their own use. The wood carving of the Kondhs, metal works by the Bathudis, cane and bamboo works among the Juangs and Bhuinyas, are all symbolic of artistic creation.

RELIGION

The tribal religions are more specific to tribe or group or community, at least by nomenclature. However, in substance they do not differ much from each other. It is believed that inanimate objects as well as living beings, which are awe inspiring in nature, are endowed with indwelling spirits of various kinds. Mountains, rocks, rivers, waterfalls, trees, etc. are believed to be inhabited by deities and spirits, good and evil. It is even believed that there are spirits presiding over various diseases. The whole world is populated by a host of spirits, good and evil. These spirits can be invoked, propitiated and even forced to help or harm human beings by various magical means and practices. The good spirits generally go unattended as no one is afraid of them. For instance, the great sun god, *Sing bonga* of the Munda is seldom worshipped as he is benign and is considered harmless. The typical trait of primitive religions is that they are more concerned with evil forces, fears and frustrations.

The original religion of the tribal population in India is commonly characterised as 'animistic'. Animism is the doctrine that inanimate objects as well as living beings are endowed within dwelling spirits of various kinds. Indeed, belief in such spirits and their veneration and worship is common to all Indian tribes. Mountains, rocks, rivers, trees, etc. are believed to be inhabited by deities and spirits. The whole world is populated by a host of spirits, good and evil. These spirits can be invoked, propitiated and even forced to help or harm human beings by various magical means and practices.[14] However, not all spirits are equally favoured by the tribes. They worship and propitiate different types and manifestations of spirits. Some tribes prefer the worship of the spirits of the forest, or rivers and mountains, others concentrate on the spirits of the earth, or of the heavenly bodies, sun, moon and stars. Even spirits of disease are believed to exist, and they must be propitiated.

Besides, spirits, there is also the belief in a 'high-god'.The term 'high-god' was coined by Andrew Lang. For long the high-god is a personal god, separate from and altogether superior to all other deities and spirits, the master, and often maker, of the universe and of men, the creator and guardian of the moral code, master over life and death, himself benevolent, immutable and kind hearted. The concept of a high-god is very likely indigenous in the tribal regions of India. When they came in to contact with the Hindus, they began to identify him either with the 'absolute being' of Hindu religion, or with its main incarnation or personification. As the Hindus call this being Paramatma, Param shiva, or Bhagwan, the tribes often use the same names for their High-god. But in north, eastern and central India, he is often identified with the 'spirit of the sun' or Sing Bonga, the high god of the mundas, or of Beru Deo, the high god of the Gonds. In eastern and central India, he is also called Dharmesh, or Dharmraj, due probably to Buddhist influence.[15] Tribes mostly adopt and worship Hindu Gods & Goddesses. Various Hindu deities, like Vishnu (especially in his incarnation as Krishna), Shiva (Mahadeo, Shankar), Hanuman, Ravan, and the epic heroes such as the Pandava brothers, play an important part in the religious life of the Primitive tribes. In fact, all tribal religions have to some extent absorbed elements of higher religions, especially of Hinduism. Some of the main Hindu gods, Shiva, and Vishnu or his incarnation as Krishna are incorporated in the tribal religions or identified with former tribal gods. Favourite figures in the tribal myths and folktales of central India are the Pandava Brothers, of the Mahabharata, and especially Bhima among them. Ayyappan is widely venerated by the tribes of south India. He has been adopted by the Hindus but it is believed that he is a tribal god.

Rites of veneration occupy a key place in the religious structure of tribes. Many primitive tribes have special rites of veneration for their ancestors, on the occasion of a death, on certain feasts. Survival of the soul after death is the belief that all primitive tribes hold irrespective of their clan. Often they believe in a plurality of souls; the shadow, life-spirit, the ego. The belief in the transmigration and reincarnation of souls is fairly widespread, but need not always be the result of Hindu influence. To many tribes, the future life is determined by the good or bad deeds a person has committed in his earthly life. But more important are certain religious rites and sacrifices without which even a highly virtuous life is of no avail. It is found that many tribes, especially in central India have erected memorial pillars for their dead, of wood or stone, sometimes artistically carved.

Magic plays a crucial role in the Socio-religious life of Schedules Tribes. The tribals have developed a largely magical world outlook. They believe that the whole world and every individual life are mainly governed and directed by superhuman powers, personal and impersonal. They are very much convinced that they can effectively influence these superhuman powers by means of magic and sorcery. In particular, the cure of disease is in the hands of magicians who by their divination or while in a trance indicate the nature of the disease, its natural or supernatural cause, and means and rites by which a cure can be achieved. The tribals have an inbuilt impression that some diseases have natural causes and can be cured by natural remedies of which they know quite a lot. More or less, they are convinced that many cases of sickness or accidents are caused either by supernatural agencies or by persons who wish the patient evil.

In their daily life and day to day activities, good and bad omens have a strong significance. The tribals firmly believe that ordinary events happening during the day may have a prophetic significance. Dreams can also be omens. Their interpretation is the task of the diviner. Accordingly the clients regulate their activities. The rural Indian population widely believe that the tribals are great experts in the invention and practice of the magical arts. But in fact, magic is practised no less frequently and confidently in the low caste communities. It is not impossible that the practice of magic and witchcraft spread from the low-caste Hindus to the tribes, and not vice versa. Tribal religion is often believed to be the outcome of their fear of the spirits. Religious rites are performed and offerings made to appease them with an intention to avert the disasters which these deities and spirits may inflict on mankind.

Tribes in Assam mostly believe in one deity superior to the rest, but as this high god is passively benevolent, he is generally of little importance in cult and daily life. The minor deities and spirits are more prominent. They are near and always demanding propitiation through sacrifices and gifts or else they take revenge. Still, the tribes entertain a strong belief in the existence of a supreme beings. His supremacy over the other gods and spirits in the world is undeniable to them.

Tribes of Eastern India have a varied perception of Supreme God. Of the Austro-Asiatic tribes, the Khasis have a supreme god whom they call U Blei Nongthaw i.e. god, the creator. This deity is, however, often conceived in female form. U Pyrtat is another supreme god whose sword is lightning. The Khasis believe that U Blei Nongthaw was in early times had close contact with men. But gradually men became jealous, and U Blei Nongthaw retreated into inaccessible distance. Khasis always believe that religion is the way to find the way back to the supreme god. U Blei Nongthaw created mother earth and heaven. Mother earth had five children, the sun (female), the moon (male), the water, the air and the fire. Out of these came all living beings on earth. Bodo tribes also believe in a creator god who is worhsiped through a more or less formal cult. The Garos call their creator god Tatara-Rabunga, while the Rabhas call him Ma-Bai who created the earth out of a pre-existing watery plain in which engulfing darkness ruled. The sacred work of creation was carried out by Nestu-Nopantu, a minor deity and a delegate of the supreme god. The Mikirs have a god whom they call the 'Great God'. But he is now a mere household god. He receives a sacrifice every third year. A pig is sacrificed to propitiate him and on the occasion of the sacrifice, feast with rice beer and wine is prepared. The Abors and Galongs also believe in a supreme god whom they call the 'All-Loving.' But their knowledge about this supreme god is very hazy.

Other tribes of eastern India like the Naga tribes believe in a supreme god though he is for them often a remote deity to whom no sacrifices are due. The Ao Nagas, for instance, call the supreme god Lungkijinga (deity of the stone house). They strongly believe that he lives high up in the sky; therefore, they also call him 'Spirit of the Air Room'. He sits on his stone house as on a throne. He usually dispenses the fates of human beings in the form of leaves. Besides dispensing fates of people, he occasionally commands the other deities to punish some men and to leave others in peace.

Besides the Supreme God, there are also the Minor Deities and Spirits. While most tribes of Assam have some conception of a personal divine being creating the world and directing its destinies, they also believe in a great variety of minor deities and spirits, demons and ghosts who rule the world, the earth as well as the world above and the world below. They are always nearer to man than the supreme god who is generally conceived as a distant divinity. He is less concerned with the fate of man and leaving the world to the mercy or malice of these superhuman spiritual beings.

South Indian tribes have a different concept of god and religion. Wild animals and forces of nature are their objects of worship. They practise a religion which, to some extent, can be characterised as animistic. Most tribes venerate the forces of nature and find their gods on the hills and in the forests of their habitat. They venerate tiger and snake gods, and also the sun and the moon. Their ancestors occupy a predominant place in their religious structure. But their religion has been more or less strongly influenced by the religion of the Hindu peoples who live around them. However, the degree of Hinduisation is perhaps less noticeable among the food gathering tribes, but has made more progress among the tribes which are shifting cultivators and settled agriculturists. Many tribes of south India venerate hill gods whom they locate on the crests and tops of hills. Mala Deivom, god of the hills is the popular god of the Adiyar, agricultural labourers. The Mala Arayar worship five hills which, in their opinion, possess superhuman powers. Five stones, symbols of the hill gods, are installed in a shed, or in the open. The shed is purified and the stones are given a bath. Raw rice grains, sandal-paste and leaves of the basil plant (tulsi) are offered on a plantain leaf, while five coconuts are offered on another leaf. Then a fowl is sacrificed and the coconuts broken. A dinner is served. A little rice is placed on twenty-one leaves and offered to the ancestors. The Palliyar and Manar consider the crests of hills as their gods and believe that these hills are haunted by spirits. They used to preserve a portion of the primeval forest and dedicate it to the forest spirits. The Uralis, on the other hand, believe that the hills are in-habited by evil spirits. The Mala Kuruvar believe that their hills are inhabited by spirits and they sacrifice to them before making a clearing and again after sowing. The Muduvar venerate Kottamala Swami, Vadaganatha Swami and other gods and believe that they reside on hill crests. The Irular woship three gods whom they believe to inhabit the Mallesvaram peak in the Attapady area. They avoid climbing the hill.A characteristic feature of Ullathan religion is the worship of spirits residing on certain hill peaks. The Allar are known to revere various kinds of plants, trees, rocks, hillocks and streams in the jungle. The Eravallar are said to do the same. The Mudugar, too, are at times seen standing in silent veneration at the foot of large trees or rocks in the forest.[16]

Many of the south Indian tribes venerate the sun and the moon. The Kanikkar, for instance, believe that the sun is the creator of all things. The sun is a female deity, while the moon is a male god. The spots in the moon represent a hare. The Kanikkar worship the sun on Fridays. Early at sunrise they place a lighted lamp in front of the hut, and also betel and fried rice, and fruits. They pray that God may accept their offerings. Then they take the offerings and make a meal of them. Almost all the tribes venerate and worship their ancestors. Thus the Adiyar worship the spirits of their ancestors and believe that those who have led a good life are reborn as human beings. The same belief is held by the Eravallar. Among the Mala Vedar, the worship of the ancestors is their principal form of religion. It is performed in a solemn form. The Kadar believe that their ancestors and the dead are their best protectors in danger and come to their assistance when they are in misery and difficulties. Some of the south Indian tribes do not seem to have a well organised priesthood. Nor do they regularly perform sacrifices. Offerings are made and sacrifices performed by the head of the family. Sometimes the village headman acts as a priest as well. The majority of the tribes, however, have professional priests. The priest is distinguished from the exorciser or shaman, though he may also act in these capacities. The exorciser uses white or black magic. First he must divine the nature of the sickness or misfortune that has befallen his client.[17]

It is a fact that the tribes of south India have no definite and clear concept of Supreme being or a so-called high-god, a god above all the other gods and spirits, kind, benevolent, just, the creator, the lord of life and death and above all lord of the Universe. Wherever such a deity appears, he bears a Hindu name and his characteristics are also that of the Hindu supreme god, Vishnu, Shiva, or one of their incarnations. Hinduised concept of High God predominates their religious customs. The Kanikkar tribes venerate a high-god by the name of Padacha Thampuran. He is the sole creator of the World. Invariably every morning on waking up, the Kanikkar tribes invoke his name and the names of other gods to ward off evil spirits and protect them. Like Hindu people, the Mudugars worship the god Shiva in the Malleswaram peak rising steeply from the Attapady valley. On Shivaratri day,they once a year climb the mountain top and offer prayers. The Kurichchiyars also prefer the worship of Shiva under his manifestation as a hunter; they call him Muttappan. They worship him in the form of a heap of stones in various jungle places and pray him to save them from bad and dangerous spirits. The god Subramania is the Supreme God of the Muthuvans. They worship him and offer prayers. A thatched shed erected for the god in each hamlet. It is at some distance from their settlements and every where outside their villages. South Indian tribes also worship various goddesses. Important and prominent among the female deities is Kali or Bhadrakali i.e. Kali with many arms. She is also venerated as Bhagavati, the wife of Shiva. The tribes also worship the goddesses of disease, the 'Seven Sisters' or 'Seven Mothers'. They call them as Kannimar. Besides, Mariamma, the goddess of cholera and smallpox, gets special veneration. All over south India she is worshipped with reverence. The tribes of central India worship high god and minor deities. They also offer sacrifices in the form of animals to appease god and goddesses.

The concept of high-god is also widely prevalent among the central Indian tribes. 'The high-god of the central Indian tribes', according to Stephen Fuchs, 'is known mainly by Aryan names: Thakur deo, Burha deo, Bara deo, Bhagwan, Dharmesh, Param deo, Narayan deo, Parmeshwar, Parmatma etc. Only the Mundari-speaking tribes (Santals, Mundas, Hos, Bhumiji, Birhors, Turis and Asurs) call him Sing Bonga (sing means sun, bonga, originally the moon, now a spirit). The high-god is indeed often identified with the sun. The high-god has no wife or brother; he does not require food, like the lower deities and spirits. He is saluted at sunrise. During public sacrifices he is addressed first. In the funerals service he is mentioned as the master over life and death. He is reproached in misfortune, and called to witness in oath-taking. A periodical sacrifice is performed in his honour every third, fifth, or twelfth year. The priest officiating in this sacrifice is the head of the celebrating family, not the village priest.

The minor deities of the central Indian tribes are of various types. One category could be called mountain or vegetation gods. Thus the Santals, Mundas, Hos and Bhumij venerate Marang Buru (the great mountain): the Oraons and Kharias call the same god Barnda, the Savars and Korkus worship Dongar deo (hill-god). This mountain-god is mainly a vegetation and rain god. Each village has its special god represented in a stone slab. Put up in a grove or under a tree, this deity is worshipped mainly after the harvest through public worship, much feasting and drinking; sexual excesses also occasionally take place at this feast. These tribes also worship female deities; prominent among them is the Earth-mother. Sacrificial victims are mainly animals, such as cattle, goat, fowl and pig. The central Indian tribes also make offerings of liquor and of morsels of food to the ancestors. They burn curdified butter and incense in these offerings. Coconuts, too, are often given in sacrifice. The tribes also believe in the existence of many evil spirits who have never been human beings. There are also spirits animating trees, rocks, rivers and springs, hills and mountains. They may harm a human being if they are offended or if offerings due to them are omitted. If a person gets sick or has a misfortune, or rather a number of misfortunes within a short time, diviners, soothsayers, exorcists and magicians are consulted to discover what deity or spirit has been offended and how to appease it. In almost every village community shamans can be found who easily fall into a trance. The tribals believe that the gods and spirits take possession of them and speak and prophesy through them. They are firm believers in the efficacy of witchcraft and magic. Black magic can only be counteracted by white magic. Witches are mostly women, when found out they are often killed.

The primitive tribes of central India are generally known for their honesty, truthfulness and generosity. This is so because they firmly believe that God has given men the order to be honest, truthful and generous; that he rewards them for their good deeds and punishes them for their sins, in this life and in the life after death.'

However, 'the religion of the Scheduled Tribes is an admixture of animism, nature worship, fetishism, shamanism, anthropomorphism and ancestor worship'. Near every tribal village there is some rock or tree, which is associated with some divinity and legend. The 'Santals', the 'Hos', the 'Mundas' and the 'Oraons' have at one end of their village a grove of trees known as *Sarana* or *Jahira* which is a place of worship.[18] The shrine of 'Bir Khumba', is worshipped by the Bhumiyas. The tribes often use various names for their 'high-God'. Both the Hos and the Mundas call their supreme deity, 'Sing Bonga'. The Hos and the Santals use the alternative word *Thakur*, the Lord, which is equivalent to the Supreme God. The Oraons name their high-God as 'Dharma' and the *Juang* call it *Mahaprabhu*.[19] The deities worshipped by the Banjaris are Banjaridevi, Mithu, Bhukia, and Siva Bhaia. Cattle worshipping is prevalent among the Banjari as they provide the means of transportation. The tribes worship a host of other deities who seem to be more important for the emotional and ceremonial side of tribal religion '*Jakari*, the Goddess of Kondhs, Earth-God called as *Basudha* by Juang, *Dharani Debta* (*Tana Penu*) by Kondhs, 'Sun-God' known as *Dharma Devata* by Juangs and *Thakur* (*Gando Bonga*) by Santals are only a few of a number of examples. The Saharas who were originally worshippers of Siva-Linga whom they adored as *Sthanu*[20] or 'Branches of Trunk'. The Kondhs worship eighty-four Gods and Goddesses, the chief among whom is *Dharani Debta* or Mother Earth. In the Koya villages, there happens to be one *Bajagudi* or 'House of Gods'. *Sindihur* is the centre of religions and social life in a Bonda village. As regards the Saoras, their Gods are legion–the God of the health, the God of the pathway, the God of grain baskets, etc.[21] There is social sanction against violation of religious norms in a tribal community. Deification tends to keep their community close and binding in the tribal societies. However, under the onslaughts of modernity and economic change such beliefs and their practises are being loosened.[22]

The aboriginal deities are usually worshipped by priests belonging to hill tribes with offerings of buffaloes, goats, pigs and fowls, and much burning of resin. It has been documented that as late as the second half of the Nineteenth century, the Kuttia Kondhs immolated human beings to the Earth Goddess *Tari Pennu* in the belief that the victim's blood would fertilise the earth. In return for the life of the human beings, the Goddess could bless them with abundant harvest.[23] Historians generally agree that the man or woman to be sacrificed, called a *meriah* and had been dedicated for this purpose from birth. The children were also regarded as *meriah*. When the time for the celebration of *meriah* festival drew near, *meriahs* were either brought or exchanged between villages.[24] Now the practice of human sacrifice has come to an end among the tribes. Much worshipped are also the Goddess of disease. *Thakurani* or *Sital Mata* or the Goddess of Small Pox is the most powerful deity and is worshipped especially during epidemics like Cholera,

Small Pox, Chicken Pox, Plague, etc. Every village has a Shaman (*Disari* or Soothsayer), an ignorant person who lives on superstition of the villagers. The hill people are extraordinarily superstitious. Every illness that befalls on them is attributed to witchcraft. The impostors, tribal medicine man and magicians are known in different areas and among different tribes by different names, such as *Jaris, Disaris, Bejus* and *Gunians.*

Christianity has slowly and gradually penetrated in to the tribal areas. It has undoubtedly brought the message of modern life, a wider companionship and a new sense of dignity of the converts. Fragments of Western lifestyle spread among some tribals with the advent of Christianity among them. Education, improved habits of living and reliance on modern medicine got some foothold with the spread of Christianity in some areas. Hinduism has also made its inroads. Many tribes are accepting Hindu religion and adopting their religious practices. The religious beliefs and practices of Bathudis are similar to the Hindus of the neighbouring villages. Bhottaras have a great belief in spirits, gods and goddesses. *Budhi Thakurani, Bharabi, Budhi Pardesi, Basumata, Bana Durga* and Sun are a few of their deities. They are propitiated during the festivals of *Chaitro Parb, Akhitrutiya, Srabana Ambasya, Nuakhia, Dasahara, Diwali, Punia* and *Suriya Jatra.* Mata, the deity for cholera and small pox is worshipped every year by the Bhunjia tribes in the month of *Chaitra* (March) and is offered a goat and cocoanut, liquidation of debt is considered to be a primary obligation by the Bhunjias and they worship the Sun for gratitude by offering cocoanut. The Bhunjias are cultivators[25] and their religious practice is more akin to Hinduism.The Binjhals worship the Gods and Goddess of Hindus besides their own deities. *Bindhy Basini* is their principal Goddess. The Dal tribes have separate sacred houses for the Gods and Goddesses. They follow the Hindus in worship. The Dharuas worship the Gods associated with their clans. Their supreme Gods are known as *Bar Deo* and *Dhulla Deo.*The Koras claim to be Hindus, worship Hindu gods and call themselves Saktas or Vishnavas. The most important deity of the Kotia tribe is 'Mauli Debta' whose shrine lies under 'Kendu' tree.

'Nisaniguda' is their goddess who protects them from small pox. Both the deities are worshipped in the month of Chaitra (March-April). Besides, they are adapted to Hinduism to a certain extent. They worship many Hindu Gods and Goddesses. The Koyas have incorporated a number of Hindu Gods and Goddesses into their pantheon and the local Hindu Gods and Goddesses are worshipped by the Koyas. The religion of the Kulis presents no special features. They worship all Hindu Gods and especially Goddesses *Mahalakshmi*. It is said that they care more for money than moral virtues. The Oraon religion represents a combination of indigenous beliefs and practices of Hinduism. Christianity as a new religion has received the favour from Oraons. Other neighbouring tribes such as Kisan, Kharia, Munda and Ho have also been converted in large number.

CONCLUSION

All that is stated in the preceding chapters and sections about the socio-economic conditions of the tribes and their commonalities mostly relate to the traditional tribal societies. But their lifestyle, religion and culture have been undergoing a change. Some changes are due to socio-religious movement from within, some changes are due to external agencies like governmental and voluntary organisations working for their development and a series of changes are being brought about through the laws, protective policies and political modernisation.

The economic status and position of Scheduled Tribes is determined from their income and the scale of employment. The development programmes have generated opportunities for the Scheduled Tribes. They are, however, coming to the forefront and are trying to be assimilated in the main process of development. They have been gainfully employed and their income has been increased. Their political participation is being taken care of through the introduction of Panchayati Raj system. They are gradually participating in the political process of the country. In general, their dignity and self-image are not properly articulated. The development process is not being properly framed to take care of the socio-economic status of the Scheduled Tribes in India.

NOTES AND REFERENCES

1. S. Mohanty and B.M. Jena, "Barriers to Educational Development Among the Tribals", in H.C. Upadhyay (Ed.), *Scheduled Castes and Scheduled Tribes in India: A Socio-Economic Profile*, Anmol Publications, New Delhi, p. 216.
2. P.K. Bhowmick (1975), "Essential Primary Considerations for Rehabilitation Schemes", *Vanyajati*, October.
3. Lang, Andrew (1898), The making of Religion, London.
4. Fuchs, Stephen (1973), The Aboriginal tribes of India, Macmillan India, pp. 264-266.
5. Verrier Elwin (1998), "Notes on the Juang", *Man in India*, Vol. XXVIII.
6. Ghruye, G.S. (1959), The Scheduled Tribes of India, Bombay.
7. Fuchs, Stephen (1973), The Aboriginal Tribes of India, Macmillan India, p. 75-76.
8. F.M. Sahoo (1989), "Study of Tribal Cultures in Orissa, From Descriptive Data to Experimental Innovations", in B.C. Ray (Ed.), *Tribals of Orissa, Changing Socio-Economic Profile*, Gian Publishing House, New Delhi.
9. Fuchs, Stephen (1973), The Aboriginal tribes of India, Macmillan India, p. 38.
10. K. Mohapatra, "Tribal Languages of Orissa", in *Tribes of Orissa*, Government of Orissa, p. 27.
11. S.K. Chatterji (1973), *Tribal Languages and the Tribal People of India*, Publications Division, Government of India, pp. 66-67.
12. Elwin, V. (1951), The tribal Art of middle India, Oxford University Press, p. 1-8.
13. *Ibid.*
14. Fuchs, Stephen (1973), The Aboriginal tribes of India, Macmillan India, p. 65.
15. Sachidananda (1965), "Directed Change Among the Birhors", *The Eastern Anthropologist*, Vol. 9, No. 1.
16. Fuchs, Stephen (1973), The Aboriginal tribes of India, Macmillan India, p. 261-262.
17. M. Haque (1986), "Height and Weight Among the Upper Bonda of Koraput", *Vanyajati*, Vol. XXXIV, No. 4, October, p. 17.

18. G.S. Ghurye, *The Scheduled Tribes*, p. 260.
19. *Adivasi*, Government of Orissa, 1963-64.
20. D.D. Kosambi, *Myth and Reality*, p. 91.
21. A. Neville Watts, *The Half Clad Tribals of Eastern India*, Orient Longmans, Calcutta, 1970, p. 16.
22. S.C. Patnaik and S. Patel, "Impact of Modernisation on Tribals: Economic Dualism and Path of Change", p. 37-54.
23. For details, see R.C.S. Bell, *Orissa District Gazetteers, Koraput*, Chapter–III, Meriah Sacrifices.
24. A. Neville Watts, *op. cit.*, p. 48-49.
25. T. Patnaik, "Bhuyan", in *Tribes of Orissa*, Government of Orissa, p. 61.

6 Backwardness and Underdevelopment

With second highest concentration and numerous groups in the globe, tribal communities in India have multilateral culture, multiplicity of languages, manifold religions, multitude social structures and multilateral but maladroit economic systems. These scheduled tribes (STs) or Adibasis(Primitive settlers) or Girijans(HillMen) or JanaJatis or Banabasis (Forest castes/ People) as they are differently called in different regions and communities of around 573 groups many of which are overlapping, reside in many of the States and Union territories. Most of them are backward and underdeveloped economically, socially and educationally. They settle far away from the general settlements in remote inaccessible and backward areas without any facilities and amenities of a civil life and still keep themselves immune from the national mainstream. Many of them are primitive and geographically isolated. These tribal communities in India constituting around 8 per cent of the total population live in roughly 15 per cent of areas of the country most of which are hills and dales, forests and plateaus. Their primitive way of life, economic and social backwardness, low level of literacy, hackneyed system of production, absence of value system, inaccessible areas with sparse physical infrastructure and their demographic quality coupled together make the tribals of India backward and under developed.[1] The demographic quality of tribal areas is unique in as much as there is ethnic diversity, economic backwardness and low level of technological development. They do not generally seek economic prosperity. Their source of happiness lies elsewhere. They are essentially satisfied if their bare necessities of life are fulfilled. Their institutions are mostly informal socio-cultural and unquestioned traditional loyalty and obedience.[2] Stephen Fuchs believes that 'it is still largely unknown what exactly hinders the cultural progress of certain tribal communities. Is it congenital low intelligence? But this can be true in only a few instances for a large part of the tribal children who were given the opportunity of an educational advancement showed largely the same intellectual abilities as children of other communities. Perhaps a more relevant factor may be the adverse environmental and geographical conditions which impair their cultural advance, the isolation which follows from living in remote and inaccessible hills, and the lack of stimulating contacts with people of a superior culture. But many tribals do live in proximity to people of a superior culture, and still remain backward and aloof. The reason for such behaviour might be less an extreme innate conservatism of which they are often accused, but more the bad experience they have had with members of the superior culture. Often they have been hurt and oppressed and mercilessly exploited and unjustly treated by these outsiders. The schemes proposed by the various welfare and development agencies not only often disturb the tribals' economic equilibrium, they also entail changes in their social life for which the tribals are mentally unprepared. For they set a high value on personal freedom and they will reject any proposal, however, advantageous economically, that this will let them down to a life of dull routine. Deeply attached to the free and exciting life as hunters and food collectors on the jungle, or at least to the clearing of the forest and the sowing in virgin soil, they will reject any occupation that leaves no room for an occasional breakaway from the drudgery of daily life.'[3] It is mainly the mentality and outlook of the tribals and their view about the outside world which are not still ready to welcome and adopt any form of merger into the mainstream or national life of India. Moreover, the tribal regions mostly have predominantly peasant economy with barter and isolation as its characteristics.[4]

One of the basic features present in every class of tribal is their backwardness and poverty. It is for this reason the areas in which they inhabit are also called backward.[5] The backwardness of these groups of people is due to their prolonged isolation from the mainstream of the society and exploitation by some advanced groups of the society. Besides, their outdated tools and technology have pegged them to a perpetual backwardness. Being unable to exploit the natural resources to their advantage and to meet the various needs of life, they have been compelled to remain in their forest abodes in continued isolation.[6] The non-farm household industry sector in these areas is caught in the poverty syndrome[7] with less labour absorption possibilities. Again, the standard of living of these people being very low, it becomes necessary for many of them including adolescents and old people to work[8] and a greater proportion of these backward people work in order to earn a living.[9] The income which they earn is substantially low[10] and their per capita income is much below the country average.[11] Stephen Fuchs very aptly described their primitive way of life and precarious living conditions leading to their backwardness and underdevelopment. 'To passing tourists, the life of the aborigines may appear beautiful and romantic: the country with its gurgling hill streams, its dense jungles abounding with game, the smiling fields basking in bright sunshine, the villages perched on steep declines, the well-swept village lanes and courtyards in front of the houses, the house walls painted with artistic designs and quaint figures, the gardens at the back with fruit trees and vegetables, the chatter of the women walking early in the morning in single file to the village well, the carefree and exciting life of hunting and collecting of jungle produce; the strange ceremonies of birth, marriage and death, the picturesque rites on feast days and occasions of sacrifice, the tireless shuffling of dancing feet on full-moon nights to the rhythm of the drums, accompanied by the singing of simple but appealing melodies, interrupted occasionally by hoarse yells in the ecstasy of the dance; the narration of folk-tales and myths, at night in the fields, to watchmen sitting around a warming fire, the impressive tribal art kept alive by the habit of adorning doors and walls with drawings and by the remodelling of dancing costumes-all these things make the life of the aborigines appear happy and exciting. There is, however, a reverse to this bright picture: the poor condition of the soil on the steep hills, the danger of erosion through ever-recurring torrential monsoon rains, the primitive and indigenous methods of cultivation, the back-breaking work during the agricultural implements, the ravaging of fields by birds and wild animals, the danger from snakes and beasts of prey, the severe restriction on hunting and collecting of jungle produce, the abject poverty and penury of aboriginal life, the near-starvation in many houses during times of unemployment or failure of crops, the exploitation through usurers and government servants, the heavy drinking, the clash of temper and lure of passion at dances, the loose morals and easy divorce, the suppression of individual enterprise and prevention of progress through over-conservative caste-elders, the frequency of death in child-birth and in infancy, the ravages of disease like tuberculosis, epidemics like small-pox and cholera, venereal diseases, the superstitions and the abject fear of witchcraft and black magic, of the spirits of evil, disease and death, the absence of the higher forms of religion, the ignorance of higher values and privation of spiritual pleasures and the lack of education. Add to all this a general feeling of insecurity and loss of mental balance, the hurt pride and impotent anger when the aboriginal has to face the contempt, ridicule or oppression of the superior classes, are impartial pictures of the true situation which today confronts the aborigines of India.'[12] Daily life of the aboriginal are all dancing and enjoyment. S. Barkataki describes the daily life of a Hillman in Assam in the following words: "One can hardly imagine the difficulty with which a Mizo or a Zemi Naga has to eke a livelihood out of his little patch of land. From before daybreak the womenfolk of a village march in processions, carrying a number of bamboo tubes in a cane or bamboo basket, hundred of feet down to a spring or a stream to collect water for the day's use. The return journey uphill with the load of water on their back is strenuous. Immediately after their return they have to get busy preparing food for the family before they accompany their husbands to help them in their work in the jhum (cultivation). About half-an-hour is spent at mid-day in eating the pack-lunch (consisting of rice, salt and chillies) they carry with them to the jhum and then work goes on again till sun-down-hoeing, sowing, weeding, whatever work at a particular stage it might be. In the evenings the men-folk snatch a few moments of leisure and relaxation which they devote to zu (rice-beer or spirit) drinking and singing, while the women have to carry on with their household chores-cooking and attending to the pigs, the fowl and their own little ones. On special occasion, there is dancing both by men and women in addition to zu-drinking and music. This is, or at least was, till very recently the normal routine of the average tribal's life in the hills.'[13] And needless to mention the conditions of the food gathering nomadic tribes. They have a tendency to resign their fate to nature, hills and dales. They are always half-fed and on the brink of starvation. Faraway from minimum social amenities, they mostly depend on jungle roots and tubers. They never try to come in contact with the people leaving outside who, despise and under estimate them. They are constantly looked down upon by the civilised people and hence are helplessly exposed to the vagaries of nature. A sense insecurity and a sort of fear psychosis has kept them away from acquiring knowledge on social values and systems and leading a descent life.[14] Let us analyse intensively some important forces and factors which directly or indirectly account for the backwardness and underdevelopment of Indian tribes.

DEMOGRAPHIC PATTERN

The Demographic Pattern of scheduled tribes of India is extremely complex and intricate. On the one extreme are the Gonds whose number is more than fifty lakhs. On the other extreme are the Onges numbering only about one hundred and twelve; the great Andamanese are barely nineteen strong.[15] However, the scheduled tribes of India constituted only 6.86% of total population during 1961 census which increased to 8.2%

during 2001. Thus, the growth percentage of scheduled tribe population to total population was only 1.16% over a period of more than four decades. The scheduled tribe population as a percentage to total population during different census periods is indicated in Table 1.

Table 1
Percentage Growth of ST Population

Census Period	*Percentage of ST Population to Total Population*
1	*2*
1961	6.86
1971	6.82
1981	7.76
1991	8
2001	8.2

Source: Census Reports.

There are 573 different tribal groups[16] most of which are divided into several subgroups. Among them are nine tribal groups namely, Bhil, Gond, Ho, Khond, Mina, Munda, Naga, Oraon and Santal, which are most numerous[17] and, therefore, are called major or large tribes. The Bhils and the Gonds, with their sub-tribes, together constitute more than one-fourth of the total tribal population. The Bhils are mostly inhabited in Rajasthan, Gujarat and South-Western Madhya Pradesh. On the other hand, the Gonds stay in South-Eastern Madhya Pradesh. Next to these two tribal groups comes the Santal, which is the third largest tribe in the country. They are found in Santal Parganas of Bihar, Birbhum district of West Bengal and Mayurbhanj district of Orissa. Among the other six tribal groups, Mina of Rajasthan, Munda of Bihar and Orissa, Oraon of Orissa had each a population of more than one million. The remaining tribes namely Ho, Khond and Naga are found largely in Bihar, Orissa and Nagaland respectively. In contrast, there are as many as 109 tribal communities having each less than 1000 population and among them there are 43 tribes, which had a population of less than 25 persons. Most of these small tribes are found in Arunachal Pradesh, the Andaman and Nicobar Islands and the South India. Different tribes, as notified under article 342 of the Constitution of India, spread over different States and Union Territories of the country, the largest number of tribal communities being in the State of Orissa. The main concentration of tribal population is in central India and in the North-eastern States. However, they have their presence in all States and Union Territories except Hayrana, Punjab, Delhi, Pondicherry and Chandigarh. The predominantly tribal populated States of the country (tribal population more than 50% of the total population) are: Arunachal Pradesh, Meghalaya, Mizoram, Nagaland, Union Territories of Dadra & Nagar Haveli and Lakshadweep. States with sizeable tribal population and having areas of large tribal concentration are Andhra Pradesh, Assam, Chhattisgarh, Gujarat, Himachal Pradesh, Madhya Pradesh, Maharashtra, Orissa and Rajasthan.

Total population and scheduled tribe population of the Country with male/female break up during 1961 census is presented in Table 2. Whereas tribal females constituted 6.98 per cent of the total females, tribal males were 6.65 per cent of the total males and total tribal population was only 6.81 per cent of the total population of the Country.

Table 2
Tribal Population of India (1961Census)

Total Population/ Tribal Population	*Persons*	*Male*	*Female*
1	2	3	4
Total Population	438,608,104	225,990,667	212,617,437
Tribal Population	29,883,470	15,040,707	14,842,763
Percentage of ST Pop. to Total Pop.	6.81	6.65	6.98

Source: Series–I, Part–II B (iii)
Census of India–1981, Primary Census abstract, Scheduled Tribes.

About seven per cent of India's population belongs to tribal communities, according to the 1971 census.[18] Mizoram had the highest percentage of tribal population (94.28%) followed by Lakshadweep (93.75%), whereas Uttar Pradesh had the lowest percentage of tribal population (0.23%) followed by Goa, Daman and Diu (0.82%). The 1981 Census shows that the population of tribal communities was little less than 8 per cent.[19] The highest concentration of tribal population was seen at Lakshadweep (93.82%) followed by Mizoram (93.55%) and Nagaland (83.99%). Total and tribal population including male and female during 1971 census is exhibited in Table 3. 1981census, however, presents a different picture. Tribal population constituted 7.76 per cent of the total population with 7.5 per cent males and 7.96 per cent females (Table 4) of the total male and female population.

Table 3
Tribal Population of India (1971 Census)

Total Population/ Tribal Population	*Persons*	*Male*	*Female*
1	*2*	*3*	*4*
Total Population	533,534,500	276,335,036	257,199,464
Tribal Population	36,408,514	18,361,797	18,046,717
Percentage of ST Pop. to Total Pop.	6.82	6.64	7.02

Source: Series–I, Part–II B (iii)
Census of India–1981, Primary Census abstract, Scheduled Tribes.

Table 4
Tribal Population of India (1981 Census)*

Total Population/ Tribal Population	*Persons*	*Male*	*Female*
1	*2*	*3*	*4*
Total Population	665,287,849	343,930,423	321,357,426
Tribal Population	51,628,638	26,038,535	25,590,103
Percentage of ST Pop. to Total Pop.	7.76	7.57	7.96

* Excluding Assam.
Source: Series–I, Part–II B (iii)
Census of India – 1981, Primary Census abstract, Scheduled Tribes.

The population of 573 different tribal communities constitute about 8 per cent of the total population of India as per 1991 Census. The Scheduled Tribes population of India *vis-a-vis* total population is shown in Table 5.

Rural concentration of tribal population is, thus, more than the urban concentration. A little less than 8 per cent of total tribal population reside in urban areas. Further, male population is slightly higher than female population of Scheduled Tribes.

Table 5
Tribal Population of India (1991 Census)*

Total Population/ Tribal Population	*Rural Urban Total*	*Persons*	*Male*	*Female*
1	2	3	4	5
Total Population	R	622,812,376	321,279,405	301,532,971
	U	215,771,612	113,936,953	101,834,659
	T	838,583,988	435,216,358	403,367,630
Tribal Population	R	62,751,026	31,755,930	30,995,096
	U	5,007,354	2,607,341	2,400,013
	T	67,758,380	34,363,271	33,395,109

* Excluding Jammu and Kashmir.

Source: Series-I, Paper-2 of 1991
Census of India-1991, Final Population, Brief Analysis of Primary Census abstract.

Though there was increase in tribal population over the years, no perceptible rise in tribal population was noticed during 2001 over the previous census periods. Tribal population constituted a mere 8.2 per cent of the total population. Total population and tribal population with Rural/Urban and male/female break up during 2001census is displayed in Table 6.

Table 6
Tribal Population of India (2001 Census)*

Total Population/ Tribal Population	*Rural Urban Total*	*Persons*	*Male*	*Female*
1	2	3	4	5
Total Population	R	742,490,639	381,602,674	360,887,965
	U	286,119,68	150,554,098	135,565,591
	T	91028610328	532156772	496453556
Tribal Population	R	77,338,597	39,045,650	38,292,947
	U	6,987,643	3,595,179	3,392,464
	T	84326240	42640829	41685411

Source: Table F PT.1, Census of India-2001, Series-I: India, Final Population totals, Registrar General and Census Commissioner, India, 2004.

State-wise total population and Scheduled Tribe population for census periods 1961,1971,1981,1991and 2001 is shown in Appendix-1, 2, 3, 4 and 5 respectively. Analysis on state wise population of scheduled tribes during different census periods reveals a complex, curious and intriguing picture. Scheduled tribes were conspicuous by their absence in some states whereas they constitute a dominant proportion in many states. For example, states like Punjab, Haryana have no tribal population whereas Mizoram (94.46%), Meghalaya (85.94) and Nagaland (89.15) have significantly higher percentage of population than all India average. A close and cursory look on the state wise population for different census periods also indicate that the pattern of growth of tribal population during different census periods was uneven in different states.

Percentage variations of total population and tribal population during the last four decades i.e., between 1961 to 2001 is shown in Table 7. Remarkably there was a decreasing trend in percentage increase of total population between the four decades whereas in case of Scheduled Tribe population, there has been an upward trend in the percentage increase only during 1971-81. Over a period of time, thereafter, percentage increase of population showed a downward trend.

Table 7
Percentage Decadal Variation of Total and Tribal Population

Census Periods	*Total Population*	*S.T. Population*
1	2	3
1961-71	25.5	25.3
1971-81	24.3	30.6
1981-91	23.79	25.67
1991-2001	21.54	24.45

Source: (i) Series-I, Paper-2 of 1991, Census of India-1991, "Final Population, Brief Analysis of Primary Census abstract"
(ii) Series - I, Paper - 2 of 2001
Census of India-1991, Final Population, Brief Analysis of Primary Census abstract.

Density of population i.e. number of people per sq. Km., in case of STs is abnormally low as compared to general population though it has increased to 28 during 2001 from 22 in 1991 census. The density of general population is much higher i.e. 266 which increased substantially (303) during 2001 as the Table 8 indicates.

Table 8
Density of Tribal Population of India

Census Periods	*Total Population*	*Scheduled Tribe Population*
1	2	3
1991	266	22
2001	303	28

Source: Census of India, 2001,Schedule Tribes Atlas of India, Devendra Kumar Sikri, IAS, Registrar General and Census Commissioner, India.

The child population are mostly non-working population. The percentage of ST child population is higher than the general population which is 18.43 and 16.03 respectively as per 2001 census. Though there was reduction in percentage of child population from 1991 census in both the cases, surprisingly reduction was higher in case of tribal child population (Table 9). Thus, demographic composition of tribal population as presented in preceding sections was extremely complex and unfavourable for their growth process in general terms.

Table 9
Percentage of Tribal Child population of India

Census Periods	*Total Population*	*Scheduled Tribe Population*
1	2	3
1991	17.97	20.18
2001	16.03	18.43

Source: Census of India, 2001,Schedule Tribes Atlas of India, Devendra Kumar Sikri, IAS, Registrar General and Census Commissioner, India.

PRIMITIVE TRIBAL GROUPS

There are certain tribal communities which have a low level of literacy, declining or stagnant population, a pre-agricultural level of technology and are economically extremely backward. 75 such groups in 16 States/UTs have been identified, and have been categorized as Primitive Tribal Groups (PTGs). The total population of the PTGs as per the 1991 Census was about 24.12 lakh. Since the PTGs constitute the most vulnerable section and are characterized by a pre-agriculture level of technology, a stagnant or declining population, extremely low literacy and a subsistence level of economy. Hunting and food gathering as food seeking activities constitute the pre-agricultural economy. Similarly, shifting cultivation is a prior stage of economic development. The communities who carry on pre-agricultural economic activities may be called primitive groups. Besides, the criteria of hunting, food gathering and shifting cultivation, low level of literacy, declining or stagnant growth rate of population may be taken as the characteristics to identify the primitive groups. In defining primitive groups some more distinguishing features have been identified. Literacy is one such feature, which may indicate the level of social development of the community. Similarly, seclusion of the community may be taken as the important criterion to identify a tribal community as primitive. Many tribal communities inhabit in remote and inaccessible areas. A few salient features of the primitive groups are listed below.

(1) The sole implements used by the primitive tribes for digging roots & tubers and carrying on cultivation are digging stick, billhook, hoe & axe. The primitive tribes who have raised their economic standards used bullock drawn country plough & simple tools in agricultural operations.

(2) Bow and arrow is the main weapon of chase & snares and traps are used for catching birds & small animals.

(3) Wearing apparel consists of an apron made of fibbers and course cotton threads.

(4) Material belongings are very few & simple.

(5) A primitive society rests on a communalistic economic base.

(6) The hut is either a windbreak or a little better shelter made from locally available materials.

(7) Staying in remote & inaccessible areas.

(8) Conservative & slow in adopting change because of face to face nature of interpersonal relationship & high degree of integration in society.

(9) Speaking languages of their own without having any or little knowledge of the neighbouring languages.

In brief, a primitive community is characterized by such qualities as distinctiveness, smallness, homogeneity and all pervading self-sufficiency. All these qualities with their ramifications are not found in full form in all primitive tribes. They are found in different degrees in different communities. But, illiteracy is the most redeeming feature of these tribes. The Level of literacy is one distinguishing feature, which indicates the proportion of social development of the PTGs. It is, therefore, generally agreed that the success of any plan for socio- economic reconstruction or for that matter, any endeavour for development of primitive tribes depends on the education and understanding of these masses. Various committees and working groups on tribal development recommended that education should be given the highest priority in the areas dominated by PTGs for the reason that education holds the key to their development. The question of tackling the problems of the more backward tribal communities has also received the attention of various commissions and study teams. The Dhebar Commission (1961) identified four different layers.[20] At the base, they identified a class of tribals in an extremely underdeveloped stage. The study team on tribal development programmes (1969) known as Shilu Ao team discerned marked development imbalance among the tribal communities.[21] They reiterated the view of the Dhebar Commission that the 'lowest layer' needed the utmost consideration and should be made the special concern of the state governments. The study team included in its report a list of backward tribal communities. At the time of review of tribal development programmes on the eve of the Fifth Plan, it was recognised that special programmes for the primitive groups should be taken up on the basis of proper identification on the lines suggested by the Shilu Ao Team. As a preliminary step, a workshop on primitive tribal communities was held in the Ministry of Home Affairs in January 1975. Detailed guidelines were issued for identification of primitive tribal groups. Based on these guidelines, nine tribal communities of the state were identified as primitive tribes by the end of 1979-80. During the Fifth Five-Year Plan, a decision was taken by the Government of India to the effect that the primitive tribal communities should be taken as a special category for whom specific programmes have to be initiated for their all-round development. Diagnostic research should be undertaken among them to evolve suitable strategies for their development and also for helping them in adjusting themselves to the new socio-economic forces of change. As a first step for ensuring this policy of the Government, the primitive tribes were identified on the criterion of pre-agricultural economy, low level of literacy and inhospitable and isolated habitat.[22] Micro projects were started and family-oriented income generating schemes were taken up for their development. On the basis of experience gained, the Working Group on Tribal Development during the Sixth Plan, recommended[23] that:

(i) High priority to the programme of primitive groups;

(ii) Identification of primitive tribal groups in accordance with the guidelines issued;

(iii) Completion of project reports for the tribal groups during 1980-81.

(iv) Incorporation of essential features like unique programme for each group, consideration of ecosystem and conservation of traditional skills in the project reports.

Accordingly, the state governments conducted a survey on socio-economic and ethnographic aspects of the primitive tribes and suggested suitable action plans. Steps were taken for implementation of the programmes. For execution cf the schemes/programmes, the schematic approach was discarded and an integration of programmes truly germane to the concerned primitive groups was executed. Since it is the human touch of the individual that will determine the quality of the programme and the future of the community, the administrative structure and the personal policies were paid the closest attention for the work.[24] A holistic approach aiming at all-round development of the primitive groups living in the project areas was made during the Seventh Plan period. The principle was supplemented as is generally adopted for and other tribal development programmes was emphasised. Instructions were issued to ensure larger investment of funds from different sectors for the development of primitive tribes residing in the Micro Project areas. As per the recommendations of Working Groups on Tribal Development, important strategies for development of primitive tribes[25] were devised. They include family-wise economic development plans and programmes, spread of education, improvement of nutrition and immunisation programmes, restoration of resource base, ban on purchase of tribal land, etc. Though a number of programmes and projects are being implemented for development of primitive tribes, the fact remains that they are still in a state of primitiveness and not quite receptive to the extraneous interventions.

Diminutive and Lesser Tribes

Some tribal communities in India, though a few in number, are in the process of extinction. Their population is either stagnant or declining over decades. These tribes are on the verge of extinction. They are very small in number. There is constant decline in the population of their community. Jarawas of Andaman Islands, Chenchu of Orissa etc. are a few such tribes. Since there is a downward trend in the growth of their population over the years, it may so happen that after a decade or two these tribes will be totally wiped out if concerted and careful efforts will not be initiated on war footing basis. Dr.B.D. Sharma has defined small populations[26] that a tribe to be considered small if its population is below 1500 of which further categorisation could be made of (i) diminutive group having population less than 1000 and ii) small group with 1000 to 1500 population. N.C. Choudhury (1982)[27] believes that there are only 50 to 60 truly small tribes with a population of 1000 who form a single homogeneous group residing in a compact area. However, in an atmosphere of general inertia, there is hardly any serious attempt in anthropological literature to define a small tribal group. The sole exception is perhaps DR. B.D. Sharma who has taken a tribe to be small if its population is below 15,000. As a matter of fact he subdivides the small tribe into two categories; diminutive groups with less than 1,000 population and small groups with 1,000 to 15,000 population. But his classification on the basis of population is quite arbitrary as there is no agreed criteria to define the size of a small tribe[28]. Historically, it is evident that the Aryans invaded ancient India through the North West frontiers. The early settlers who resisted them were either completely annihilated or under compelling circumstances some of them merged with them. The rest were pushed into interior jungles to the dales and forest side inhospitable regions of our country where some of them were able to preserve their twin culture and traditions.[29] This is perhaps one major reason which led to conspicuous absence of any small tribal group in North-West. Hinduisation process in tribal communities fares the way for their amalgamation with caste Hindus. The tribals of India have been influenced by certain traditions of communities around them. The major neighbouring communities in all areas have always been Hindus. As a result, from the very early periods, there have been several points of contacts between the Hindus of the areas and the tribal communities living along with them. In central India, for example, some of the tribal population have been greatly influenced by caste Hindus and they have adopted their 'style of life'. Thus, the tribal customs and rites are often modified in the processes of social absorption. There are numerous other tribes or their sections which have undergone selective acculturation and have added selected traits or features of the regional Hinduism to their respective traditional cultures. In this process of acculturation, most of them have failed to occupy any rank in the caste hierarchy, while a few are being integrated into the lower strata of those Hindu social system. Many of them have already reached a point of no return and they are not accepted by the caste groups for commensality and connubial relations at all. This has endangered the very survival of there groups.

Christianisation of tribals is also responsible for doing away their own culture and adopt a better standard of living. Christianity penetrated in tribal areas as the Christian Missionaries could establish themselves very easily in tribal areas by rendering help in various forms. The situation led to a large scale connection of tribals into Christianity and a widespread dissolution of innate culture among the converts. The same economic pursuits might be followed, but the institutions, benefits, outlooks and attitudes of life of the people have been completely changed. The Christian tribals are now ashamed of thief former mode of life. Other forces like altruism process is responsible for disturbing the stable culture of scheduled tribes. At times, high caste Hindus residing with the tribal people have accepted the morals, rituals and beliefs of the tribes. It has already been established that the Dravidian concept of worship and customs have been accepted by the Aryans and they have been integrated in the course of time during the evolution of Hinduism. It is evident, in this process as accepted by anthropologists that the representatives of the great tradition may succumb to the 'little tradition' which seems to have happened occasionally and the same has been reflected in most of the diminutive tribes. While the Christianity has functioned as a force of fission in disintegrating the indigenous tribal organisation in terms of the emergence of caste like groups, it has also worked as a force of fusion to consolidate inter-tribal social and religious affinity on the various denominational and religious levels. Contemporary process is also greatly responsible in disturbing the equilibrium of tribal culture. Industrialisation and urbanisation have literally made topsy-turvy of the tribal life. During the present century and specially after independence, the pace of mining and manufacturing industries, as well as the exploitation of power and forest resources have been greatly accelerated in the hilly and forested belts of tribal areas. This release of 'pull factor' during the last four decades in the hither to neglected tribal belts gets reflected in the growth of the largest percentage of urban population. The industrialisation led to rapid urbanisation comparatively in a short span of time, leading this region to an 'Industry-based-urban-explosion. Such an explosion in the heart of tribal belts of central India had led to 'cultural mutation' and the once isolated, homogeneous folk and primitive communities were exposed and thrown upon to get assimilated in the global network at urban Industrial Civilisation. Presence of non-tribes in tribal areas results in net outflow of resources from the tribal areas leaving them impoverished. This is illustrated by instances of zones inhabited by the so-called primitive groups. One tends to presume that, on account of the small numbers comprised in each of such groups, the proportion between natural resources and human beings would be favourable. This is not borne out from experience of such small communities like the Chenchu in the districts bordering Andhra Pradesh and Orissa, the Juang in the district of Keonjhar, the Kutia Kondh of the district of Phulbani (both in Orissa), the Pahadia of the district of Santal Parganas (Bihar), the Saharia of Rajasthan. Such communities suffer from under-nourishment. At the conceptual level the patterns of change due to various forces and factors can be analysed from various angles. The tribals are identified with simplicity, self-reliance, homogeneity, co-operation, distinctiveness, optimism, honesty etc. but their values of tribal culture are being transformed at a very fast pace in to complexity, heterogeneity, competition, Individualization, conflict, frustration etc. The foregoing processes have released a set of faces, which are leading tribal communities from the 'phase of acculturation of the accelerated cultural mutation[30]. George Rich, a leader among the Innu of the Labrador Quebec peninsula very aptly described the conditions of the Jarwas of the Andaman Islands *vis-à-vis* the Innu Community of north-eastern Canada.[31]

"The Jarawa tribe of the Andaman Islands has long captured the imaginations around the world, especially among other tribal peoples like my people, the Innu of north-eastern Canada. Since the final years of the twentieth century, when they stopped resisting with lethal arrows, any contact with outsiders, the world has watched the Jarawa with fascination. We don't know why they stopped shooting at the settlers and poachers encroaching on their land. Perhaps they felt overwhelmed by the sheer numbers of settlers from the Indian mainland now living on their islands. But for indigenous peoples who have already lost their land, the drama unfolding before our eyes is far too familiar. We are holding our breaths as we watch the future of this strong, proud people balancing on a knife-edge. We, Innu, know only too intimately the devastation that results when a tribe of hunters loses its land, its way of life and its independence. When these things are lost, self-respect and a sense of who we are also disappear, and for many, the reason for living is gone. For the Innu, all of this happened within a generation. Not so long ago-within the last 50 years, in fact-our parents and grandparents lived on the land. Survival was, for them, part of daily life as a hunting people. They depended on the movements of the caribou, the abundance of small game, and predictability of the weather. A small thing- a simple mistake, a run of bad weather, or a shift in the wind-could mean the difference between starvation and survival. Our parents learned to be attentive to what was happening on the land and among the animals. These were the skills that enabled us to survive as we have for thousands of years in a land so harsh the Europeans called it the 'land given to Cain'. Survival was something different for my generation. We grew up in the communities to which the government lured our parents in the 1960s with promises of houses, health care, and a better way of life. Within a few short years of settlement, most of our parents were reduced to alcoholism and idleness, many of our brothers and sisters were sexually abused by teachers and priests, and almost all of us were caught up in a system that seemed to be designed to destroy us as a people.

Over a span of perhaps 20 years, we were reduced from self-reliance to a situation of almost total dependency. Our parents, hunters all their lives, were branded as poachers and prosecuted by wildlife officers for trying to feed their families; our teachers tried to make us ashamed of our identity and our culture. It was life we'd suddenly become unwelcome guests in our own land. At the time, we didn't have the skills we needed to survive as colonised people. Few of us spoke English or French. We depended on the priests to deal with the outside world on our behalf, but they were as much a part of the system as were the government officials. As young people, we found that our grandparents could teach us little about talking to the government, or negotiating a land claim, or dealing with proposed mining and hydro developments. We didn't understand how the Canadian system worked-only that we had somehow ended up at the bottom of it. The devastation wrought by these changes is evident in the shattered self-esteem of my parents' generations of Innu growing to adulthood today. The evidence of this damage is in the epidemic of suicides and solvent abuse among our youth. Children as young as 12 have hung themselves; others have lost themselves in solvents and drugs. Our communities have some of the highest suicide rates on the planet. But among this wreckage are the survivors. This is perhaps our people's greatest strength: we know how to survive. It is what we have always done. The Jarawa may be luckier than we have been. It seems that some in India have learned from the mistakes of colonial history. The Indian government promises that it will not try to assimilate the Jarawa into mainstream society- at least for now- and that the Jarawa will be able to remain on their forest land, hunting and gathering, and developing as they themselves choose. Yet reports from the ground suggest that the reality in the Jarawa's forests is sadly different. The Jarawa are not being settled like the Innu in villages far from their hunting grounds-but poachers are stealing the animals they depend on, depriving them of an independent livelihood and of a central part of their culture. Alcohol, drugs and sexual abuse, all of which have ravaged my people, are being introduced by local settlers and sometimes, as with the Innu, by the very people the government has sent to 'look after' them.

And the Jarawa, much more than the Innu, are in danger of being wiped out by new diseases brought by outsiders". Likewise the 'Chenchu' tribes of Orissa, though a developed community are very less in number and there is no appreciable growth in their population for last two decades though special care has been taken by the government for their development through establishment of special project for their systematic development.

The accelerated phase of transformation has definitely disturbed the equilibrium in the traditional societies, to a large extent. The mega population were able to sustain this but the micro ounces are perishing numerically as well as culturally. Development is a long drawn process but its success depends primarily on a proper appreciation of the problem. The small tribes being varied in number and culture, pose a special problem for the planners and administrators. As more often these people are subjected to pressure from longer communities their survival is often at stake. It is therefore, incumbent upon planners to take note of the situation, prepare plans and programmes specially catering to their needs[32]. The foremost requirement is to promote the production system of the tracts concerned and to provide off-season employment for means of sustenance of members of such communities for the entire year. The primitive tribal groups, nomadic groups, shifting cultivators, forest villagers, families displaced by development projects and migrant tribal labourers coming under such category need special attention. Special and appropriate programmes for tribal women of such groups are called for. The disability, from which these vulnerable areas and groups suffer from, needs to be identified for remedial action. There is, thus, an urgent need for appropriate and effective development programmes to check extinction of lesser tribes.

Superstition and Sorcery

Scheduled Tribes are steeped in superstition. They practise witchcraft, sorcery and exorcises. Practice of witchcraft is widely prevalent in most of the tribal communities of India[33].

Due to their superstitions and strong belief in unscientific practices, tribal communities are not receptive to most of the measures and alleviative actions of government and other extraneous agencies meant for their Development. They often practice exorcises for treatment of contagious and even dreaded diseases. Due to superstition, they are hesitant to take patients suffering from malaria, dysentery or diarrhoea to nearby hospitals rather worship the local Gods or Goddesses to cure them. Such cases galore in tribal areas. Bonda women shaving off their heads or covering their faces with tattoos might point to a legend- Sita had cursed them that they would never look beautiful nor have enough cloth to cover themselves. Such age-old superstitions and evil practices might fade in the years to come through proper research and education as some anthropologists and personnel in charge of SC and ST welfare believe. More research projects on different aspects of tribal life need be taken up to zero in on the reasons for such superstitions. Tribes have different blind beliefs which adversely affect their living conditions and hamper their merger with the mainstream. Bondas in Koraput district of Orissa are not the only ones affected by supersition. The Lodhas of eastern india also carry out highway robberies with the belief that their god will be angry and wipe out their families if they do not practise this social evil from any civilised society. As a result, even well to do Lodhas have been resorting to robbery and theft. The Mankadia community feasts on monkey meat because they believe that it helps them foray into forests like the simians. Mushahar tribal communities living in U.P. and Bihar have a different superstition. They eat rats and believe that it is preordained. There tribes also practise of ferreting out grain from rat's burrows. They are most often stigmatised because of this association with rats. Eating of rats has become a part of their tradition due to blind beliefs and age old superstitions.

The prevalence of witchcraft among different tribal groups very often leads to the killing of suspected practitioners. The killing of suspected practitioners is also due to the superstition and blind belief that the occurrence of diseases or any kind of misfortune faced by any member or their family of the community is the handiwork of the sorcerer or the practitioner of the witchcraft. Such type of killings of fellow tribals is common in different tribal communities particularly of Orissa, M.P, Jharkhand and Chhatishgarh.

Sorcery is also a ticklish issue to tackle with. According to a report[34] under the caption "WITCH-HUNTING TAKES ITS TOLL IN ORISSA", Killing over sorcery are on the rise in tribal pockets. The trend is a great cause of concern for rationalists, state police and psychologists. The report reads as follows. March, 2008: Despite being innocent, 40-year-old Samu Soy from village Ranibhola in Mayurbhanj was branded a witch. His cousins strangulated him when Samu walked inside Simlipal forest last Sunday. His wife and son were also murdered the following day in a similar manner when they went in search for Samu. August, 2007: A group of tribals gave death sentence to four persons, including three women at Pratappur village in Balasore district. They were suspected to be witches. The tribals beheaded them before dumping them into a river. Besides these two incidents, there are many cases tht are unreported. Police sources said, at least 15 people were killed in Balasore and Mayurbhanj districts in the last seven months. "We don't have a compiled data of how many have been killed due to witch-craft, sorcery and voodoo. But, child sacrifice and sorcery deaths are common in tribal pockets due to lack of awareness". Circle inspector of police (Karanjia), Orissa Raj Gopal Kar said. "The accused held in Samu's murder said the family practiced black-magic. But we don't have any such evidence," Kar added. Police sources said such incidents are common in Ganjam, Sundargarh, Jharsuguda, Koraput, Jajpur and Mayurbhanj districts of Orissa. Some families are even ostracized and banished from their villages due to superstition. According to an estimate, superstition has led to the death of over 60 people in the last eight years in parts of Orissa. Sundargarh and Mayurbhanj are the most vulnerable districts, which recorded 50 deaths. Ganjam has reported more cases of torture due to sorcery. "The actual figure might be more because some cases are unreported. IT boom has hardly helped the Poor tribals free themselves from the pre-historic beliefs. "Interestingly, the tribals don't regret for the inhuman acts. In many cases, when tribals suffer from any prolonged disease, they suspect someone who practices witch-craft. And, when the patient dies, they kill the suspect." Despite strict police vigilance, such practices are still existing. Superstitious people kill and torture others in the name of sorcery.

Another interesting incident regarding Tribal toddler marrying to a dog was reported in Times of India.[35] The report goes like this. "This would have made even Amy Hempel, author of the Dog of the Marriage thrilled. A two-year-old tribal toddler of Mundasahi village in Jagatsinghpur was married to a female dog on Sunday to ward off the evil spell on him. The wedding was a normal one with the only aberration that the bride was a female dog and the groom Gudulu, son of Radhamohan Singh of Mundasahi, was brought in a flower-decorated auto-rickshaw to the village temple. The villagers organized a feast after the marriage and about 150 people had a sumptuous meal, including *handia* (country liquor). A village priest fixed Sunday to tie the knot as it was an auspicious day according to the tribal almanac. Many people from neighbouring villages attended the wedding which was performed among reneditions of Sanskrit and Santhal sloka chanted by temple priest Sarakari Munda. Said Radhamohan Singh, father of the two-year-old child, "Arranging marriage of a dog with a tribal child is one way of pleasing the village deity and to ward off the evil spell on my son. Such marriages have been held in the past in many villages of the state and neighbouring states of Jharkhand and Chhattisgarh". Bandhu Naak, whose dog was the groom, said, "We haven't done anything wrong. This is just a ceremony to please the tribal deity. In the great epic Mahabharata, a dog helped Pandavs to reach heaven. If this is superstition, even wearing a stone or a talisman means the same". Superstition rules the roost in tribal areas sometimes harming and claiming the lives of innocent tribes and thus retarding the progress and prosperity of the community.

Gender Dimensions

Gender dimension of tribal communities of India also has a bearing on the backwardness of tribal people. In some tribal communities, female members are the chief bread earners for the family in addition to their household works. In some other communities, tribals take pride in having more than one wife. More number of women a tribal man marries, more economic support he gets from them. Here the earning capacity and support to the family determines her position and status in the family.

The trend shows that the sex ratio of total population during census periods is declining whereas for that of tribal population it was increasing till 1981 and from 1981 to 1991 census it has declined from 983 to 972 (Table 10).

Table 10
Sex Ratio of Tribal Population of India, 1961-2001

Census Periods	*Total Population*	*Tribal Population*
1	2	3
1961	941	937
1971	930	982
1981*	935	983
1991*	927	972
2001	933	977

* Excludes Assam, Jammu and Kashmir.

Source: (i) Series–I, Paper–2 of 1991, Census of India–1991, "Final Population, Brief Analysis of Primary Census abstract" and other Census Reports.
(ii) Census 2001

A wide Gender gap in literacy is another important facet which need immediate attention. Tribal Women constitute roughly around 50 percent of the total population of Scheduled tribes. Their role in domestic as well as economic activities can hardly be overemphasized. In tribal societies, women are mainly responsible for maintenance of families and look after Socio-economic activities. But their literacy level is far below the male population. Gap in literacy between male and female among scheduled tribes is 24.4 per cent scheduled tribes and

21.6 for total population.The educational level of tribals is very low.[36] Further, the insignificant literacy rate among tribal women is of great concern. Illiteracy gripping the tribal female-folk distorts the female role models. It perpetuates ignorance and superstition among them.[37]

The female literacy rate among tribals during the period 1991 to 2001 increased from 18.19% to 34.76% which is lower by approximately 20% as compared to literacy rate of the females of the general population.

Child Sex Ratio is more favourable in case of STs in both 1991 and 2001 census periods. The child sex ratio is 972 in case of STs but it is only 933 for General population during 2001. Though there was a reduction in child sex ratio in both the cases during a decade period, the reduction was more (16 nos.) in case of General Population than the tribal population (13 nos.) as revealed from the Table 11.

Table 11
Child Sex Ratio of Tribal population of India

Census Periods	*Total Population*	*Scheduled Tribe Population*
1	*2*	*3*
1991	949	985
2001	933	972

Source: Census of India, 2001,Schedule Tribes Atlas of India, Devendra Kumar Sikri, IAS, Registrar General and Census Commissioner, India.

Apart from low sex ratio and pronounced illiteracy among tribal women, there is another dimension responsible for their backwardness. Among the Banchhara and Bedia tribes of Madhya Pradesh, there is widespread prevalence of caste-based prostitution.[38] It is even ritually sanctioned. In their social system, a married girl is not engaged in prostitution but her sister and mother could practise this. Among the Bedias, the father may marry off some of his daughters but others are introduced into this profession. Among the Banchharas, at least one daughter is pushed into prostitution and others could be married off. The prevalence of this practice prevents them from getting into the national mainstream. The Madhya Pradesh government has started a scheme called "JABALI' for rehabilitation of these tribes.

Lack of Basic Minimum Services in Tribal Areas

Tribal areas lack certain basic services like drinking water, health, housing, nutrition, rural roads etc. One of the long-term needs of tribals development is improvement in their quality of life. The problem of drinking water in tribal areas is acute on account of the *ab initio* paucity of drinking water. Further, some villages suffer from contaminated water supply. Sanitation and hygiene are major casualties on account of these handicaps in tribal areas. Therefore, apart from the provision of food, provision of safe drinking water should be accorded highest priority.

Tribals suffer from poor health conditions.[39] The present state of health of tribals is the cumulative result of under-nourishment compounded by several other factors which include incidence of chronic endemic diseases such as malaria, filarial, tuberculosis, venereal diseases, yaws, leprosy etc. The present health status of tribals is a contributory factor to their numerical decline. There is, therefore, an urgent need to bring such tribal communities within the fold of genetic, preventive and curative medical sciences concomitant with the attempt to improve their nutritional levels. However, the health treatment of tribal communities should be undertaken with a fine degree of perception without which the delicate natural balance in which they are set today may be upset. According to the National Commission on STs, 'it is widely accepted that malnutrition among tribals is wide spread, which is largely attributable to abject illiteracy, environmental conditions, difficult terrain, traditional beliefs and customs and, above all, the non-availability of basic health services. The ill-nourished tribals live in an environment, which has been degraded, and, as a result, diseases such as malaria, filarial, tuberculosis, and goiter are endemic in most of the tribal areas. The tribal people, however, in the course of their isolated existence, have developed alternative systems of medicines. They have a rich store of knowledge of various herbs, plants, insects and animals, which have medicinal value. These drugs and practices have sustained the tribal communities for generations. Now due to change in medical system, the modern method of medicine has also made inroads into the tribal areas. But the tribals, being rooted to their culture, generally prefer to have their own system of medicine and only when they find that it is ineffective, they go in for the allopathic system of medicine. Once the tribals decide to make use of allopathic medicines, they face another problem, which relates to non-availability of doctors and other paramedical personnel. It is commonly known that posting of doctors and other paramedical staff in tribal areas are treated as punishment posting with the result that most of the posts in the centres and sub-centres are generally vacant in tribal areas. There are no private practitioners in these areas as it is not lucrative due to non-viability of this profession in the interior tribal areas. There is a general lack of hygiene and sanitation which aggravates the health problems of the tribals and, therefore, on the whole, tribal people have a lower level of health as has been seen by various health indices like low birth-weight, life expectancy at birth, maternal mortality rate, infant mortality rate and prevalence rate of various communicable diseases, genetic disorders, alcoholism and drug addiction. It has to be accepted that the traditional system of using herbal medicines and the tribal medicine man is not sufficient to take care of all health problems of the tribal people and they have to get access to the modern system of medicine. It is also true that more and more numbers of the tribals are taking to the allopathic and other systems of medicines. However, on account of several factors, health and medical care services are not easily accessible and affordable and, wherever they are available, tribals have not been able to take full benefit of these health services due to illiteracy, ignorance and innate shyness of tribal communities'[40]. Besides, poor health, another important concern is Poor Housing. A comfortable house, which the tribes used to construct with local available materials, is difficult to find in some areas now. Sometimes local material is not available because of depleted forest resources. In some cases the relevant species have been replaced by commercial species and the tribe has no longer free access to forests. Housing condition has, as a result, deteriorated. Housing facilities, therefore, should be provided to tribals in tribal areas. As per the provisional estimates made available by 2001 Census and reported by the commission, the housing shortage in the rural areas is about 149 lakhs as compared to 137 lakhs housing shortage as per 1991 Census. Under the Indira Awaas Yojana, during the last three years, on an average, about 14-15 lakhs houses are being constructed every year whereas the annual requirement is about 30 lakhs house per annum as per the 2001 Census. In addition to this, it is estimated that about 10 lakhs shelterless households are being added every year. Thus, against the total requirement of about 40 lakhs houses, only 14-15 lakhs houses are being constructed leaving a gap of about 25 lakhs houses every year in the rural areas.[41]

Nutrition programmes should have been implemented vigorously and should have universal coverage in tribal areas. On account of the prevalent low level of nourishment, midday meals should be provided to all the children in the age group 6-11 and supplemental feeding programmes for all under-nourished in the age group of 0-6, pregnant women and nursing mothers.[42] Besides these, adequate and safe drinking water is a major problem in tribal areas. In the opinion of the National Commission on STs, 'coverage in terms of access to drinking water, proper upkeep of water supply schemes has been a problem. Many factors like sources going dry, increase in quality problems, systems becoming defunct due to poor maintenance, demand from other competing sectors like agriculture, industry, etc. pose threat to sustainability of drinking water supply schemes. Putting in place an effective operation and maintenance system calls for huge investments. The rural electrification programme is one of the important components in rural development and as important as rural drinking water supply, health, nutrition, primary education, shelter and rural connectivity. The availability of power in rural areas will lead to economic development and its attendant spin-off benefits like food security, better health, literacy, etc. With this in view, the Government has been focusing on village electrification since the beginning of the planning process. While this has resulted in the electrification of around 86 per cent of the country's villages, the use of electricity in villages for productive and subsistence needs is still very limited. About 70 per cent of the rural households are yet to get electric connections and, therefore, power-based economic activities in the electrified villages are minimal. The actual benefits of the investments made in the rural electrification programme can only be realized if the people are in a position to use electricity for their day-to-day activities as well as for industrial and commercial activity. The existing definition of an electrified village is not in order as it does not meet the requirements of the rural people. The existing definition states that 'A village will be deemed to be electrified if electricity used in the inhabited locality within the revenue boundary of the village for any purpose whatsoever.' The Commission is of the view that this definition needs to be changed so as to declare a village as electrified only if a minimum number of households, say 50%, in that village are provided with electricity connections. Around 80,000 villages in the country are yet to be electrified even on the basis of the current definition of village electrification. Thirteen States have declared 100 per cent electrification of their villages. The villages yet to be electrified are mostly in Assam, Arunachal Pradesh, Bihar, Jharkhand, Madhya Pradesh, Meghalaya, Orissa, Rajasthan, Uttar Pradesh, Uttaranchal and West Bengal. Of these 80,000 villages, it may be feasible to electrify only around 62,000 through the conventional grid expansion. The balance 18,000 villages are located in remote areas, hilly terrains, islands, deserts etc. and are also thinly populated. Such villages can be electrified more economically through decentralized and non-conventional energy sources like solar, wind, small hydro and biomass'[43]. Thus, tribal areas in general, lack basic minimum services like health, housing electricity and drinking water both in terms of availability and quality.

Lack of Supportive Infrastructure

It is a fact that the tribal areas have sparse physical infrastructure. Barring a few exceptions, there is no Supportive Infrastructure in these backward areas. Whatever exists might not be able to support beneficiary oriented programmes. These are poor in the matter of physical and mass communication. Adequate infrastructure is required for production, anti-poverty, education and anti-exploitative programmes. Supportive infrastructures have to be legislative, physical, institutional and administrative. Among items of physical infrastructure, special emphasis should be given on minor as well as lift irrigation, soil and water conservation, cooperation and land reforms, which support beneficiary oriented programmes. Capital intensive sectors like large and medium industries, roads and bridges, mining, power, road transport may be given somewhat lower priority unless their spin off effects as such will have a great economic impact on the tribal economy. It is important to remember that, it is the human element that makes or mars the development of any region or group. Steps should, therefore, be taken to improve the quality of the development functionary working at various levels. In addition to all these, more resources, better utilisation and management of the incentives are needed to make tribal people equal partners of larger society. This aspect has not been given adequate attention while planning for tribal development. It has been studied that corruption and inefficiency siphons off a larger mount of resources. This keeps the tribal people where they were. In order to make efficient use of the resources, all steps need to be taken to remove corruption and inefficiency. The corrupt officials should be taken to task. And the committed officials should be rewarded amply. Necessary changes could be brought about in the existing laws to get rid of this social evil. The administrative structure needs to be simplified. Financial procedures warrant simplification. No appreciable measures has so far been taken in this regard. Besides, necessary steps have not been taken to involve the tribal people where it is possible while taking up major industries, power projects, etc. Guidelines in clear terms have not been prepared for giving them adequate rehabilitation and compensation. No monitoring mechanism has been put in place to ensure that the novice tribal people do not get exploited and harassed by the government officials for getting their compensation. There is a need for provisions for the development of the tribals along with the development of the areas. This will accelerate tribal development process.[44] But such harmonious fusion is yet to happen.

Incidence of Poverty

Of late, tribals have been fast losing the areas traditionally under their possession and also the rights to exploit these areas. Poverty, indebtedness and the malafied mechanisms of the more advanced groups who have been extending their influence over the tribal areas are the reasons behind it. The tribals are gradually becoming tenants or working as labourers on the land owned by them earlier. This, no doubt, indicates gradual pauperisation of the tribals. The incidence of poverty is more acute in case of Scheduled Tribes. Old and outdated methods of production, chronic unemployment and serious underemployment contribute, to a great extent, to their poverty condition. Reduction of the incidence of poverty of tribals through raising the levels of productivity and off-season employment is, therefore, an important factor for tribal development.

According to 1991 Census figures, 42.02% of the Scheduled Tribes population were main workers, of whom 54.50% were cultivators and 32.69% were agricultural labourers. Thus, about 87% of the main workers from these communities were engaged in primary sector activities. These disparities are compounded by higher dropout rates in formal education, resulting in a disproportionately lower representation in higher education. The cumulative effect has been that the proportion of Scheduled Tribes below the poverty line is substantially higher than the national average. As per a statement provided by the Planning Commission, it is observed that ST people living below poverty line in 1993-1994 was 51.94% in rural areas, and 41.14% in urban areas respectively. The percentage of ST population living below poverty line has decreased to 45.86% in rural areas and 34.75% in urban areas as per the estimation of below poverty line in the year 1999-2000. Though there is a decrease of STs living below poverty line by about 6% in rural areas and 4.5% in urban areas during the last five years, around 46% rural and 35% urban tribes are still extremely poor.[45]

According to the data, as high as 52 percent of STs are Below Poverty Line (BPL) and the corresponding figure for the total population is only 37.3 percent during 1993-94 but it was substantially higher in 1977-78 i.e. 72.4 and 53.1 percent respectively as the Table below (12) reveals.

Table 12

Persons Below Poverty Line (Rural : 1977-78 to 1993-94)

	Percentage of People in BPL Category	
Years	*Total*	*STs*
1	2	3
1977-78	53.1	72.4
1983-84	45.6	58.4
1993-94	37.3	51.9

Source: Tribes in India, A Data Sheet, Planning Commission, Backward classes and Tribal Development Division, Government of India, New Delhi, July, 2000.

There is wide variation of percentage of ST population *vis-à-vis* general population living below poverty line in different States. BPL percentage of the population, both STs and general, in rural areas for all the States is exhibited in Appendix-6. State-wise estimation of BPL percentage of tribal dominated States in rural areas during 1993-94 has been displayed in Table 13.

Freny Manecksha[46] meets one of India's poorest tribes whose children make themselves ill by eating raw bhindi to keep their hunger at bay. His report about mushhars in Uttarpradesh is as follows. Starvation deaths are headline grabbers. But when an entire community lives on the brink of starvation through the year it rarely merits a mention. One such group, the Musahars in Uttar Pradesh light their Chula

Table 13
Scheduled Tribes of India below Poverty Line

	Below Poverty Line (Rural- %) 1993-94	
States/Union Territories	*Total*	*STs*
1	*2*	*3*
INDIA	**37.27**	**51.94**
Arunachal Pradesh	45.01	NA
Assam	45.01	41.44
Madhya Pradesh	40.64	56.69
Manipur	45.01	NA
Meghalaya	45.01	NA
Mizoram	45.01	NA
Nagaland	45.01	NA
Orissa	49.72	71.26
Sikkim	45.01	NA
UNION TERRITORIES		
A & N Islands	32.48	NA
D & N Haveli	51.95	NA
Daman & Diu	5.34	NA
Lakshadweep	25.76	NA

Source: Tribes in India, A Data Sheet, Planning Commission, Backward classes and Tribal Development Division, Government of India, New Delhi, July, 2000.

once a day, in the evening, and live on one meal. Last month, when I visited a Musahar tola (settlement) of some 25 families in Barrachawar Block of Ghazipur in eastern UP, the families were waiting for the meals-the only earning members-to return with the daily wages. Rajmunna, one of the women explained, "We have no land. My family of eight is entirely dependent on daily wages of around Rs.10 to Rs.25. We eat two chappatis per head. A quarter kilo of dal must suffice for us all. Occasionally we get some vegetables like green peas that we make into a gravy'. Rajmuna describes her chronic hunger as a "burning pit in the abdomen". She is unable to walk any distance without getting breathless. Rinku, a teenager, is noticeably ill and has been diagnosed with TB of the bones. She has not received any treatment. The Musahars claim that a health worker makes the rounds but demands Rs. 10 per injection. Things get grimmer in August and September when there is low demand for agricultural labour. The Chula is then lit one in two days. Basi (leftover) rotis are given to the children the next morning. "We have to give the children something to eat because if the hunger pangs get too much for them they run into the fields and gobble raw bhindi, which makes them ill", says an elder Ram Prasad Vanbasi. A 2003 study by a student of the Indian Institute of Rural Management found that 90 percent of the Musahar children below six suffer from malnutrition. Tuberculosis and rheumatic fever are common. There is no electricity in the tola. It gets waterlogged every monsoon forcing the families to shelter in the Block Development Offices premises. Shifting their possessions is easy-all they own are string charpoys, kitchen utensils and a few tattered garments. One of India's most marginalised communities, the Musahars live largely on the banks of the Gandak and its tributaries in eastern UP and Bihar. They are believed to be tribals evicted when the British cleared forest lands. Small plots given in compensation were usurped by powerful landlords. A project conducted under the Poorest Area Civil Soceity programme (a development programme for India's 100 poorest districts) found that 60 per cent of Musahars were landless. Others own waterlogged, infertile plots. The Musahars social and political isolation was heightened when the British tagged them as a criminal community. In independent India, they have remained vulnerable targets with the police forcing them to do beggar or forced labour. Consequently, Musahars have a great fear of authority. This is why they find it difficult to get Below Poverty Line cards. Forced to away from upper-caste villages, Musahar children who attend school are made to sit separately. Many do not even have the necessary papers to vote. An important landmark took place in May this year when, before the UP elections, two voluntary bodies-the Musahar Vikas Pahal and Musahar Manch-organised a dialogue between the voiceless community and different parties. All the candidates acknowledged the necessity of speedy land reforms to enable Musahars to earn a decent livelihood. But it will take much more that to help these 'dalits of the dalits.

Case of Mushahars of U.P. is just a tip of the iceberg. They are not the only tribe with acute poverty and pauperisation. Many other tribes residing in different parts of the Country are also extremely poor. Anecdotes of the following tribes of Orissa, M.P., Jharkhand, Chhatisgarh etc. may be taken to illustrate the point.

BAIGA: Shifting cultivation is practised by them. They live on wild fruits, roots and animal meat. They are darkish in complexion. They have no permanent homes as they move from place to place looking for fresh cultivable lands. The Baigas of the plains work as labourers.

BANJAR: Formerly they were migratory in their habit and sold commodities in various places moving in large groups. History supports the fact that the Banjari were employed by the Hindu as well as Muslim kings to carry necessities for the soldiers to the war front. In course of time they have migrated to different places. They live in abject poverty.

BATHUDI: The main occupation of the Bathudis is settled agriculture. Amount of land owned by most of the families is not sufficient to meet their requirements. There are landless Bathudis who solely depend on wage earning or petty business. Consequently, most of them work as part time labourers and do petty rice business. They grow paddy and other cash crops such as pulses, sugar, potato, groundnuts, etc. Hunting and fishing are no more practised as gainful economic pursuits.[47]

BHOTTARA: The Bhottaras are agriculturists.[48] They work as wage earners when there is no work in the fields. A few of them also serve in firm.

BHUIYAN: The sources of living of the Pauris are food gathering, hunting and shifting cultivation.[49] They collect edible roots, fruits and worms (Kai) from the nearby streams. As agriculturists they practise shifting cultivation.

BHUMIA: The Bhumiyas prepare implements like *Kula* and *Duti*. From various kinds of fibres like jute, sabai and siali, they weave a large net for catching fish and *Kudarjal* for entrapping rabbit. From Siali leaves they prepare *Talari,* which is a country umbrella. They prepare other agricultural implements. In addition to agriculture work, the Bhumiyas prepare implements like *Kula* and *Duli*. From various kinds of fibres like jute, sabai and siali, they weave a large net for catching fish and *Kudarjal* for entrapping rabbit

BHUMIJ: The Bhumijs are agriculturists. Their main occupation is cultivation supplemented by wage earning, collection of jungle products and hunting. After harvest when they do not have openings for wage earning, the Bhumij men go to work in the mining quarries and in tea gardens of Assam. As land holding is not sufficient for livelihood for most of the families, they work as part time labourer for the neighbouring cultivators when agricultural operation is in swing. Hunting as a gainful economic pursuit has been given up due to depletion of forest and restrictions imposed by the government.

BHUNJIA: Bhunjias are a small tribe. According to R.V. Russel and R.B. Hiralal, "the term Bhunjia may perhaps signifies one who lives on the soil, from Bhum the earth and Jia, 'depended on'. The word Binjia, a synonym for Bhinjhwar, is similarly a corruption of Bewar Jia, and means one who is dependent on dahia or patch of cultivation. They are not an advanced community in the sense that majority of them are illiterate.

BIRHOR: The Birhors are one of the earliest nomadic tribes in India. As the very name implies, they are the people belonging to the forests. They not only belong to the forests but are in close association with the basic features of the forests and the connected environments from time immemorial.[50] The Birhors fall to the category of hunting and gathering group. Instead of being settled up in a particular place permanently, the Birhors wander from place to place within a circumscribed area and, therefore, known as a nomadic tribe.[51] The Birhors are skilled monkey catchers. They use nets made of siali creepers for catching monkeys and consume the flesh of the monkeys.[52] The skin is sold to the local scheduled caste people. Although the Birhors tap different sources for their livelihood, they run deficit in their food supply many a times. During scarce period they eat mango kernels, which are preserved at home for use in difficult times.[53] They collect various types of green leaves and mushrooms, fruits such as 'Kendu', palm and mango from the forest for their consumption. While collecting barks from the forest, they dig out roots, fibres and collect honey, which supplements their principal cereal diet.[54]

BONDA: They are extremely aggressive. Age-old isolation, poverty, intoxication and fear of sorcery are the chief reasons of their aggressiveness. Gruel of ragi and rice are the chief food of the tribe. They collect wild vegetables, bamboo shoot, mushrooms, etc. They keep cattle, goats, pig and poultry. They drink enormous quality of wine called salap, the juice of Sago palms. They have their own hill cleanings where they practise Podu. According to customary practices, these clearings become individual property and each household owns a number of sites on the hillsides, which are cultivated in rotation.

DAL: Each Dal owns a number of Mahul trees. Mahul is collected and stored by each family on which they depend for their food. Mostly Mahul is exchanged for Ragi and Kondu with the contractors who bread liquor in the neighbourhood. The Kultas, Bhuitiyas and Marwaries also exploit by advancing loans before harvest. The Dals sell their products at a nominal rate as a precondition of getting loan.

DESUA BHUMIJ: The Bhumij have taken to wage earning as the main source of income. Most of them are landless and only a few families have got land which is not sufficient to meet their requirements. Almost all of them work as labourers for the neighbouring cultivators. Children are employed to tend cattle. The depleted forest in the neighbouring area does not provide much scope for collecting green leaves, roots and fruits as in the past. With much difficulty, they can bring fuel and Sal leaves for sale. In leisure time they manufacture bricks. During summer, a few Bhumij men go to work in the tea gardens of Assam or in Calcutta or in the Mining Quarries. Although rice is their staple food, they hardly get full meals throughout the year. They eat beef, pork, fowl, white ant, mouse, termites and other unclean food. Rice-beer and Mohua liquor are taken too.

DIDAYI: The Hill Didayi practice shifting cultivation whereas the plain people have adopted settled agriculture. The hill Didayis collect a variety of roots and fruits during the entire year to supplement their food. The Didayis are voraciously addicted to juice or salap tree which is available in abundance in the forests. The hill Didayis live on subsistence level.

GADABA: They practised shifting cultivation in a localised area. Each family divides its holding for shifting cultivation in two parts and cultivates a part, when the other remains barren. The places are alternated once in every three years. Since their production is insufficient they resort to food collection in the jungles. Mango Kernel, edible roots, etc. support them for two months in a year.

HO: Hunting and collection of edible roots and tubers are a part and parcel of their economy. Rice is their staple food. The females collect the roots, tubers, green leaves, mushrooms from the jungle. The Hos go for wage earning to earn their livelihood. They prefer to wage in terms of kind rather than wage in money terms.

HOLVA: Their main occupation is agriculture. They cultivate the land as owner and on share basis. Many of them remain as labourers with the people who own land. They collect jungle products.

JATAPU: The Jatapus are mainly agriculturists but the poorer sections earn their bread by wage earning or being employed as labourers. Rice and gruel constitute the staple food of the Jatapus.

KULI: It is said that the name 'Kuli' has been derived from the word 'Kula', a dumb bell of the cow used for the process of guarding. They are engaged as cattle rearers by the the rich people of the vicinity but earn a scanty wage. But many of them work as labourers. The list of the aforesaid tribes is only illustrative. There are many primitive classes whose economic conditions are also precarious.

Exploitation and Indebtedness

Indebtedness and exploitation are the harrowing features of the tribal economy. The tribals appear to accept indebtedness as an inevitable and inescapable aspect of their existence. Most of the tribal families are born in debt, live in debt and die in debt. They, irrespective of their occupations, wallow in poverty. The tribals are improvident in their habits and always need money to fulfil social obligations and rituals which results in exploitation by the unscrupulous and egregious moneylenders. Small amounts of money borrowed at high rates of interest from time to time multiply into a sum beyond his capacity to repay. Finally, the small land holding he possess goes to the moneylender in partial satisfaction of the debt. Traders in tribal areas are found using substandard weights and measures. Cheating and intimidation are freely used by the traders and local non-tribal merchants. Land alienation by the non-tribal immigrants and dominant groups is also a regular feature. Merchants, moneylenders, landlords and liquor-vendors work havoc with their economy. Modern economy has entered into the area in the form of "Traders frontier" with concomitant backwash effects of exploitation and land alienation.

Elimination of exploitation and enforcement of protective and anti-exploitative measures are the basic needs of tribal development. Exploitation of tribals' forms a *lait motife* in the tribal canvas of today. Sometimes, the unscrupulous elements under one cover or another exploit the simple tribal situation.[55] Exploitation in tribal areas mainly occurs in the fields of liquor vending, land alienation,[56] money-lending, forestry, trade including collection and disposal of minor forest products and labour including forest labour. While generally the passing of lands from the ownership and control of the tribals is ascribed to the lacunae in the law, due to faulty implementation, rapacious exploitation by unscrupulous traders, moneylenders etc., sometimes the tribals are overwhelmed by a sense of alienation from the socio-political system itself, which they think is responsible for their massive dispossession.[57]

There are numerous problems that the tribals are facing today of which economic crisis and poverty come to the forefront. It is through the traditional money-lending system that the tribals are greatly exploited. Indebtedness is, thus, the next pressing problem of these areas.[58] The tribal economy is characteristically a subsistence type of economy. Due to their traditional hedonistic type of world view, they have very little savings. Naturally, when they are in need of money, they are forced to depend on others particularly on the non-tribal moneylenders. Under this system, a person who takes a loan from a moneylender or landowner is required to serve him just like a slave according to the terms and conditions of the loan. Quite often, if he is unable to repay the loan, slavery descends to his son or even to the third generation.[59] This system is known by various names in different parts of the country–in Rajasthan it is called Sagri, in Orissa Gothi, in Andhra Vetti, in Mysore Jeetha, in Madhya Pradesh Naukarinama and Mahidari etc.[60]

Countering exploitation through more vigorous enforcement of the various anti-exploitative measures and protection of the interests of the Scheduled Tribes through appropriate legal and administrative support is one of the basic needs. Article 46 of the Constitution specifically enjoins on the states the special responsibility of promotion with special care of the education and economic interests of weaker sections of the people and in particular of the Scheduled Cates and Scheduled Tribes and of protecting them from social injustice and exploitation. The Constitution provides adequate authority to a state for achieving these objectives. The Fifth Schedule to the Constitution provide, "the Governor may make regulations for the peace and good government in any area in a state which is for the time being a scheduled area". Be that as it may, the tribals were hard-pressed to repay their loans due to lack of organised marketing facilities for their agricultural and forest produces at remunerative prices. As a result, they had to fall back into the clutches of the money lenders and traders who advance money for production, consumption and marketing and in the process continue the exploitation.[61]

Tribal-landlord strife are common features in tribal dominated areas. A report in an English daily says, "Clashes between the landed gentry and the landless tribal community in Bisama Katak area of Rayagada district have escalated as at least a dozen people from both sides were injured and many houses razed in violence spread over the past 10 days. Fear stalks the area amid allegations that police and the district administration were supporting the "mighty" landlords. Trouble began in the erstwhile peaceful tribal dominated Bariguda village on July 9, 2007 when supporters of the CP (M-L) Liberation launched a "land free" campaign in the area. ....The goons hired by the landlords attacked two party leaders who were subsequently arrested. The police action has encouraged the landlords to attack the poor tribals", the party's state secretary Khitish Biswal said. A delegation of the tribals, led by Biswal, met the Governor of Orissa and apprised him how the landlords had retained hundreds of plots "illegally". Nearly 48,000 acres of land reportedly remained under the landlord's clutches, while more than 50 percent of Rayagada's population was landless. According to government rules effective in Orissa since 1978, no person can own more than 18 acres of land. "But the ratio is totally different in the tribal-dominated districts," Biswal said. The party requested to Governor to rescue the "Innocent" tribals who were starving due to lack of land and selling their children to combat poverty. We have freed at least 4,380 acres of land from the clutches of several landlords in Rayagada," party leader Radhakanta Sethi said. Besides Rayagada, the party has been carrying out its "land free" campaign in Gajapati and Koraput districts of Orissa from July, 2008"[62]

Illiteracy

The prevalent paradigm of economic development of scheduled tribes is not sustainable if social development in the form of minimum level of education is not properly imparted to them. Programmes of economic development for and the spread of education among STs should go side by side if both are to succeed.

The socio-economic development of Scheduled Tribes depends on educational advancement. Education is a cardinal basic social input for economic Development of Primitive tribes. Education is more than a mere asset for some tribal communities;[63] investment in education is, in a way, crucial for their existence. Kaun-tsu very aptly pointed out;

> "By sowing seed, you will harvest once,By planting a tree, you will harvest tenfold,By educating the people, you will harvest one hundred fold."

The role of education as an instrument of socio-economic transformation has been well established. This will not only inculcate a sense of urgency and involvement of STs for rapid economic development but also ensure bringing them to the mainstream of national consciousness. Education can attack and revolutionize the basic thinking and attitudes of the primitive people. Education is regarded as one of the most effective and forward looking instrument of tribal social transformation. Hence, their educational development is closely related to their economic development. The very meaning of 'education', which is derived from the Latin word 'educase', means to nourish, to cause to grow. 'And it is this original meaning of the word as a developing agency that most closely correspond to the transformation of an infant into a full member of a specific human society, sharing with the other members a specific human culture. Education, therefore, gives him the key to a fuller and richer life and helps the primitive tribal communities to satisfactorily negotiate with the transitional phase of socio-economic change. Hence, it is considered as a key parameter in generating a new awareness among the people by disseminating the knowledge and information for promoting change. Emancipation from ignorance and illiteracy is the sine qua non for Economic emancipation. It is no luxury, no academic fad and no political stunt. It is necessary to individual happiness and social well-being. It is an inalienable and integral part of their all-round development. In the words of Neal Jacoby (1970): "Education holds the key to development. Development is not just change in terms of saving-income ratio, or export-GNP ratio; development is an enormously complex process involving changes in customs, habits and ways of doing things". Continued economic exploitation has brought them to a state of helplessness exemplified by migrant labour, debt bondage, etc. A medium of education will equip them to deal with middlemen, merchants and traders on a better footing. The adults need to undergo citizenship training to understand the process of law, revenue, police, forest and in fact, of the entire administration to remove their present disadvantage. Literacy, to quote Dr. Huxley, 'is a pre-requisite for scientific and technical advance, and for better health, more efficient agriculture and productive industry, for democracy and national progress and for international awareness and knowledge of other nations.' Dr. Huxley's definition envisages a long-range programme having a two-fold purpose, material and spiritual. So far as the material aspect is concerned, it seeks to improve the standard of living in the backward and underdeveloped people by imparting education to the individual in the essentials of health, nutrition, improvement of agricultural production, healthier and happier home-life and useful recreational activities. On the spiritual side, the programme aims not only at making the individual aware of the larger world community and his relations therewith but also enabling him to exercise his right of having his way in the determination of the destiny of a man.

The 1950 World Census definition on literacy is mere 'ability to read and write a simple message'. According to the latest definition of census of India, persons of age 7 years and above, who can both read and write with understanding in any language, is considered as literate. Let us have a cursory glance on the literacy scenario of scheduled tribes of India in general.

Table 14 presents literacy rate of Scheduled Tribes *vis-à-vis* General Population of different categories (male, female, total populations) for the last five census periods. In rural areas literacy rate of general population is 58.47% whereas, literacy rate of STs is only 45.01%.

Table shows that literacy rate of general population increased from 24.0 during 1961 to 64.83 in 2001 registering an increase of about 41% for the last 40 years. On the other hand, tribal literacy increased from 8.5 to 47.08 during the same period i.e. an increase of about 39%. But none the less, there is a discernible gap of approximately 18% in the literacy rate of tribals and the general population according to 2001 census. In case of female population there is a yawning gap of around

Table 14
Tribal Literacy Rate of India, 1961-2001

Population	*Year*	*Persons*	*Males*	*Females*
1	*2*	*3*	*4*	*5*
Total	1961	24.0	34.4	13.0
	1971	29.5	39.5	13.7
	1981*	36.2	46.9	24.8
	1991*	52.11	64.13	39.29
	2001	64.83	75.62	53.67
Tribal	1961	8.5	13.8	3.2
	1971	11.3	17.6	4.9
	1981*	16.4	24.5	8.0
	1991	29.60	40.65	18.19
	2001	47.08	59.14	34.75

* Excludes Assam.
Source: Collected and compiled from Census Reports.

19% but for male population it is nearly 16%. The difference between male literacy and female literacy is about 22% in case of total population but approximately 25% in case of tribal population. However, female literacy in general presents a dismal scenario. It is only around 35% in case of Scheduled tribes. Literacy rate of Primitive Tribal Gropus (PTGs) presents even more dismal picture. In almost all cases of primitive tribes, their literacy percentage is far behind the literacy percentage of Scheduled tribesin general. Also wide Gender gap in literacy is another important facet which need immediate attention. Tribal Women constitute roughly around 50 percent of the total population of Scheduled tribes. Their role in domestic as well as economic activities can hardly be overemphasized. In tribal societies, women are mainly responsible for maintenance of families and look after Socio-economic activities. But their literacy level, as indicated above, is far below the male population. Thus, the educational level of tribals is very low.[64] Further, the insignificant literacy rate among tribal women is of great concern. Illiteracy gripping the tribal female-folk distorts the female role models. It perpetuates ignorance and superstition among them.[65]

Gross Enrolment Ratios (GER) in India during 1997-98 in classes 1 to V is 89.7 in case of total children but this is higher i.e. 90.7 in case of ST children. But in higher classes this GER sharply declined in case of ST children. It was 58.5 in case of total children and only 43.2 in case of ST children in classes VI to VIII. Thus, in higher classes GER is significantly lower in case of ST children than the General Children. Coming to the Dropout Rate (DOR), it was exceedingly higher in case ST children. DORs in classes I to VIII during 1993-94 was as high as 77.7 percent but this was only 52.8 percent in case of General children. GER in classes 1 to V and VI to VIII of total and ST children during 1997-98 and DOR in classes 1 to VIII during 1993-94 of total and ST children in different tribal dominated States and Union territories of India has been displayed in Table 15.

Table 15
Gross Enrolment Ratios and Drop-out Rates of Scheduled Tribes of India (1991)

	Gross Enrolment Ratios (1997-98)				*Drop-out Rates (1993-94)*	
	Classes I-V		*Classes VI-VIII*		*Classes I-VIII*	
States/Union Territories	*Total*	*STs*	*Total*	*STs*	*Total*	*STs*
1	2	3	4	5	6	7
INDIA	**89.7**	**90.7**	**58.5**	**43.2**	**52.8**	**77.7**
Arunachal Pradesh	97.2	99.2	65.8	69.2	68.7	73.6
Assam	109.1	NA	69.3	NA	67.6	66.3
Madhya Pradesh	102.3	82.4	64.9	38.1	44.7	76.0
Manipur	80.8	91.6	70.5	55.5	72.3	51.3
Meghalaya	93.3	86.4	52.7	48.9	57.7	84.3
Mizoram	113.6	113.8	70.6	73.5	52.4	71.6
Nagaland	94.3	97.2	65.6	73.3	38.1	67.7
Orissa	90.5	88.3	53.4	31.9	61.2	86.5
Sikkim	113.3	107.3	59.0	56.9	78.4	75.7
UNION TERRITORIES						
A& N Islands	86.8	75.6	93.9	65.2	27.3	23.6
D & N Haveli	96.1	96.7	59.1	51.9	62.2	67.8
Daman & Diu	99.1	109.8	69.5	71.8	-	39.3
Lakshadweep	104.5	105.1	69.1	66.5	52.2	46.7

Source: Tribes in India, A Data Sheet, Planning Commission, Backward classes and Tribal Development Division, Government of India, New Delhi, July, 2000.

voluntary workers also constitute a serious impediment to the progress of literacy and mass-education. A.H. Halsey (1970) outlined the social determinants of educability as–inequalities of school provision, social class and cultural ingredients such as language, the social distance between the teacher and the pupil, the level of educational aspiration, the definition of roles in the school and the nature of peer groups in childhood and adolescence. Thus, the educational gaps in various communities may be viewed as due to the differences in the provisions of educational facilities, socio-economic status of the parents lack of motivation of education which mainly arise among the tribal groups as a result of isolation-lack of communication and social distance. Because isolation affects in many contexts–the community as a whole, the school within the community, the pupil within the class-room and the teacher within the educational system.

The country had in the past only traditional method of educational system imparted mostly by religious institutions. Formal education was introduced by the British. After independence, Article 46 of the Indian Constitution lays down a Directive Principles of State Policy which provides that the State shall promote with special care, the educational and economic interests of the people and in particular of Scheduled Castes and Scheduled Tribes. Article 47 and Article 30 of the Constitution have some provisions for educational interests of the scheduled tribes. In the first two Five-Year Plans, not much emphasis was laid on education. The policy of government emphasised on providing the immediate basic necessities like food and shelter to people. It was only during the Third Five-Year Plan that the states were allotted good amount of money towards education of Scheduled Tribes. However, the strategy adopted during the Seventh Plan period was to a considerable extent successful in highlighting the problems of education of the primitive tribal groups. The Eighth Plan accorded top priority for strengthening the economic base of the primitive tribes in the framework of their socio-economic and cultural context. The local persons having knowledge of tribal language were given preference in the appointment of school teachers. The curriculum was redesigned keeping in view the requirement of the tribal people. Large number of residential schools were opened. Adult education programmes were expounded. Hostel facilities were expanded to give boarding facilities to the tribal students at the primary, middle and high school levels. Besides providing reading and writing materials to these students, Pre-matric scholarships are awarded to students at pre-matric level. Post-matric scholarship is awarded to post-matric students. Graduate students in general courses, medical, engineering, agriculture, veterinary science students etc. are provided scholarships. A scheme has been introduced for giving cash Award to the Head Sevaks for Increasing Enrolment and Checking Dropouts of Tribal Children at Primary Level. During the Ninth Plan, special care was taken for development of education in micro project areas in conformity with the recommendations of the Working Group on Tribal Development. During the Tenth Plan (2002-2007), it has been programmed to invest funds out of the General Education Schemes of the Education Department for education development programmes of ST students including children of primitive tribes.

But not withstanding all these efforts and despite our stepping into the 21st century, development of tribals in the state remains a distant dream. The primitive tribes remain primitive. Literacy among the tribals is at a low ebb. Female literacy among them is negligible.[68] Hence, education of tribals is one of the cardinal basic inputs, the importance of which cannot be over emphasized. To-day there is universal recognition of the supreme importance of Fundamental Education as the only means to elevate mankind emotionally and intellectually, morally and materially. In the words of Joad: "To a man of trained and developed tastes, the world becomes literally a larger place, larger and more exciting. He is able to see in it more of beauty, more variety, and more scope for his sympathy and understanding. The world is transformed from a humdrum scene of workshop, factory and of office to a Universe of meaning and mystery and a treasure-house of beauty. Hence, it is considered as a key parameter in generating a new awareness among the people by disseminating the knowledge and information for promoting change. It is universally admitted that the success of any plan for social and economic reconstruction or for that matter, any national endeavour whether in peace-time or in war depends on the education and understanding of the masses. The purpose of education is the humanization of mankind, which begins emotionally and not intellectually. Schooling can correct "infantile dehumanization" and can humanize the child. Education is now recongnised as the principal vehicle of social change, since it is no longer simply a matter of mastering the three R's–reading, writing and arithmetic–nor is it merely a matter of skill acquisition, of preparing for a vocation or profession. Rather, it is the means to improving the quality of life, achieving social mobility and participating in the world's affairs[69].Therefore, in order to correct the pitfalls and mitigate the tribal problems in educational front, some policy challenges are warranted.

The scheduled tribes have some peculiar characteristic features. The schemes for educational development that are being introduced for the development of the others will not be applicable to them due to their cultural specialities, ecosystems and aptitudes. Around 50% of boys and barely more than a third of the girls belonging to STs who enter school make it past after two/three years of schooling. Hence, reduction of dropouts is a major challenge for enhancing the literacy rate of STs. According to Olsen (1945): "Ever more clearly it becomes apparent that school education must be projected out of the sheltered class room and into the living community which is the child's primary scene of the present, and future life-activity".Hence,it is imperative that education must reach these people living in inaccessible areas[70].

Discouraging teacher's absenteeism may, in the short run, be a remedial measure.Government teacher absenteeism is high in the areas predominated by PTGs. In some cases, some teachers run businesses and others skip school in the morning but give paid tuitions to richer students in the afternoon.

Stringent rules must be made and strict supervision be introduced for cheking the absenteeism of teachers in these areas. Adequate infrastructure under both overheads and services should be made available in the tribal areas because most of the tribal population of the state is found in the hill region, dense forest and inaccessible areas of the state. The tribal people who have specially suffered from relative isolation for centuries, suffer from backwardness, superstitions and many of the impediments. They need all types of encouragement and incentives for pursuing studies. Sometimes when the government comes forward to provide adequate educational opportunities and incentives for the educational development of the tribal people, satisfactory results are not seen. All those incentives and facilities have failed to attract the girl children in particular. The tribal people are obviously newcomers in the race of literacy[71]. Majority of them are yet to enjoy the benefits of modern education and assistance provided by the government. However, the efforts made by certain non-government organisations have proved beneficial. Keeping this in view, the government should encourage some committed voluntary organisations to undertake the task in the remote tribal areas. Besides this, appropriate policy should be developed to check dropout rates. More emphasis has to be given on elementary education. There is a need to open a good number of residential schools for tribal girls in particular. There is a need to upgrade the primary schools. Special vocational education is to be imparted to tribals in crafts like tailoring, typewriting, embroidery or other traditional skills. Besides, emphasis has to be laid on various types of incentives both for the teachers as well as the students. Undoubtedly, incentives play a major role in removing the educational backwardness among the tribals. The government's commitment to social justice is directly related with that of development of education among them. Considering the vastness in terms of geographical area and bulging population size and backwardness, policymakers cannot ignore the educational grievances of other sections of our society.[72]

Shifting Cultivation

Practice of the shifting cultivation[73] is another important retarding factor for tribal development. Tribals were perhaps the original settlers of the Indian soil, hence called primitive or and aborigines. For a long period, dependence of the tribals on the forest for their sustenance was undisputed.[74] Forest is intimately connected with tribal life and economy. To a vast majority of the tribal people, the forest is their well loved home and their livelihood. Their very existence depends on it. It gives them food, fruits of all kinds, edible roots and leaves. Forests are a source of minor products, which are sold or exchanged. It provides them with materials to build their houses or to practice their arts, which are often financially gainful. By exploiting the natural products, they supplement their meagre income. It keeps them warm with its fuel and cool with its graceful shade.[75] They enjoy the rights of exploitation of the forest produce for their own benefit. The barriers and regulations imposed on them with the advent of Government control over forests resulted in a conflict in their lives in economic, physical and psychological terms.[76] The forest contractors exploited the tribal labourers in several ways and illegally collected fees from them for the use of flowers and fruits. Gradually, the dependence of the tribal economy on the forests decreased with a corresponding increase in agriculture. The agricultural situation in forest villages has become far from satisfactory. These forest villages are labour camps of the forest department, which are settled under the byelaws of forest manuals placing these labourers on the borderline of slavery.[77] Although, each family living in a forest village is allotted some land for cultivation, no tenancy rights are conferred on the tillers. Neither *Patta* is given to this effect nor can they enjoy any permanent right to cultivate the land.[78] Once the villagers migrate from the village, they lose their land, which is taken over by the forest department. During the decade from 1951-61, the promotional increase in the landless agricultural labourers belonging to Scheduled Tribes had been quite substantial.[79]

Land is not of much significance to the tribals as the symbol of social status but as a means of livelihood. An analysis of the tribal workers in various occupations shows that tribal economy revolves round farming. But it is primitive or rudimentary in nature adopting only a few known direct methods of production. Shifting cultivation is one such example.[80]

The age-old method of land use on the slopes of hills[81] necessitates the trees and bushes to be cut down and fired after drying. Seeds are then sown in little holes dug in the ground is known as 'shifting cultivation'. Such a field whose fertility is not replenished by manuring (except through ashes obtained from burn-out vegetative cover) yields a diminishing return and is practically exhausted in 2 or 3 years time.[82] The farmer then moves over to a new patch of forest area allowing the abandoned plot to recoup.

Jhum cycle depends upon the density of population of a particular area and availability of suitable hill slopes. As population increases, a vicious circle stands. The Jhumming cycle becomes shorter and soil fertility is not fully restored. Consequently yields decline and further areas are brought under the Jhumming. The Jhum cycle is further shortened.[83] In Orissa, of late, with the increase in the pressure of population, the Jhum cycle which was about 10 to 22 years has reduced to 5 to 12 years now.[84] It came down to 4 to 6 years in 1973. With further decrease of the period it stands at 2 to 5 years now.

Similar is the trend found in other parts of India. The Jhum cycle which was 30 to 40 years previously have shrunk to 1 to 17 years in Arunachal Pradesh, 4 to 5 years in Meghalaya, Mizoram and Tripura, 5 to 10 years in Assam hills, 6 to 8 years in Manipur and 6 to 15 years in Nagaland.[85] The immediate consequences of rapid rise in population are extension of areas of Jhum cycle resulting in low productivity, out migration to some rich villages in search of jobs as hired labourers at low wage and indebtedness.[86] There are 109 tribes in India alone who practise shifting cultivation.[87] Excepting in extreme climatic regions like Polar or Tundra or deserts where conditions are unfavourable for quick growth of plants, this practice is prevalent with minor variations even now throughout the world.[88]

In India Shifting Cultivation is widely practised in North Eastern Region of the country comprising of Assam, Manipur, Meghalaya, Nagaland and Tripura and Union Territories of Arunachal Pradesh and Mizoram, Kerala, Madhya Pradesh, Andhra Pradesh and Orissa. This practice is known as 'Jhum' in Assam, Pendo, Bewar and Dahi in Madhya Pradesh, Tekunglu in Nagaland, Hookismong in Tripura, Adiabik in N.E.F.A. and Biringa, Podu and Dahi in Orissa. In Orissa, this method is practised by the tribes of 'Bonda', 'Didayi', 'Koya', 'Gadaba' and 'Paraja' of Koraput, the 'Kutia Khonda' and 'Dangria Kondh' of Koraput and Phulbani, the 'Langia Saora' of Ganjam and Koraput, the 'Kondh' and 'Pengo Kondh' of Kalahandi and Sambalpur, 'Juang' and 'Pauri Bhuyan' of Keonjhar District.[89]

It has been estimated by the Taskforce on Shifting Cultivation set up by the Ministry of Agriculture that approximately 9.95 million hectares in the tribal and hilly areas of the country are under shifting cultivation. About 223 development blocks in 62 districts in 16 states are affected by this practice. Shifting cultivation is a dominant production activity for approximately 12 per cent of the tribal population of the country. The shifting cultivators lived in below subsistence level. The period of rotation has dangerously come down from around 7 years a few decades back to about 3-4 years in several forests and hilly areas in the country.

Shifting cultivation is a wasteful activity from environmental and forest wealth point of view. It has deleterious effects on soil and water regime. The effects of prolonged shifting cultivation are starkly in evidence in certain areas like Koraput district of Orissa where the barren rounded reddish brown hills are unable to grow a blade of grass and the soil has been reduced to ferruginous laterite due to continual erosion and leaching. Ecologists and environmentalists have expressed their concern and demanded its discontinuation. It destroys the fertility of the soil as well as the forest products on which the tribal people depend for their subsistence. The hill slopes have been fully denuded and are completely barren due to the impermanent land husbandry. Besides destroying the valuable forests for the sake of less valuable crop or grain, it leads to acute soil erosion and causes the springs below the hills to dry up. Podu is, therefore, wasteful, unproductive, unscientific and self destructive. It is inherently defective and economically unsound. A major chunk of forest land area is affected by this practice of shifting cultivation and millions of tribal people are involved in this. However, a number of control measures have been undertaken by the Government during the Five Year Plans.[90] Emphasis has been laid on their settlement and resettlement. A comprehensive development package has been framed and undertaken for prevention of shifting cultivation but have only a limited impact.

FOREST

Forest is an inalienable part of tribal life & culture. Forest holds the promise of their very existence and growth. Both forest and tribal people are inseparable and interdependent for their survival. Many of the tribal people dwell in the forest. The conservation of ecology and forest resources by tribal people who inhabit there have been aptly mentioned in ancient scriptures. But the britishers, in colonial pre independence era did not pay heed to this stark reality for their vested interests. Of course the forces and factors prevalent at that time compelled them to avoid this fact and adopt a stern policy. In post independence era, in our zeal and vigour to protect and preserve natural resources and habitat, Government of India promulgated some conservation measures blissfully ignoring the fact that the very concept of conservation is strongly embedded in the culture and ethos and ways of life of tribal people. From time immemorial, the aborigines have been living in the forests. Their life is intimately linked with the forests which is their well-loved home and source of livelihood. The tribals have enjoyed freedom to use forests and hunt animals.[91]

These direct benefits, they feel, are their 'natural rights.' Forests give food and shelter to the tribal population of the State. Edible fruits of all kinds, leaves, roots, tubers, animals, birds and insects, and fish from the streams and rivers of the forests constitute the items of food for the tribal people. Forests provide raw material for erecting their houses. Their cattle graze in them. Herbs cure their diseases. Forests keep them warm with fuel and cool with shade.[92] These are a source of ingredients for alcholoic drinks. Hunting and fishing are their common pastime. Such associations of the tribals with the forests from the prehistoric days have given them a 'conviction that remains even today deep in their hearts that the forest belongs to them. They used the forest lands for cultivation the way they wished. A variety of agricultural practices are prevalent in the tribal economy depending upon the terrain, soil and climate. Shifting cultivation, however, is the main system of tribal agriculture. This is regarded as the oldest method of agriculture man has employed from the time when he first learnt the use of land and fire in the Neolithic period.[93] But the traditional natural rights started to shrink when gradually people from outside moved into the forests in the middle of the 19th century.[94] Many of the tribal customs and habits, particularly in respect of cultivation and hunting, were found to be inconsistent with conservation and detrimental to society. The government policy, therefore, exercises closer control over the use of forests and regulates the rights and privileges of the users.[95] In the process the tribals have been deprived of some of their natural rights. Still they enjoy a variety of privileges and concessions. A number of those advantages have never been codified. Nor has the Forest Departments of the States given 'adequate publicity to the privileges and concessions granted to the tribals.'[96] With consequent misgivings and misunderstandings among the latter. Only hunting is fully prohibited. In the Reserve Forests, freedom to use forests has been restricted. The National Commission for Scheduled tribes observe that 'the reservation processes for creating wilderness and forest areas somehow ignored the bona fide interests of the tribal community in respect of the legislative framework in the regions where tribal communities primarily inhabit. The simplicity of tribals and their general ignorance of modern regulatory frameworks precluded them from asserting their genuine claims to resources in areas where they depended upon. The modern conservation approaches also advocate exclusion rather than integration. It is only recently that forest management regimes have in their policy processes realized that forests have the best chance to survive if the tribal communities living in them participate in its conservation and regeneration measures. It is a well known fact that the forest dwelling scheduled tribes have been residing on their ancestral land from times immemorial and that their exists a symbiotic relationship between the forest dwelling scheduled tribes (FDSTs) and the biological resources in India. They are integral to the very survival and sustainability of the forest eco-systems, including wild life. The non-recognition of the rights of the FDSTs over the land on which they have been living in forests since ages has been attracting public attention since pre-Independence period. The non-recognition of their rights have come to be erroneously looked upon as encroachers of forest lands and the threat of eviction has always been looming large in their psyche. Insecurity of tenure and fear of eviction from these lands where they have lived and thrived for generations are perhaps the biggest reasons why tribal communities feel emotionally as well as physically alienated from forests and forest lands. All these factors have resulted in historical injustice to them. Inadequate implementation of the Provisions of the Panchayats (Extension to the Scheduled Areas) Act, 1996, by non-transfer of control/ownership over the natural resources, including the Minor Forest Produce to the local communities and by non-extension of PESA Act to the entire scheduled areas, including forest areas, have further compounded their miseries. Although the provisions of the Panchayats (Extension to Scheduled Areas) Act, 1996 (PESA) gives the rights of ownership of MFP to the respective local communities, the collection and trade of most of the high value MFP is largely monopolized by the Corporations of the Forest

Department of the States and poor FDSTs are just employed by the contractors only as wage earners.[97] Regardless of the harmful effects, it can be safely hold that in the immediate present the poor tribals are forced to eke out their existence from this evil practice and forests thus do help them to live on, uneasily though. The scheduled tribes consider themselves as sons of the forests and their right over forests is absolute and inviolable. The tribal economy and their economic organisation are, in many ways, interlaced with the forests. It is interesting to note that tribal population is concentrated in those areas where forests cover is high. The scenario relating to non-recognition of the rights of the scheduled tribes over the land on which they have been living for generations is in existence notwithstanding the Government taking a consistent view on the central theme of integrating FDSTs living in and around forests into every aspect of managing forest and, all policy statements, including Forest Policies, circulars, guidelines and Govt. Orders issued and Forests have been espousing the cause of tribal communities and emphasizing the need for putting these communities at the centre of any conservation measures. Thus, the genuine rights of the tribes dwelling in forests have not been recognized despite all the legislative/policy framework. However, recently the Ministry of Environment and Forest and the Ministry of Tribal Affairs, Government of India have decided to formulate a comprehensive Central legislation to redress the historical injustice done to the tribal communities and for clear assertion of their legal rights on the land. Accordingly, the Scheduled Tribes and Forest Dwellers (Recognition of Forest Rights) Bill was promulgated.

Minor Forest Produce (MFP) is the major source of income to many tribals. This activity both procurement and sale is not a continuous activity since the period from July to October is a lean period during which only a meagre MFP can be procured. But majority of tribals depend on this for their sustenance. The poor tribals has also another possible source of wresting benefit from forests. They try to dispose of their Slender surplus agricultural produce (SAP) in the market in order to acquire some necessities of life. Ragi, maize, a variety of oil seeds like mustard, niger, castor, gingelly; pulses like red gram, black gram and cash crops like turmeric, etc. are some of the agricultural products which the Adibasis sell are impoverished mainly produced from the forest lands cultivated by them either under shifting or settled cultivation, both of which are rigorous considering the return and yield. The minor forest products which the tribals are allowed to collect and sell are Mohua flowers, Mohua seeds, Sal seeds, Tamarind, Myrobalans, Broom Sticks, Kochila seeds, Petmuri fibre, Siali fibre, Kusum seeds, Siali leaves, arrowroot, genduli gum, honey and wax, etc. The tribals are, by nature Simple and gullible. They are thus prone to exploitation by the petty traders and contractors. They Soldom use money in the remote and inaccessible areas. They are mostly ignorant of any type of weights and measures. They are subject to exploitation in the exchange process in both the ways, that is, at the time of selling their products and also when they purchase their basic requirements. A meagre and throw-away prices are offered for their sales and exorbitant prices are charged for their purchases by the traders. Thus, contractors, middlemen, egregious as they are, constantly try to exploit the poor and gullible tribes. Moreover, the prices of MFP and SAP are also subject to the fluctuations depending upon the season and market conditions. Poor tribals also incur loss due to such price fluctuations. It in this connection that the National Commission on Scheduled tribe observe in their report that 'it is universally recognized that the tribals for generations have been dependent on forests for their livelihood requirements. Studies have shown that Minor Forest Produce (MFP) account for 50 to 70% of the food requirements of certain tribal communities. They collect a variety of MFP for their own use and to sell them in the market either for cash or kind. Traditionally the tribals were forced to sell their MFP to private traders at very unremunerative prices. In order to overcome this problem, cooperative societies and corporations were set up. These corporations/cooperatives were meant to protect the tribals from the exploitation by middleman. These steps, however, have so far met with limited success only on account of a number of factors arising from inadequate working capital, imperfect organization, poor management, and lack of participation of Scheduled Tribes. The tribal corporations purchase forest produce from the tribals at reasonable prices and provide them with necessities like Ragi, rice, salt, kerosene, cloth etc. at fair prices. The LAMPS (Large-Size Multi-Purpose Societies) were also created during the Sixth Five Year Plan period for procurement of MFP and surplus agricultural produce, supply of essential commodities, agricultural inputs, provision of credit facilities for production and consumption either by converting the existing primary agricultural cooperative societies or by organizing new LAMPS at block levels so as to to cover a population of at least 10,000 in a compact group of villagers with minimum coverage of 10,000 acres of agricultural land and annual short term credit potential of Rs. 51.00 lakhs. This experiment also met only with a very limited success on account of LAMPS running into losses due to poor recovery of loans provided by the National Bank for Agricultural and Rural Development (NABARD) for further disbursement among the tribals. The Tribal Cooperative Marketing Development Federation (TRIFED) was set up as an apex body of cooperatives by Government of India (under the administrative control of Ministry of Tribals Affairs) to ensure fair economic price for the produce grown/collected by the tribals and to check their exploitation by the vested interests. TRIFED has its network for collection, processing and marketing of forest and agricultural commodities of tribals. The management of the TRIFED has taken certain new initiatives in the recent past (i.e. 2002-2003) by way of shifting the focus from trading activities concerning procurement and sale to the marketing and development of tribal products. However, the TRIFED has not come up to the expectations of the Government both in its earlier role connected with procurement and sale of Minor Forest Produce and in its new role of market developers for tribal products in providing effective assistance to the tribals. The limited success of this organization is principally accountable to diverse factors including poor management. A diagnostic study commissioned by TRIFED in January, 2002 detailed the following reasons for the Federation's unsatisfactory performance:

(i) Organizational deficiencies, arising out of limited focus on procurement, lack of market intelligence, ad hoc approach to project execution and poor work culture.

(ii) Systemic failure, resulting from a lack of planning framework, monitoring procedures, and the ad hoc nature of purchase and selling operations.

(iii) Operational weaknesses, brought about by poor storage facilities, high inventory costs, huge fixed expenses and unprofitable procurement activities. The study, in view of the above factors, suggested that the TRIFED needed a complete overhaul.[98] The ownership of MFP was still a distant dream of tribals. The first formal proposal to confer ownership rights in respect of MFP to the Scheduled Tribes was passed in a Conference of Tribal and Forest Ministers held in 1976 as a part of the Tribal Sub-Plan strategy adopted during the Fifth Five Year Plan. Madhya Pradesh was the only State, which followed up this recommendation and formally declared that the tribal was the 'owner' of MFP. This decision was, however, operationalised only in case of tendu patta, which is a nationalized item through a Government resolution. No decision has been taken by the State in respect of other minor forest produce. No other State Govts. took any action in pursuance of the 1976 recommendations of the Government of India. This speaks of the apathetic attitude by the State Governments to confer rights to tribals in respect of MFPs. The next major step, however, was taken in 1996 with the enactment of the Provisions of Panchayats (Extension to the Scheduled Areas) Act, 1996 (PESA) which, inter-alia, envisages conferral of ownership under Section 4(m) (ii) which is reproduced below: "(m) while endowing Panchayats in the Scheduled Areas with such powers

> and authority as may be necessary to enable them to function as institutions of self-government, a State Legislature shall ensure that the Panchayats at the appropriate level and the Gram Sabha are endowed specifically with the ownership of minor forest produce". But ironically, Most of the States have simply defined the MFP products as per Indian Forest Act, 1927. Only a few States like Gujarat and Maharashtra have made legal provisions regarding ownership of MFP in pursuance of the above-cited provisions of PESA Act, 1996.

In some States, there are two groups of cooperative organisations operating in the tribal economy for marketing the forest produce of the Adibasis. One group of cooperatives deal in a number of minor forest products. The other group work specifically for the tasar cocoons. Some States made a modest beginning in 1936 when the State Governments established the Marketing Cooperative Societies in their states. Subsequently, particularly during the Second Five-Year Plan, a number of Forest Marketing Cooperative Societies were registered in the tribal areas.[99] The number of societies, however, came down in later years. Members of these societies are mostly tribals.[100] These societies take lease of the forest areas for collection of different minor forest products. Members of the societies collect the products from the interior forests. The societies purchase the products from the members at fair prices on certain days of the week at various places where weekly markets take place within their area of operation.[101] They also directly purchase from the members in the interior villages. Some of the societies have their own collection depots. Value of the purchases and sales of these societies has increased during in initial years of its operation. Sale of forest produce also increased manifold. As per the recommendation of the Study Team on Cooperatives in Tribal Development Projects (Bawa Committee) set up by the Government of India, a number of Forest Marketing Cooperatives have been converted to Large-sized Agricultural Multipurpose Societies (LAMPS) which provide a package of services like credit, purchase, sale, supply of seeds and agricultural implements to the tribals.[102] In order to coordinate the activities of these societies and assist them in marketing their produce in and outside the states, apex organisations were formed in States. Accordingly, the State Forest Produce Marketing Cooperative Societies were registered. The Apex Societies had difficulties of working capital and organisation. Because of low turnover, it had to run at a loss. Some State Governments like Orissa therefore, decided to expand its activities and after a thorough change of its Bye-laws, formed the Orissa State Tribal Development Cooperative Society Ltd. (OSTDCS) On 7.4.1972. Meanwhile, Government in T.R.W. Deptt. had initiated the Purchase, Sale and Fair-Price-shop Scheme (PSFS) in 1964. 12 such schemes were operating in 8 districts with 80 purchase centres and 94 sale centres. These Schemes encountered difficulties of inadequacy of working capital, lack of flexibility in financial matters and absence of a system to prepare market reports. As objects and functions of these schemes were very similar to that of the O.S.T.D.C.S., government decided to merge the P.S.F.S. schemes with the latter. After the merger of the schemes towards the end of 1972, the share capital base of the society was strengthened, Bye-laws were amended and it re-registered itself with a new name Tribal Development Cooperative Corporation of Orissa Ltd. In 1975. Later on its activities expanded and after several amendments and modifications, the Tribal Development Cooperative Corporations (TDCCs) were formed. Its main objectives, interalia, are to procure the surplus tribal produce and to arrange marketing of the produce of the primary societies and the tribals. The other objectives of the Corporation are-disbursement of production-cum-consumption loans to the tribals and supply of basic consumer goods and other necessities to the tribals. The Forest Marketing and Labour Cooperative Societies, and other Credit Cooperative Societies functioning in the scheduled areas of the state are the primaries of the T.D.C.C. However, the number of primary member societies, and value of purchases and sales have increased to a great extent. The Corporation every year takes lease of the forest areas (except the areas leased out to the Forest Marketing and Labour Cooperative Societies) for collection of minor forest products. Tribal people bring their collection of minor forest produce to the fair price shop-cum-procurement centres of the corporation. The Corporation also purchases 'directly from the villagers, interior village markets, regular village markets in semi-urban areas as also from village leaders of tribal areas and itinerant dealers'. But in many cases, the corporations, have not started functioning through its primary societies; they operate via its own branches and shops which is a significant drawback of these marketing Co-operatives. Another such Co-operatives deal with tassar cocoons. Tasar rearing is an important profession of the Adibasis in the areas dominated by Scheduled tribes. Tasar cocoon which is used for manufacture of silk is woven by some wild species of silkworms belonging to the family 'Saturniidae'. The original home of the worms is on Sal trees.The seed cocoons are collected from Sal trees and laid on Asan trees where they lay eggs and multiply. After the worms grow to a certain size, they weave cocoons which are collected by the rearers. Tasar has, however, become important as a foreign exchange earner.[103] Some tribal people who rear Tasar believe that Tasar rearing must be done only with loans advanced by traders and not from one's own savings'.[104] With this superstition they let themselves be exploited by the traders. To save the rearers from the extortion of the middlemen, the state governments took steps to bring them into the cooperative fold. Tasar Rearers' Cooperative Societies were established in some States doing such activities during the Second Five-Year Plan. But, they have their own limitations of non-availability of funds and mismanagement leading to their sickness or closure.

The tribal people are now being exploited in the process of procurement and price fixation of minor forest products. In most of the cases, the traders who are private people are hand in gloves with the government officials. The government people take extra interest to protect the interests of the traders than the interest of the tribal people. The policies of the government in this regard should be modified in order to safeguard the interest of the tribals. The minor forest products play a vital role in the day-today living of the tribals. Cooperatives have their merits and demerits. Rampant corruption in these organisations existing in tribal regions of has led literally to their closure. Consequently, the tribals have become victims of middle persons. Concerted efforts should be made by the government to reorganise and revitalise these cooperatives, to benefit the tribals.[105]

DISPLACEMENT

Extensive areas of land have been acquired by the central as well as State Governments for Commissioning of Mega steel and other factories, giant industries, mining activities, dams, hydroelectric and irrigation projects. As these industries and enterprises are being established in mainly in tribal areas, the poor tribals lost their land in most cases.[106] Displacement and resettlement of tribals *vis-à-vis* general population in India in various projects activities for the period from 1951 to 1990 indicated in the Table below (16).

Table 16
Displacement of Tribals (1951-1990) (Persons in lakh)

Types of projects	*Total Displaced*	*Tribals Displaced*	*Total resettled*	*Tribals resettled*
1	2	3	4	5
Dams	164.0	63.2	41.0	15.8
Mines	25.5	13.3	6.5	3.3
Industries	12.5	3.1	3.8	0.8
Wild life	6.0	4.5	1.3	1.0
Others	5.0	1.3	1.5	0.3
Total	213.0	85.4	54.1	21.2

Source: Tribes in India, A Data Sheet, Planning Commission, Backward classes and Tribal Development Division, Government of India, New Delhi, July, 2000.

As revealed from the aforementioned table, whereas 213.0 lakh total persons displaced, 85.4 lakh tribals were displaced, 54.1lakh and 21.2 lakh respectively were resettled during the period from 1951 to 1990. Thus, tribals constitute more than forty percent of the total persons displaced. The Dhebar Commission found that in Gujurat, for instance, due to the changes and defective execution of land revenue Laws, 20 percent of the tribals had lost their land. The tribals were given indemnification in cash after an often very arbitrary and unfavourable evaluation of the property they lost. The tribals most often squandered the cash which they received. They seldom bought new land. This further accentuated their pauperisation.

Displacement disrupts long established social networks, and with them the social support systems through which the very young, the very old, the poor and other at-risk members of the community are sustained. People were forced to replace the socio-cultural fabric and eco-systems which had given meaning to their lives for thousands of years by alien places and were reduced to 'nomads' or 'misfits'.The interface between the tribal people and mining activities was first considered in the Tribal Sub-Plan strategy in 1974. The guidelines issued by the Government of India and the Planning Commission acknowledged that adequate benefits from these projects had not flown to the tribals. These guidelines emphasized the need for identification of the zones of influence of the existing industries and also those likely to be established. It was further envisaged that the future policy should be so evolved that the local community became co-sharer in the benefits of mining and industrial activity in the region. In pursuance of this policy, the Union Government while clearing the Malanjkhand Copper Project in Madhya Pradesh in 1976 made it a pre-condition that a plan for the zone of influence shall be prepared and implemented as an integral part of the project. This policy has, however, not been pursued systematically[107]. There is, however, another factor, which necessitates development is that there are vast natural resources waiting to be tapped in shape of water, soil, forest, minerals in contradiction to some developed areas of the country, where they have already been tapped or where such natural opulence is hardly seen. These abundant natural resources should be tapped for all round development of tribal areas. But the tribal displacement should be minimized as for as practicable and R & R polices, should tuned favourably towards ST evacuees.

Land Reforms

Land reform measures were implemented to ensure personal cultivation and discourage tenancy and absentee-landlordism, which were detrimental to agricultural reorganisation. It is a prerequisite to give benefit to the tribals under the land reform laws. In the absence of land records, moneylenders and vested interests usurp land belonging to tribals. Civil courts also find it difficult to uphold the rights of tribals whenever settlement records are outdated or not available. Absence of land records makes it difficult for the tribals to avail of institutional credit. Land is one of the most crucial and vital resources of tribals, their economy being predominantly limited to land and forest. It is also an important factor determining socio-economic status and power in society. Making the tribal people owners of land can be the most effective way of empowering them. Possession of land gives status, stability and determines the life style of every community, social, economic and political equations. Land ownership by tribals enables them to stand on their own feet for the purpose of livelihood, and also deprives the rich of their free or cheap labour. Land disputes have been one of the most important causes of atrocities on tribals.[108]

According to an estimation by the Ministry of Rural Development, Government of India, as of January, 1999 there was a huge difference of area in Acres between tribal land alienated and area restored in their favour. Figure for some of the tribal dominated States is indicated in Table 17.

It can be seen from the table that Andhra Pradesh topped the list of States followed by Madhya Pradesh and Karnataka whereas Rajasthan is at the tail end followed by Assam in case of tribal land alienated and restored. But in case of almost all States listed in the table, area restored in favour of tribals is much lower than their land alienated.

Table 17
Tribal Land Alienated and Restored (As of January, 1999)

Name of the States	*Tribal land (in Acres)* Alienated	Restored
1	2	3
Andhra Pradesh	279419	106315
Assam	5174	448
Bihar	104893	47034
Gujurat	116629	100492
Karnataka	130373	69465
Madhya Pradesh	158398	48398
Orissa	95015	53245
Rajasthan	3446	364
Tripura	24243	6221

Source: Tribes in India, A Data Sheet, Planning Commission, Backward classes and Tribal Development Division, Government of India, New Delhi, July, 2000.

Unemployment

Employment scenario of STs presents a dismal picture. A very few and a handful members of their community are employed in organised sector and others are either chronically unemployed or underemployed or seasonally unemployed (disguised unemployed). Raising their productivity in agriculture, horticulture, animal husbandry, forestry, cottage, village and small industries and provision of employment in all seasons will go a long way in reducing the incidence of poverty of Scheduled Tribes. However, creation of employment potential during the slack season is a prime need to ward off starvation for a few weeks in a year, which is a normal feature in some tribal areas. There should be provision of capital inputs, technology, marketing, training etc. to augment production in tribal areas. Implementation of effective programmes may help in removing poverty to a great extent. There is, thus, a continued emphasis on raising the levels of productivity and creation of employment opportunities. This, in turn, will call for higher investment by way of special central assistance, flow from state plan, from financial institutions and central sector projects. This is inevitable as with increased price levels a much higher investment would be necessary for a family in order that the assistance can have a dent on poverty and enable the family to have a sustained but reasonable level of income to cross the poverty line. However, massive unemployment of scheduled tribes can be substantiated from a glance on their work participation rate and occupational status.

Work participation rate, percentage of main workers, percentage of female main workers etc. is more unfavourable in case STs. A cursory glance on the data presented in the corresponding tables are pointers of their unemployment position and consequent underdevelopment and backwardness. The work participation rate of STs remain more or less stagnant during 1991 to 2001 though in case of the general population it increased by around 1.5 percent as revealed from Table 18. During 1961, Work Participation Rate (WPR) of total population was 42.9% whereas for scheduled tribes (STs) it was as high as 56.9%. However, WPR substantially declined during 1991 for both general as well as STs which stood at 37.5% and 49.3% respectively. Table 18 indicates WPR for both total and ST population right from 1961 to 2001.

Table 18
Work Participation Rate (1961-1991)

	Work Participation Rate	
Census Period	*Total*	*STs*
1	2	3
1961	42.9	56.9
1971	32.9	38.5
1981	36.8	49.8
1991	37.5	49.3
2001	39.23	49.07

Source: (i) Tribes in India, A Data Sheet, Planning Commission, Backward classes and Tribal Development Division, Government of India, New Delhi, July, 2000.
(ii) Census of India, 2001,Schedule Tribes Atlas of India, Devendra Kumar Sikri, IAS, Registrar General and Census Commissioner, India.

It can be seen from the table that in all the census periods, WPR of Scheduled tribes is higher than that of the total population. WPR of STs was almost 14% higher during 1961 which was of course slightly declined in 1991 (around 12%). A list indicating State-wise WPR and occupational status of total population and ST population of tribal dominated states during 1991 is displayed in Table 19. Among the States, M.P has the highest WPR of STs (52.7) followed by Orissa (49.4) and Mizoram (47.6). Among the Union Territories, Dadra and Nagar Haveli has the highest WPR (55.6) followed by Damn and Diu (47.4) as revealed from the table. WPR of all the States

Table 19
Work Participation Rate of Scheduled Tribes of India (1991)

	WPR (1991)	
	Total Workers	
States/Union Territories	*Total*	*STs*
1	2	3
INDIA	**37.5**	**49.3**
Arunachal Pradesh	46.2	45.9
Assam	36.1	41.2
Madhya Pradesh	42.8	52.7
Manipur	42.2	46.7
Meghalaya	42.7	43.2
Mizoram	48.9	47.6
Nagaland	42.7	41.9
Orissa	37.5	49.4
Sikkim	41.5	40.5
UNION TERRITORIES		
A & N Islands	35.2	39.2
D & N Haveli	53.2	55.6
Daman & Diu	37.6	47.4
Lakshadweep	26.4	24.1

Source: Tribes in India, A Data Sheet, Planning Commission, Backward classes and Tribal Development Division, Government of India, New Delhi, July, 2000.

and Union territories of India of total and ST population has been indicated in Appendix-8. The Percentage of main workers substantially reduced to 33.84% during 2001 from 42.03 during 1991 in case of STs but it was reduced to around 4 percent only during the same period in case of general population (Table 20).

Table 20
Main Workers of Tribal Population in India (in %)

Census Period	*TotalPopulation*	*Scheduled Tribe Population*
1	2	3
1991	34.35	42.03
2001	30.39	33.84

Source: Census of India, 2001,Schedule Tribes Atlas of India, Devendra Kumar Sikri, IAS, Registrar General and Census Commissioner, India.

In case of male main workers reduction was only 6 percent for general population whereas it was around 10 percent in case STs as the Table 21 indicates.

Table 21
Male Main Workers of Tribal Population in India (in %)

Census Period	*TotalPopulation*	*Scheduled Tribe Population*
1	2	3
1991	50.89	53.72
2001	44.96	43.52

Source: Census of India, 2001,Schedule Tribes Atlas of India, Devendra Kumar Sikri, IAS, Registrar General and Census Commissioner, India.

But in case of female main workers, the reduction during the same period was 6 percent for STs but only around 2 percent for general population (Table 22).

Table 22
Female Main Workers of Tribal Population in India (in %)

Census Period	*TotalPopulation*	*Scheduled Tribe Population*
1	2	3
1991	16.56	29.99
2001	14.85	23.93

Source: Census of India, 2001,Schedule Tribes Atlas of India, Devendra Kumar Sikri, IAS, Registrar General and Census Commissioner, India.

Occupational Status is also unfavourable for STs compared to general population. More number of STs are marginal workers, their percentage as cultivators and agricultural labourers are abnormally high whereas their percentage in different other services is perceptibly low which are the contributory factors for the backwardness and under development of the community. During 1991 census, percentage of marginal workers of general population is around half of the ST marginal workers. The trend was almost similar during 2001. Percentage of ST marginal workers is slightly less than the double than that of the general population in 2001 as revealed from the Table 23.

Table 23
Percentage of Marginal Workers of Tribal Population in India

Census Period	*TotalPopulation*	*Scheduled Tribe Population*
1	2	3
1991	3.49	7.28
2001	8.84	15.23

Source: Census of India, 2001,Schedule Tribes Atlas of India, Devendra Kumar Sikri, IAS, Registrar General and Census Commissioner, India.

Under occupational Status, a substantially higher percentage of Scheduled tribes are cultivators and Agricultural labourers than the total population as can be seen from the Table 24 below.

Table 24
Occupational Status (1991) (in Per cent)

Category	*Total Population*	*ST Population*
1	2	3
Cultivators	38.7	54.5
Agricultural Lab.	26.1	32.7

Source: Tribes in India, A Data Sheet, Planning Commission, Backward classes and Tribal Development Division, Government of India, New Delhi, July, 2000.

In both the categories of occupation, STs form a significantly higher percentage than the total population. A list indicating State-wise (major states dominated by STs) occupational status of total population and ST population during 1991 has been displayed in Table 25.

Table 25
Occupational Status of Scheduled Tribes

States/Union Territories	*Occupational Status (1991) (in %)*			
	Cultivators		*Agri. Lab.*	
	Total	*STs*	*Total*	*STs*
1	*2*	*3*	*4*	*5*
INDIA	**38.7**	**54.5**	**26.1**	**32.7**
Arunachal Pradesh	60.4	85.0	5.1	1.4
Assam	50.9	77.9	12.1	10.3
Madhya Pradesh	51.8	63.2	23.5	29.5
Manipur	61.8	84.1	6.7	2.3
Meghalaya	55.3	61.5	12.5	13.1
Mizoram	61.4	66.7	3.3	3.3
Nagaland	72.6	81.6	1.4	0.5
Orissa	44.3	50.8	28.7	38.3
Sikkim	57.8	62.9	7.8	4.8
UNION TERRITORIES				
A & N Islands	16.0	0.1	5.5	Nil
D & N Haveli	59.7	71.9	10.3	12.2
Daman & Diu	10.2	8.8	3.7	18.1
Lakshadweep	Nil	Nil	Nil	Nil

Source: Tribes in India, A Data Sheet, Planning Commission, Backward classes and Tribal Development Division, Government of India, New Delhi, July, 2000.

Arunachal Pradesh has the highest percentage of cultivators (85%) followed by Manipur (84.1%) and Nagaland among the states. So far as Union territories are concerned, Dadra and Nagar Haveli has the highest percentage (71.9) against the All India average of 54.5 percent. Among tribal dominated States, Orissa has the dubious distinction of highest percentage of Agricultural labourers (38.3%) followed by M.P (29.5%) against All India average of 32.7 percent. Occupational status of scheduled tribes and general population for all the states is displayed at Appendix-9.

The percentage of cultivators to main workers is as high as 51.03 percent in case of STs which is only 33.85 per cent in case of general population during 2001. Moreover, the percentage reduction of main workers to cultivators from 1991 to 2001 was almost 5.50 per cent for general population but it was only around 3.50 percentage in case of STs as the Table 26 indicates.

Table 26
Cultivators to Main Workers of Tribal population in India (in %)

Census Period	*TotalPopulation*	*Scheduled Tribe Population*
1	2	3
1991	39.35	54.50
2001	33.85	51.03

Source: Census of India, 2001,Schedule Tribes Atlas of India, Devendra Kumar Sikri, IAS, Registrar General and Census Commissioner, India.

Moreover, as many as 28.35 percent of ST main workers are agricultural labourers representing more than 7 per cent higher than the general population as per 2001 census which was also higher (6.40%) in 1991 census (Table 27).

Table 27
Agril. Labourers to Main Workers of Tribal Population (in %)

Census Period	*TotalPopulation*	*Scheduled Tribe Population*
1	2	3
1991	26.56	32.96
2001	21.00	28.35

Source: Census of India, 2001,Schedule Tribes Atlas of India, Devendra Kumar Sikri, IAS, Registrar General and Census Commissioner, India.

Percentage of main workers engaged in household industries is much less in case of STs in both the census periods. An increase in the percentage is noticed in case of general population than the ST population as the Table 28 reveals.

Table 28
Main Workers Engaged in Household Industries (in %)

Census Period	*Total Population*	*Scheduled Tribe Population*
1	2	3
1991	2.43	1.04
2001	3.97	1.77

Source: Census of India, 2001,Schedule Tribes Atlas of India, Devendra Kumar Sikri, IAS, Registrar General and Census Commissioner, India.

Census figures in the last two consecutive census periods also show an interesting revelation that the percentage ST female workers engaged in household industries far outweigh their general counterpart (Table 29).

Table 29
Female Workers Engaged in Household Industries (in %)

Census Period	*TotalPopulation*	*Scheduled Tribe Population*
1	2	3
1991	33.74	43.56
2001	39.02	48.71

Source: Census of India, 2001,Schedule Tribes Atlas of India, Devendra Kumar Sikri, IAS, Registrar General and Census Commissioner, India.

This amply speaks of the contribution of ST females in household works besides their participation in general economic activities. Besides, as many as 41 percent of general main workers are engaged in various services whereas a very miniscule segment of STs i.e. only 18.85 percent of STs are engaged in other services.

Table 30
Main Workers Engaged in Other Services (in %)

Census Period	*TotalPopulation*	*Scheduled Tribe Population*
1	2	3
1991	9.77	4.07
2001	41.17	18.85

Source: Census of India, 2001,Schedule Tribes Atlas of India, Devendra Kumar Sikri, IAS, Registrar General and Census Commissioner, India.

Moreover, the increase in the percentage of main workers in other services is far more higher in case of general population than the ST main workers in the census periods 1991and 2001 as the Table 30 indicates.

POLITICAL REPRESENTATION

Representation of STs in various political forums from highest level to grass root levels i.e. from Lok Sabha at the Centre, Legislative Assemblies at the State Level and PRIs at the Duistrict, Block and Gram Panchayat Level is extremely low. Members of Parliament (MPs) from Lok-Sabha is only 7.5% of the total members i.e. 41 members of STs of the total 543 MPs during 1999. It is, however, slightly higher in legislative assemblies of different States. 530 tribal leaders constituting 13.2% represented in legislative assemblies of States during the year 2000 of the total 4072 Members of Legislative Assemblies (MLAs). In case of Panchayati Raj Institutions (PRIs) which includes Gram Panchayats, Panchayat Samities and Zilla Parishads, of the total 1792332 members, 225090 members constituting 12.6% belong to STs during 1997. State wise (tribal dominated states) list of number of ST representatives out of the total representatives in Lok-Sabha during 1999, in Legislative Assemblies during 2000 and in PRIs during 1997 is indicated in Table 31. It is startling to note that there is no ST representative of MPs and MLAs in a number of States.

Table 31
Political Representatiion of Scheduled Tribes of India

States/Union Territories	Political					
	Lok Sabha (1999)		*Leg. Assembly (2000)*		*PRIs (1997) (Includes G.P., P.S & Zilla Parisad)*	
	Total	*STs*	*Total*	*STs*	*Total*	*STs*
1	2	3	4	5	6	7
INDIA	**543** (7.5 %)	**41**	**4072**	**530** (13.2%)	**1792332**	**225090** (12.6%)
Arunachal Pradesh	2	Nil	60	59	7015	7015
Assam	14	2	126	16	28140	3607
Madhya Pradesh	40	9	320	75	453472	135685
Manipur	2	1	60	19	944	325
Meghalaya	2	Nil	60	55	NA	NA
Mizoram	1	1	40	39	NA	NA
Nagaland	1	Nil	60	59	NA	NA
Orissa	21	5	147	34	87224	NA
Sikkim	1	Nil	32	12	980	229
UNION TERRITORIES						
A& N Islands	1	Nil	Nil	Nil	NA	NA
D & N Haveli	1	1	Nil	Nil	NA	NA
Daman & Diu	1	Nil	Nil	Nil	NA	NA
Lakshadweep	1	1	Nil	Nil	NA	NA

Source: Tribes in India, A Data Sheet, Planning Commission, Backward classes and Tribal Development Division, Government of India, New Delhi, July, 2000.

Political representation of STs in India in Lok Sabha, Legislative Assemblies and PRIs for all the states is displayed at Appendix-10.

REPRESENTATION IN ADMINISTRATION

Representation of STs in premier Civil Services of India is very discouraging. As on 1.3.2000, out of total 5227 Indian Administrative Service Officers only 258 officers are from STs representing a shocking percentage of 4.9%. The representation of STs is slightly higher in case of Indian Police Service (IPS). Out of total 3207 IPS Officers, 231 Officers belong to STs constituting 7.2% as on 1.11.1999 as indicated in Table 32 for major tribal dominates States. A list indicating State-wise numbers of IAS and IPS Officers of General and ST categories has been indicated in Appendix-11.

Table 32
Representation of Indian Tribes in Administration

	Administration			
States/Union Territories	*I.A.S (As on 1.3.2000)*		*I.P.S (As on 1.11.1999)*	
	Total	*STs*	*Total*	*STs*
1	2	3	4	5
INDIA	**5227**	**258 (4.9%)**	**3207**	**231 (7.2%)**
Arunachal Pradesh	259	18	156	13
Assam	216	27	131	25
Madhya Pradesh	406	14	278	20
Manipur	156	26	95	16
Meghalaya	xx	xx	xx	xx
Mizoram	x	x	x	x
Nagaland	54	13	37	27
Orissa	207	7	133	4
Sikkim	41	10	23	6
UNION TERRITORIES				
A & N Islands	x	x	x	x
D & N Haveli	x	x	x	x
Daman & Diu	x	x	x	x
Lakshadweep	x	x	x	x

Source: Tribes in India, A Data Sheet, Planning Commission, Backward classes and Tribal Development Division, Government of India, New Delhi, July, 2000.

x-Included under Arunachal Pradesh, xx-Included under Assam in States.

However, compared to All India representation of STs in Administration, State wise representation display a wide variation. The representation in advanced States is somewhat better as compared to tribal dominated States.

A CONCLUDING NOTE

Government of India has promulgated different laws and policies, devised several plans and initiated a number of programmes and schemes for improving the conditions of ST communities and bring them to the mainstream. But the results do not commensurate the objectives envisaged. The tribal sub-plan strategy was launched to streamline the development efforts meant for STs. But the main limitations of the tribal sub-plan strategy are absence of proper organisation, faulty process of identification of target groups and above all lack of proper coordination between different departments. These programmes were unsuitable for environmental realities and failed to transmit their effects through functional linkages of a spatial hierarchical system. All these led to haphazard implementation of many programmes. An evaluation study made on the working of the Malkangiri ITDP of Orissa indicates that programmes like soil conditioning, soil improvement and green manuring, farmer's training and publicity were not taken up. Ineffective implementation of other programmes could not benefit the tribals in raising their levels of living.[109] The draft Five-Year Plan 1978-83 emphasised to continue the sub-plan strategy with suitable modifications to remove the present inadequacies in programme implementation.[110]

Due to historical reasons, the tribal people, until recently, were generally in a state of educational and economic backwardness and socio-cultural distinctiveness. Scheduled Tribes speak a number of tribal dialects. Their cultural heritage, which is rich and varied, acts as a unifying force. The skills, aptitudes and inclinations of different tribes are different. On the one hand, they are nomadic food gatherers, hunters and shifting cultivators. On the other hand, they are also agriculturists and horticulturists. The tribal scenario of the country, therefore, presents an extremely complex socio-economic panorama. No scheme or programme can be uniformly prescribed for the whole country as far as development of STs is concerned. Only such schemes, which are in tune with the agro-climatic conditions of the region/ area and socio-cultural ethos of particular tribal community, can be successful. Accordingly, local planning at the level of districts/ITDAs/MADAs/ Micro Projects/Cluster Projects has to be given adequate emphasis.

Various development programmes have been implemented in the tribal areas for the welfare of the tribal people. The programmes are on family basis, community basis and on area basis. Further, they have been implemented without any regard to the people's propensity to adopt them. Main of them, therefore, failed bitterly on all fronts. Area development approach has been adopted on the pretext that since the tribal areas have remained isolated for long due to inaccessibility, the tribal people living in such areas could benefit them.[111] They could not receive exposures of the developed societies. Hence, various state governments, central government and voluntary organisations have undertaken the development programmes of time bound nature. For want of awareness, family programmes do not make headway and so are the community programmes for want of initiative and leadership. Some area development/ infrastructure development programmes and people's development/ income generating poverty eradication programmes have not fared well.

The functional system in which the tribal people operate sustains and breeds poverty. The village artisans and traders encounter bleak marketing prospects in view of the low demand for their products. Flow of products from the urban manufacturing sector and the inaccessibility of these people to the doorsteps of modern manufacturing technology fails to extricate them from their limited economic horizon.[112] The tribal poor are most unfavourably affected by the deteriorating terms of their trade relationships. The inadequacy of infrastructural facilities compels them to fall easy prey to the middlemen. The inefficiency, corruption and operational rigidity in the Government agencies have been detrimental to the interests of the rural poor. The production system, the economic and social framework in which the rural people work, insures them by and large, against a vertical rise in productivity asset accumulation.[113] The functional basis emanating from such a situation not only breeds poverty among them but also perpetually sustains them at that level. Therefore, unless the rural poor is freed from the quagmire of their narrow economic base and the various functional system, there is no possibility of a positive change in the poverty scenario of the tribal areas.

Moreover, allocation in itself does not guarantee in any way the attainment of lofty objectives proclaimed by the Constitution.[114] The proper execution must keep pace with the allocation so that the desired results can be expected. In some cases, there is mismatch between the outlay and expenditure because of the non-implementation of the programmes in time. However, with all measures taken by the various governments to promote the quality of tribal life, much needs to be enquired into. It needs to be ensured whether the development programmes have made any impact on improving the quality of life of tribal beneficiaries. There is a strong feeling that selected few well-off tribals have been bagging subsidies from the programmes.

The basic needs for any developmental effort in the tribal areas have not been fully addressed. Unless the forces of destabilisation are checked and corrective measures applied, the provision of social and economic services will not have any significance. Our concern for the development of tribals is not new. Since the promulgation of the Constitution and the implementation of the Five Year Plans, we have been making efforts for the development of these scheduled masses of people. Evaluation of the progress made so far strikes a sordid note. It appears that our package of development programmes is not compatible with the realities of the tribal society.[115]

The levels of socio-economic development vary considerably between non-tribal and tribal population, between one tribe and another tribe and even among different sub-groups of a tribal group. Besides, the tribals have the diversity of their culture and multiplicity of their languages. The disparities and diversities make tribal development and micro level planning for tribals at grassroots level imperative. Though efforts have been made during the last many years to improve the lot of the tribals, enough has not been done to bring them on par with the advanced sections of society. Both programme, planning and implementation have remained stereotyped and devoid of tribal bias. Consequently, even the little that has been invested in tribal welfare could not percolate to the intended beneficiaries in its entirety. In spite of the recommendations of the expert committees and commissions, the programmes failed to give the desired results[116]. The ultimate result of such defective planning and implementation is the emergence of an undulating socio-economic situation in which certain tribal groups and areas have progressed while others remained static.

NOTES AND REFERENCES

1. Panda (Dr.) N.K. (2006), Policies Programmes and Strategies for Tribal Development, Kalpaz Publications, Delhi, P.42
2. R.K. Mishra (1974), "Some Problems of Developmental Administration of Tribal Areas in India", Paper presented in Workshop on "Perspective on Tribal Development and Administration", April 18-20, 1974), N.I.C.D., Hyderabad.
3. Fuchs, Stephen (1973), The Aboriginal Tribes of India, Macmillan India, Delhi.
4. Basudev Sahoo, "Transforming a Tribal Economy", in *Tribal Problems of Today and Tomorrow* (Ed.), p. 56.
5. Raghunath Patnaik, "Socio-Economic and Educational Developments of the Tribals in Backward Regions of Orissa", in *Tribal Problems of Today and Tomorrow* (Ed.), p. 34.
6. P.K. Bhowmick (1986), "Reports on Scheduled Tribes, An Appraisal", in L.P. Vidyarthi (ed.), *Tribal Development and Its Administration*, Concept Publishing Company, New Delhi, p. 63.
7. S.C. Pattnaik (1984), "Rural Poverty and Planning Techniques", in K. Prasad and S.C. Patnaik (Ed.), *Rural Development Strategies for Weaker Sections*, p. 8.

8. S.C. Patnaik (1974), "Tribal Economy in Orissa and Strategy for Development", *Southern Economist*, 1 November.
9. P.C. Mohapatra, "The Strategy of Development of Tribal Economy of Orissa with Special Reference to Koraput District", in *Tribal Problems of Today and Tomorrow* (Ed.), p. 42.
10. S.N. Ray (1974), "Malphariyas of Santal Parganas", *Bulletin of the Bihar Tribal Welfare Research Institute*, Vol. XVI, Nos. I & II (Special Issue), p. 143.
11. A.N. Agrawal (1979), *Indian Economy*, Vikash Publishing House, New Delhi, p. 95.
12. Fuchs, Stephen (1973), The Aboriginal tribes of India, Macmillan India, , pp. 76-78.
13. S. Barkataki (1969), Tribes of Assam, New Delhi, p. 4
14. Panda (Dr.) N.K. (2006), Policies Programmes and Strategies for Tribal Development, Kalpaz Publications, Delhi, p. 45
15. B.D. Sharma (1978), *Tribal Development–Concept and the Frame*, Prachi Publications, New Delhi, p. 1.
16. *Final Population Totals: Brief Analysis of Primary Census Abstract*, Census of India, 1991, Series-I, Paper-2 of 1992, p. 38.
17 B.K. Roy Burman (1969), "A Preliminary Appraisal of Scheduled Tribes of India", Office of the Registrar General, Government of India, New Delhi, p. 2.
18. C. Von Furer-Haimendorf, *Recent Developments in the Position of Indian Tribal Population*, p. 1.
19. Buddhadeb Choudhury (Ed.) (1982), *Tribal Development in India, Problems and Prospects*, Inter India Publications, Delhi, p. XVII.
20. The Dhebar Commission was appointed by the Government of India in 1961 to make an in-depth study on matters pertaining to tribes and their development. It recommended suitable measures for their development.
21. The Shilu Ao team appointed by the Government of India studied the problems concerning backward communities. It suggested policies and programmes for their development.
22 Government of India, "Report of the Working Group on Development of Scheduled Tribes during 7th Five Year Plan", p. 87.
23. Government of India, "Report of the Working Group on Development of Scheduled Tribes during Sixth Plan, 1980-85", pp. 115-16.

24. *Ibid.*

25. Government of India, "Report of the Working Group on Development of Scheduled Tribes During the Seventh Five Year Plan", pp. 87-94.

26. Sharma, B.D., 1978-Triabl Development: The Concept and the frame, New Delhi

27. Chowdhury, N.C.,1982 - The problems of Development of Small Tribes, in Choudhury, B (Ed.)

28. Choudhury, N.C., 'The problem of Development of small tribes, in choudhury Buddhades (Ed.), 1982, Tribal Development in India, Inter India Publications, New Delhi, p. 236.

29. Bhowmick, P.K. (1982), Approach to tribal welfare, in choudhury, B (Ed.) Tribal Development in India, Problems and Prospects (Delhi).

30. Vidyarthi L.P. and B.K. Rai (1977), The Tribal Culture of India, Delhi.

31. An Article Punished in English Saily "*Times of India*", Date, 14. 2. 2007.

32. Sharma, B.D. (1978), 'Tribal Development, The Concept and the Facame, New Delhi, p. 118.

33. An Article Punished in English Dail,y "*Times of India*", Dated,16. 03. 2007

34. An Article Punished in English Daily, "*Times of India*" Dated, 17. 03. 2008

35. An Article Punished in English Daily, "*Times of India*", Dated, 25.03.2008.

36. M.L. Patel (1989), "Some Aspects of Educational Development of Tribes", *Bulletin of Cultural Research Institute*, Calcutta, Vol. X, No. 3 and 4; G.P. Reddy, "Introductory Agriculture in Tribal Community: The Case of Chenchus" M.K. Raha and P.C. Coomar (Eds.), *Tribal India: Problems, Development Prospect*, Vol. II, Gian Publishing House, New Delhi, p. 90.

37.S.N. Rath and D.K. Behera (1991), *A Glance at the Problems of Education among the Tribal Child in India: A Socio-Economic Profile*, Anmol Publications, New Delhi, pp. 206-2207

38. "Caste Based Prostitution Prevalence in M.P.", *Times of India*, 12 August, 1997.

39. NCAER (1963), "Report on Socio-Economic Conditions of Primitive Tribes in Madhya Pradesh", New Delhi, p. IX.
40. Report of the National Commission on Scheduled Tribes, Government of India, pp. 49-50.
41. Report of the National Commission on Scheduled Tribes, Government of India, pp. 52.
42. Panda (Dr.) N.K. (2006), Policies Programmes and Strategies for Tribal Development, Kalpaz Publications, Delhi, p. 43
43. Report of the National Commission on Scheduled Tribes, Government of India, p. 57.
44. Panda (Dr.) N.K. (2006), Policies Programmes and Strategies for Tribal Development, Kalpaz Publications, Delhi, p. 266-267
45. Report of the National Commission on Scheduled Tribes, Government of India, p. 5.
46. *"Times of India"*, An English daily Dated, 05.11.2007.
47. B. Choudhury, "Bathudi", *Tribes of Orissa,* p. 36.
48. G.N. Satapathy, "Bhattada", in *Ibid.,* p. 40.
49. B.B. Mohanty, "Bhuyan", in *Ibid.,* p. 45.
50. N. Prasad (1963), *Land and People of Tribal Birhor,* Tribal Welfare Research Institute, Ranchi, 1964; S.P. Malhotra, "Kinship Organisations of Birhors", *Bulletin of the Bihar Tribal Research Institute,* Vol. V, No. 2.
51. B. Chakrabarty (1988), "Relationship Between Ecology and Economy - A Study of the Birhors", *Bulletin of the Cultural Research Institute,* Vol. 12, No. 1 & 2, 1976; W.H.P. Driver, "Birhors", *Journal of Asiatic Society,* Vol. 57.
52. K.N. Sharma (1955), "How the Uthulu Birhors Make Their Living", Vol. 16, No. 4, 1958; B.K. Sen, "Notes on Birhors", *Man in India,* Vol. 35, No. 2.
53. L.P. Vidyarthi (1958), "The Birhors-A Study of Ecology, Economy and Wandering", in *Selected Papers of 5th International Congress,* 1960; L.P. Vidyarthi, "Cultural Types of Tribal Birhors", *Journal of Social Research,* Vol. 1.
54. L.P. Vidyarthi (1958), *Ibid.,* "Cultural Types of Tribal Birhors", *Journal of Social Research,* Vol. 1.
55. Om Mehta (1976), *Tribal Development: The New Strategy,* Government of India, New Delhi, p. 2.

56. The Problem of Unwanted Transfer of Land Ownership from the tribal to non-tribal is, in short, described as Land Alienation. For further details, see M.L. Patel, "Agro-Economic Problems of Tribal India", *op. cit.*, p. 63.
57. B.K. Roy Burman (1982), "Transfer and Alienation of Tribal Land" in Buddhadeb Choudhury (Ed.), *Tribal Development in India, Problems and Prospects*, Inter India Publications, Delhi, p. 69.
58. Government of India, New Delhi, *Tribal Development: The New Perspective*, p. 2.
59. Buddhadeb Choudhury and Sumita Choudhury, "On Some Tribal Problems", *op. cit.*, pp. 89-90.
60. *Ibid.*
61. Man and Life: *A Journal of the Institute of Social Research and Applied Anthropology*, Vol. 23, Nos. 1 & 2, Jan-June, 1997.
62. An Article Punished in English Daily, *"Times of India"*.
63. Panda, Dr. N.K .(2007), "Education: A Cardinal Basic Social Input for Economic Development of Primitive Tribes", *ADIVASI*, Vol. 47, June-Dec.
64. M.L. Patel (1989), "Some Aspects of Educational Development of Tribes", *Bulletin of Cultural Research Institute*, Calcutta, Vol. X, No. 3 and 4; G.P. Reddy, "Introductory Agriculture in Tribal Community: The Case of Chenchus" M.K. Raha and P.C. Coomar (Eds.), *Tribal India: Problems, Development Prospect*, Vol. II, Gian Publishing House, New Delhi, p. 90.
65. S.N. Rath and D.K. Behera (1991), *A Glance at the Problems of Education among the Tribal Child in India: A Socio-Economic Profile*, Anmol Publications, New Delhi, pp. 206-2207.
66. Roy, *Never too late*, orient Book Company, Calcutta, 1953.
67. Patel, S. (1991), *Tribal Education in India*, Mittal Publications, New Delhi.
68. Panda, Dr. N.K.' 'Policies, programmes and strategies of tribal Development, Kalpaz publications, New Delhi, 20-P.258-259
69. Bose, A.B, *Problems of Educational Development of Scheduled Tribes*, man in India, Vol.50; No.1 (Jan.- March, 1970) PP. 29-32.
70. Alan Sable (1977), *Education in Orissa*, S. Chand & Company Ltd; New Delhi.
71. Ralhnaiah, E.V. (1977), *Structural Constraints in Tribal Education: A Regional Study;* Sterling Publicatiions, New Delhi.

72. Durkheim. E. (1956), *Sociology & Education*, Newyork, Amerirwah Book Comp.
73. Report of the Commissioner for Scheduled Castes and Scheduled Tribes (Twenty Fifth Report), 1977-78, Part-I, pp. 96-97; For further details, see, M.L. Patel, *Agro-Economic Problems of Tribal India*, Progress Publications, Bhopal, 1972.
74. M.L. Patel (1982), "Agro-Economic Problems of Tribals in India" in Buddhadeb Choudhury (Ed.), *Tribal Development in India, Problems and Prospects*, Inter India Publications, Delhi, p. 51.
75. Buddhadeb Choudhury and Sumita Choudhury, *op. cit.*, p. 87.
76. Report of the Committee on tribal Economy in Forest Areas, 1967, New Delhi, p. 11.
77. M.L. Patel, "Agro-Economic Problems of Tribals in India", *op. cit.*, pp. 53-54.
78. Report of the Scheduled Area and Scheduled Tribes Commission, Government of India, New Delhi, p. 513. This Commission recommended that shelters in Forest villages should be granted security of land tenure.
79. B.K. Roy Burman, "Various Dimensions of Land Problems among the Tribes of India", *VANYAJATI*, Vol. XIX, No. 2, p. 70.
80. M.L. Patel, *Agro-Economic Problems of Tribals in India, op. cit.*, p. 59.
81. N.K. Jaiseal, "Barriers of Diffusion of Farm Innovations among Tribal People", A paper discussed in Workshop (April 18-20, 1974), N.I.C.D., Hyderabad, pp. 4-5.
82. B.W. Hoddev (1973), *Economic Development in the Tropics*, Methuen and Co. Ltd., London, pp. 44-45.
83. Trinath Gupta and Shreekant Sombarni, "Control of Shifting Cultivation: The Need for a Systematic Approach and Systematic Appraisal", *IJAE*, Vol. XXXIII, No. 4, Oct-Dec., 1978, p. 2.
84. N.K. Banerjee, "An Appraisal of Shifting Cultivation in India", in M.L. Patel, *Agro-Economic Problems of Tribals in India, op. cit.*, pp. 113-114.
85. F.K. Wadia (1976), "Control of Shifting Cultivation in North Eastern Region", *Prajna*, Vol. 3, July-Sept., p. 315.
86. Saradindu Bose (1967), "Carrying Capacity of Land Under Shifting Cultivation", *Asiatic Society*, pp. 131-135.

87. Majority of tribes practising Shifting Cultivation are from North Eastern Region and Union Territories of the country. Tribes of other states like Kerala, Madhya Pradesh, Andhra Pradesh and Orissa also practise Shifting Cultivation.

88. The Yoraba of cargo basin, the Bemba of Northern Rhodesia, the Yao of Southern Nyasaland, the Malasion of Solomon Islands, the Boro of Western Amazon Forest, the Bakairi Indians of Upper Xingu Region of South America, Hill Tribes of British, North Bornes and Veddah of Ceylon are still practising this Shifting cultivation. The primitive cultivators of West Africa call it 'farming' and it is known as 'Sartage' in French. The Veda of Ceylon call it 'Chena' and the Burmese hill tribe as 'Taungia'. For further details see: Nag, D.S., *Tribal Economy (An Economic Study of the Baija)*, Bharatiya Adimjati Seva Sangha, New Delhi, 1958, pp. 410-418.

89. P.C. Mohapatra (1987), *Economic Development of Tribal India*, Asish Publishing House, New Delhi, p. 130.

90. M.L. Patel, "Some Aspects of Shifting Cultivation", *The Newsletter*, July 1972, Government of India, Department of Social Welfare, New Delhi, pp. 23-29.

91. Report of the Scheduled Areas and Scheduled Tribes (Dhebar) Commission, Vol. I. 1960-61, pp. 125-142, reproduced in Background Papers for the First Course on Tribal Life and Culture for Senior Forest Officers (Hyderabad: N.I.C.D., November 9-18, 1976), Part B: Tribals and Forests, p. 1.

92. Report of the Scheduled Areas and Scheduled Tribes (Dhebar) Commission, Vol. I, 1960-61.

93. (i) P.R. Chandra, "Tribal Economy", *Adibasi* (April 1970-January 1971), Vol. XII, Nos. 1 to 4 (Bhubaneswar: T.R.B., Orissa), p. 3.

    (ii) L.C.Sharma, "Forestry", *Yojana* (July 1977), Vol. XXI, No. 11, pp. 20-23.

94. Report of the Scheduled Areas and Scheduled Tribes (Dhebar) Commission, Vol. I, 1960-61,

95. Report of the Study Team on Tribal Development Programmes-All India, (P.Shilu Ao) Committee on Plan Projects (New Delhi: Planning Commission, Government. of India, 1969), p. 41.

96. Report of the Study Team on Tribal Development Programmes-All India, (P. Shilu Ao) Committee, p. 42.

97. Report of the National Commission of Scheduled Tribes, p. 38.
98. *Ibid*, p. 42.
99. A Brochure on the Activities of the Orissa State Tribal Development Cooperative Society Ltd. (Bhubaneswar: O.S.T.D.C.S., 1974), p.1. and Statistical Outline on Cooperation in Orissa, 1963-64 (Bhubaneswar: Registrar, Cooperative Societies, Government of Orissa), p. iii.
100. Statistics on Cooperatives in Orissa, 1964-65, (Bhubaneswar: Registrar, Cooperative Societies, Government of Orissa), p.9 and Settlement of Lease of Minor Forest Produce in favour of F.M.C,.S. (converted to LAMPS) for the year 1977-78, Letter No. 15570/ MKt.-III(6)/XLV-FM-30/77 dt,4.8.77 (from Addl. Registrar of Cooperative Societies to Secretary, F.F.A.H. Deptt.).
101. Report of the Minor Forest Produce Enquiry Committee, Orissa, 1965 (Bhubaneswar: Cooperation and Forestry Deptt., Government of Orissa), p. 8.
102. Report of the Review Committee on the Working of the O.S.T.D.C.S.Ltd., *op.cit.*, p. 29: Sub-Plan for Tribal Regions of Orissa, 1974-79, *op.cit.*, p. 78 and Settlement of Lease of Minor Forest Products in Favour of F.M.C.S. (converted LAMPS) for the year 1977-78.
103. Tasar Silk Industry in India (Report of the Tasar Silk Committee, 1966, New Delhi: Ministry of Commerce, Government of India), pp. 6 & 15-16.
104. (i) S.N.Mishra, "Tasar Rearing by Adibasis of Orissa", Adibasi (July 1967), Vol. IX, No. 2, p. 4 (ii) B.B.Mohanty, "Development of Handloom and Sericulture", Special Supplement, Amrita Bazar Patrika (an English daily), Dt. 1.4.1979.
105. Panda, Dr. N.K.' 'Policies, programmes and strategies of tribal Development, Kalpaz publications, New Delhi 20, p. 267
106. Fuchs, Stephen; *op.cit.*
107. Report of the National Commission of Scheduled Tribes, pp. 34-35.
108. *Ibid*, pp. 29-30.
109. B. Nighna and P.C. Mohapatra (1980), "Evaluation Report of Malkangiri ITDP, Koraput District, Orissa", Utkal University.
110. Government of India, Planning Commission, *Draft Five-Year Plan, 1978-83*, p. 255.

111. M.L. Patel (1992), "Direction of Tribal Development", *Vanyajati*, Vol. XL, No. 2, April, p. 33.

112. M.K. Mohanty (1990), *Tribal Society, Programmes, Planning and Economic Change*, Chugh Publications, Allahabad, pp. 81-82.

113. S.C. Patnaik, *Anatomy of Rural Poverty in Orissa and Strategy of Rural Development*, p. 11

114. V.C. Kumaran, "Development of Tribal Areas", in S.G. Deogaonkar (Ed.), *Problems of Development of Tribal Areas*, p. 40.

115 Suresh Chandra Rajora, "Tribal Society and Its Differential Profile (A Case for Development Programmes), *VANYAJATI*, Vol. XXXIV, No. 1, p. 7.

116. Panda, Dr. N.K.' 'Policies, Programmes and Strategies of Tribal Development, Kalpaz Publications, New Delhi, 20, p. 184.

APPENDICES

Appendix-1
State-wise Population of Scheduled Tribes in India (1961 Census)

States/Union Territories	*Total Population*	*Scheduled Tribe Population*	*% to total Population*
1	*2*	*3*	*4*
Andhra Pradesh	35,983,447	1,324,368	3.68
Assam	11,872,772	2,068,364	17.42
Bihar	46,455,610	4,204,770	9.05
Gujarat	20,633,350	1,367,255	13.35
J & K	3,560,976	-	-
Kerala	16,903,715	207,996	1.23
Madhya Pradesh	32,372,408	6,678,410	20.63
Madras	33,686,953	252,646	0.75
Maharashtra	39,553,718	2,397,159	6.06
Mysore	23,586,772	192,096	0.81
Orissa	17,548,846	4,223,757	24.07
Punjab	20,306,812	14,132	0.07
Rajasthan	20,155,602	2,309,447	11.46
Uttar Pradesh	73,746,401	-	-
West Bengal	34,926,279	2,063,883	5.91
UNION TERRITORIES			
Andaman & Nicobar Islands	63,548	14,122	22.22
Delhi	2,658,612	152,085	-
Himachal Pradesh	1,351,144	108,194	8.01
L.M & A. Islands	24,108	23,391	97.03
Manipur	780,037	249,049	31.93
Tripura	1,142,005	360,070	31.53

Contd...

States/Union Territories	*Total Population*	*Scheduled Tribe Population*	*% to total Population*
1	*2*	*3*	*4*
Dadra & Nagar Haveli	57,963	51,261	88.44
N.E.F.A.	336,558	5,042	1.50
Nagaland	369,200	343,697	93.09
Pondicherry	369,079	-	-
Sikkim	162,189	37,170	22.92
Total	438,608,104*	29,883,470	6.81

Source: Statement-48 & 49, Census of India, 1961, Paper-I of 1962, Primary Census Abstract, Scheduled Castes and Scheduled Tribes.
* Excludes Goa, Daman & Diu

Appendix–2
State-wise Population of Scheduled Tribes in India (1971 Census)

States/Union Territories	Total Population	Scheduled Tribe Population	% to total Population
1	2	3	4
Andhra Pradesh	43,502,708	1,657,657	3.81
Arunachal Pradesh	467,511	369,408	79.02
Assam	14,625,152	1,606,648	10.99
Bihar	56,353,369	4,932,767	8.75
Goa	857,771	7,654	0.89
Gujarat	26,697,475	3,734,422	8.75
Haryana	10,036,808	-	-
Himachal Pradesh	3,460,434	141,610	4.09
Karnataka	29,299.014	231,268	0.79
Kerala	21,347,375	269,356	1.26
Madhya Pradesh	41,654,119	8,387,403	20.14
Maharashtra	50,412,235	2,954,249	5.86
Manipur	1,072,753	334,466	31.18
Meghalaya	1,011,699	814,230	80.48
Mizoram	232,390	313,299	94.26
Nagaland	516,449	457,602	88.61
Orissa	21,944,615	5,071,937	23.11
Punjab	13,551,060	-	-
Rajasthan	25,765,806	3,125,506	12.13
Sikkim	209,843	-	-
Tamil Nadu	41,199,168	311,515	0.76
Tripura	1,556,342	450,544	28.95
Uttar Pradesh	88,341,144	198,565	0.22
West Bengal	44,312,011	2,532,969	5.72
UNION TERRITORIES			
Andaman & Nicobar Islands	115,133	18,102	15.72
Chandigarh	257,251	-	-
Dadra & Nagar Haveli	74,170	64,445	86.89
Daman and Diu	857,771	7,654	0.89
Delhi	4,065,698	-	-
Lakshadweep	31,810	29,540	92.86
Pondicherry	471,707	-	-
Total	533534500	36408514	6.82

Source: Statement-2
Census of India, 1981, Series–I, India, Part–II B (iii)
Primary Census Abstract, Scheduled Tribes.

Appendix-3
State-wise Population of Scheduled Tribes in India (1981 Census)

States/Union Territories	*Total Population*	*Scheduled Tribe Population*	*% to total Population*
1	*2*	*3*	*4*
Andhra Pradesh	53,549,673	3,176,001	5.93
Arunachal Pradesh	631,839	441.167	69.82
*Assam	-	-	-
Bihar	69,914,734	5,810,867	8.31
Goa	1,086,730	10,721	0.99
Gujarat	34,085,799	4,848,586	14.22
Haryana	12,922,618	-	-
Himachal Pradesh	4,280,818	197,263	4.61
Karnataka	37,135,714	1,825,203	4.91
Kerala	25,453,680	261,475	1.03
Madhya Pradesh	52,178,844	11,987,031	22.97
Maharashtra	62,784,171	5,772,038	9.19
Manipur	1,420,953	387,977	27.30
Meghalaya	1,335,819	1,076,345	80.58
Mizoram	493,757	461,907	93.55
Nagaland	774,930	650,885	83.99
Orissa	26,370,271	5,915,067	22.43
Punjab	16,788,915	-	-
Rajasthan	34,261,862	4,183,124	12.21
Sikkim	316,385	73,623	23.27
Tamil Nadu	48,408,077	520,226	1.07
Tripura	2,053,058	583,920	28.44
Uttar Pradesh	110,862,013	232,705	0.21
West Bengal	54,580,647	3,070,672	5.63
UNION TERRITORIES			
Andaman & Nicobar Islands	188.741	22,361	11.85
Chandigarh	451,610	-	-
Dadra & Nagar Haveli	103,676	81,714	78.82
Daman and Diu	1,086,730	10,721	0.99
Delhi	6,220,406	-	-
Lakshadweep	40.249	37,760	93.82
Pondicherry	604,471	-	-
Total	665287849	51628638	7.76

Source: Statement-2, Census of India, 1981, Series-I, India, Part - II B (iii) Primary Census Abstract, Scheduled Tribes.

* Assam is excluded as census could not be held due to disturbed conditions prevailing there. Assam

Appendix-4
State-wise Population of Scheduled Tribes in India
(1991 Census)

States/Union Territories	*Total Population*	*Scheduled Tribe Population*	*% to total Population*
1	2	3	4
Andhra Pradesh	66,508,808	4,199,481	6.31
Arunachal Pradesh	864,558	550,351	63.66
Assam	22,414,322	2,874,441	12.83
Bihar	86,374,465	6,616,914	7.66
Goa	1,169,793	376	0.03
Gujarat	41,309,582	6,161,775	14.92
Haryana	16,463,648	-	-
Himachal Pradesh	5,170,877	218,349	4.22
Karnataka	44,977,201	1,915,691	4.26
Kerala	29,098,518	320,967	1.10
Madhya Pradesh	66,181,170	15,399,034	23.27
Maharashtra	78,937,187	7,318,281	9.27
Manipur	1,837,149	632,173	34.41
Meghalaya	1,774,778	1,517,927	85.53
Mizoram	689,756	653,565	94.75
Nagaland	1,209,546	1,060,822	87.70
Orissa	31,659,736	7,032,214	22.21
Punjab	20,281,969	-	-
Rajasthan	44,005,990	5,474,881	12.44
Sikkim	406,457	90,901	22.36
Tamil Nadu	55,858,946	547,194	1.03
Tripura	2,757,205	853,345	30.95
Uttar Pradesh	139,112,287	287,901	0.21
West Bengal	66,077,965	3,808,760	5.60
UNION TERRITORIES			
Andaman & Nicobar Islands	280,661	26,770	9.54
Chandigarh	642,015	-	-
Dadra & Nagar Haveli	138,477	109,380	78.99
Daman and Diu	101,586	11,724	11.54
Delhi	9,420,644	-	-
Lakshadweep	51,707	48,163	93.15
Pondicherry	807,785	-	-
Total-India (Excluding Jammu and Kashmir)	838,583,988	67,758,380	8.08
India (Excluding Assam and J & K)	816,169,666	64,883,939	7.95

Source: Table No. 5 and 6
Census of India, 1991, Series - I, Paper - 2 of
Final Population Totals: Brief Analysis of 1992 of Primary Census Abstract.

Appendix-5
State-wise Population of Scheduled Tribes in India (2001 Census)

States/Union Territories	*Total Population*	*Scheduled Tribe Population*	*% to total Population*
1	2	3	4
Andhra Pradesh	76.21	5.02	6.59
Arunachal Pradesh	1.09	7.05	64.22
Assam	26.66	3.31	2.41
Bihar	82.99	.76	.91
Chhattishgarh	20.83	6.62	31.76
Goa	1.35	.0006	.04
Gujarat	50.67	7.48	14.76
Haryana	21.14	-	-
Himachal Pradesh	6.08	.24	4.02
J & K	10.14	1.10	10.90
Jharkhand	16.94	7.09	26.30
Karnataka	52.85	3.46	6.58
Kerala	31.84	.36	1.1
Madhya Pradesh	60.35	12.23	20.27
Maharashtra	96.88	8.58	8.58
Manipur	1.17	.74	34.2
Meghalaya	2.32	1.99	85.94
Mizoram	.89	.84	94.46
Nagaland	1.99	1.77	89.15
Orissa	36.80	8.14	22.13
Punjab	24.36	-	-
Rajasthan	56.51	7.10	1.56
Sikkim	.54	.11	20.60
Tamil Nadu	62.40	.65	1.03
Tripura	3.20	.99	31.05
Uttar Pradesh	166.2	.11	.06
Uttarakhand	8.49	.26	3.02
West Bengal	80.18	4.41	5.5
UNION TERRITORIES			
Andaman & Nicobar Islands	.356	.029	9.61
Chandigarh	.901	-	-
Dadra & Nagar Haveli	.22	.137	62.24
Daman and Diu	.158	.014	8.85
Delhi	13.85	-	-
Lakshadweep	.060	.057	94.51
Pondicherry	.974	-	-
Total	1028610328	84326240	8.2

Source: Table F PT.1, Census of India – 2001, Series–I: India, Final Population totals, Registrar General and Census Commissioner, India, 2004.

Appendix-6
State-wise Scheduled Tribes in India below Poverty Line

	Below Poverty Line	
	(Rural- %) 1993-94	
States/Union Territories	*Total*	*STs*
1	2	3
INDIA	**37.27**	**51.94**
Andhra Pradesh	15.92	25.66
Arunachal Pradesh	45.01	NA
Assam	45.01	41.44
Bihar	58.21	69.75
Goa	5.34	NA
Gujarat	22.18	31.20
Haryana	28.02	Nil
Himachal Pradesh	30.34	63.94
Jammu & Kashmir	30.34	NA
Karnataka	29.88	37.33
Kerala	25.76	37.34
Madhya Pradesh	40.64	56.69
Maharashtra	37.93	50.58
Manipur	45.01	NA
Meghalaya	45.01	NA
Mizoram	45.01	NA
Nagaland	45.01	NA
Orissa	49.72	71.26
Punjab	11.95	Nil
Rajasthan	26.46	46.23
Sikkim	45.01	NA
Tamil Nadu	32.48	44.37
Tripura	45.01	NA
Uttar Pradesh	42.28	37.11
West Bengal	40.80	61.95
UNION TERRITORIES		
A& N Islands	32.48	NA
Chandigarh	11.35	Nil
D & N Haveli	51.95	NA
Daman & Diu	5.34	NA
Delhi	1.90	Nil
Lakshadweep	25.76	NA
Pondicherry	32.48	Nil

Source: Tribes in India, A Data Sheet, Planning Commission, Backward classes and Tribal Development Division, Government of India, New Delhi, July, 2000.

Appendix-7
State-wise Gross Enrolment Ratios and Drop-out Rates

	Gross Enrolment Ratios (1997-98)				*Drop-out Rates (1993-94)*	
	Classes I-V		*Classes VI-VIII*		*Classes I-VIII*	
States/Union Territories	*Total*	*STs*	*Total*	*STs*	*Total*	*STs*
1	2	3	4	5	6	7
INDIA	**89.7**	**90.7**	**58.5**	**43.2**	**52.8**	**77.7**
Andhra Pradesh	89.5	99.4	45.7	23.5	62.8	88.1
Arunachal Pradesh	97.2	99.2	65.8	69.2	68.7	73.6
Assam	109.1	NA	69.3	NA	67.6	66.3
Bihar	75.9	81.7	34.8	30.4	78.7	85.5
Goa	86.1	0.0	79.7	82.8	12.3	3.3
Gujarat	115.7	117.2	68.4	53.7	59.9	73.1
Haryana	83.9	Nil	65.9	Nil	23.9	Nil
Himachal Pradesh	90.0	93.8	78.2	72.7	19.7	43.3
Jammu & Kashmir	67.2	NA	64.4	NA	56.5	NA
Karnataka	104.6	105.8	67.6	85.7	62.9	58.0
Kerala	90.0	107.5	95.4	84.5	0.9	31.4
Madhya Pradesh	102.3	82.4	64.9	38.1	44.7	76.0
Maharashtra	112.9	112.7	86.3	62.1	49.8	70.7
Manipur	80.8	91.6	70.5	55.5	72.3	51.3
Meghalaya	93.3	86.4	52.7	48.9	57.7	84.3
Mizoram	113.6	113.8	70.6	73.5	52.4	71.6
Nagaland	94.3	97.2	65.6	73.3	38.1	67.7
Orissa	90.5	88.3	53.4	31.9	61.2	86.5
Punjab	81.6	Nil	65.0	Nil	39.2	Nil
Rajasthan	96.9	90.4	52.7	42.3	65.4	85.0
Sikkim	113.3	107.3	59.0	56.9	78.4	75.7
Tamil Nadu	108.5	96.8	93.6	70.1	36.3	71.6
Tripura	88.3	90.0	54.7	41.7	68.4	83.9
Uttar Pradesh	62.3	96.9	40.0	69.7	37.5	40.7
West Bengal	92.2	101.1	47.1	49.6	46.7	86.0
UNION TERRITORIES						
A & N Islands	86.8	75.6	93.9	65.2	27.3	23.6
Chandigarh	79.4	Nil	80.8	Nil	0.0	Nil
D & N Haveli	96.1	96.7	59.1	51.9	62.2	67.8
Daman & Diu	99.1	109.8	69.5	71.8	-	39.3
Delhi	89.0	Nil	81.0	Nil	25.4	Nil
Lakshadweep	104.5	105.1	69.1	66.5	52.2	46.7
Pondicherry	93.5	Nil	93.2	Nil	7.5	Nil

Source: Tribes in India, A Data Sheet, Planning Commission, Backward classes and Tribal Development Division, Government of India, New Delhi, July, 2000.

Appendix-8
State-wise Work Participation Rate of Scheduled Tribes in India

	WPR (1991)	
	Total Workers	
States/Union Territories	*Total*	*STs*
1	2	3
INDIA	**37.5**	**49.3**
Andhra Pradesh	45.1	54.0
Arunachal Pradesh	46.2	45.9
Assam	36.1	41.2
Bihar	32.2	45.7
Goa	35.3	37.8
Gujarat	40.2	51.7
Haryana	31.0	Nil
Himachal Pradesh	42.2	49.6
Jammu & Kashmir	NA	NA
Karnataka	42.0	47.8
Kerala	31.4	46.0
Madhya Pradesh	42.8	52.7
Maharashtra	43.0	52.2
Manipur	42.2	46.7
Meghalaya	42.7	43.2
Mizoram	48.9	47.6
Nagaland	42.7	41.9
Orissa	37.5	49.4
Punjab	30.9	Nil
Rajasthan	38.9	46.4
Sikkim	41.5	40.5
Tamil Nadu	43.3	52.1
Tripura	31.1	35.8
Uttar Pradesh	32.2	43.4
West Bengal	32.2	47.7
UNION TERRITORIES		
A & N Islands	35.2	39.2
Chandigarh	34.9	Nil
D & N Haveli	53.2	55.6
Daman & Diu	37.6	47.4
Delhi	31.6	Nil
Lakshadweep	26.4	24.1
Pondicherry	33.1	Nil

Source: Tribes in India, A Data Sheet, Planning Commission, Backward classes and Tribal Development Division, Government of India, New Delhi, July, 2000.

Appendix-9

State-wise Occupational Status of Scheduled Tribes in India

States/Union Territories	*Occupational Status (1991) (in %)*			
	Cultivators		*Agri. Lab.*	
	Total	*STs*	*Total*	*STs*
1	*2*	*3*	*4*	*5*
INDIA	**38.7**	**54.5**	**26.1**	**32.7**
Andhra Pradesh	27.7	41.2	40.9	46.6
Arunachal Pradesh	60.4	85.0	5.1	1.4
Assam	50.9	77.9	12.1	10.3
Bihar	43.6	63.1	37.1	25.5
Goa	14.7	5.7	9.2	21
Gujarat	33.4	45.9	22.9	39.4
Haryana	38.8	Nil	19.0	Nil
Himachal Pradesh	63.3	72.0	3.3	2.3
Jammu & Kashmir	NA	NA	NA	NA
Karnataka	34.2	36.8	28.9	42.9
Kerala	12.2	16.7	25.5	55.5
Madhya Pradesh	51.8	63.2	23.5	29.5
Maharashtra	32.8	37.8	26.8	47.1
Manipur	61.8	84.1	6.7	2.3
Meghalaya	55.3	61.5	12.5	13.1
Mizoram	61.4	66.7	3.3	3.3
Nagaland	72.6	81.6	1.4	0.5
Orissa	44.3	50.8	28.7	38.3
Punjab	31.4	Nil	23.8	Nil
Rajasthan	58.8	76.1	10.0	13.5
Sikkim	57.8	62.9	7.8	4.8
Tamil Nadu	24.8	37.4	34.6	43.8
Tripura	38.1	57.3	23.4	29.9
Uttar Pradesh	53.3	69.6	18.9	13.0
West Bengal	28.4	29.7	24.6	50.7
UNION TERRITORIES				
A & N Islands	16.0	0.1	5.5	Nil
Chandigarh	1.0	Nil	0.7	Nil
D & N Haveli	59.7	71.9	10.3	12.2
Daman & Diu	10.2	8.8	3.7	18.1
Delhi	1.1	Nil	0.8	Nil
Lakshadweep	Nil	Nil	Nil	Nil
Pondicherry	6.9	Nil	29.5	Nil

Source: Tribes in India, A Data Sheet, Planning Commission, Backward classes and Tribal Development Division, Government of India, New Delhi, July, 2000.

Appendix-10
State-wise Political Representatiion of Scheduled Tribes in India

States/Union Territories	*Political* Lok Sabha (1999) Total	STs	Leg. Assembly (2000) Total	STs	PRIs (1997) (Includes G.P., P.S & Zilla Parisad) Total	STs
1	2	3	4	5	6	7
INDIA	**543**	**41** (7.5 %)	**4072**	**530** (13.2%)	**1792332**	**225090** (12.6%)
Andhra Pradesh	42	2	294	15	248045	16257
Arunachal Pradesh	2	Nil	60	59	7015	7015
Assam	14	2	126	16	28140	3607
Bihar	54	5	324	28	NA	NA
Goa	2	Nil	40	Nil	1301	Nil
Gujarat	26	4	182	26	68581	10225
Haryana	10	Nil	90	Nil	56880	Nil
Himachal Pradesh	4	NIl	68	3	20171	858
Jammu & Kashmir	6	Nil	87	Nil	NA	NA
Karnataka	28	Nil	224	2	82685	7094
Kerala	20	Nil	140	1	12708	138
Madhya Pradesh	40	9	320	75	453472	135685
Maharashtra	48	4	288	22	225164	20875
Manipur	2	1	60	19	944	325
Meghalaya	2	Nil	60	55	NA	NA
Mizoram	1	1	40	39	NA	NA
Nagaland	1	Nil	60	59	NA	NA
Orissa	21	5	147	34	87224	NA
Punjab	13	Nil	117	Nil	93280	Nil
Rajasthan	25	3	200	24	119151	16574
Sikkim	1	Nil	32	12	980	229
Tamil Nadu	39	Nil	234	3	47887	NA
Tripura	2	1	60	20	5687	448
Uttar Pradesh	85	Nil	425	1	161439	923
West Bengal	42	2	294	17	71578	4837
UNION TERRITORIES						
A & N Islands	1	Nil	Nil	Nil	NA	NA
Chandigarh	1	Nil	Nil	Nil	NA	Nil
D & N Haveli	1	1	Nil	Nil	NA	NA
Daman & Diu	1	Nil	Nil	Nil	NA	NA
Delhi	7	Nil	70	Nil	NA	Nil
Lakshadweep	1	1	Nil	Nil	NA	NA
Pondicherry	1	Nil	30	Nil	NA	Nil

Source: Tribes in India, A Data Sheet, Planning Commission, Backward classes and Tribal Development Division, Government of India, New Delhi, July, 2000.

Appendix-11

State-Wise Representation of Indian Tribes in Administration

States/Union Territories	*Administration* I.A.S (As on 1.3.2000)		I.P.S (As on 1.11.1999)	
	Total	*STs*	*Total*	*STs*
1	2	3	4	5
INDIA	**5227**	**258 (4.9%)**	**3207**	**231 (7.2%)**
Andhra Pradesh	325	15	181	10
Arunachal Pradesh	259	18	156	13
Assam	216	27	131	25
Bihar	399	25	241	18
Goa	x	x	x	x
Gujarat	234	10	129	10
Haryana	211	2	96	Nil
Himachal Pradesh	131	12	73	6
Jammu & Kashmir	111	5	80	4
Karnataka	261	9	135	8
Kerala	184	4	109	3
Madhya Pradesh	406	14	278	20
Maharashtra	365	8	202	9
Manipur	156	26	95	16
Meghalaya	xx	xx	xx	xx
Mizoram	x	x	x	x
Nagaland	54	13	37	27
Orissa	207	7	133	4
Punjab	197	1	144	3
Rajasthan	244	13	145	15
Sikkim	41	10	23	6
Tamil Nadu	334	11	177	6
Tripura	xxx	xxx	xxx	xxx
Uttar Pradesh	579	15	390	13
West Bengal	313	13	250	15
UNION TERRITORIES	x	x	x	x
A & N Islands	x	x	x	x
Chandigarh	x	x	x	x
D & N Haveli	x	x	x	x
Daman & Diu	x	x	x	x
Delhi	x	x	x	x
Lakshadweep	x	x	x	x
Pondicherry	x	x	x	x

Source: Tribes in India, A Data Sheet, Planning Commission, Backward classes and Tribal Development Division, Government of India, New Delhi, July, 2000.

x-Included under Arunachal Pradesh,

xx-Included under Assam, xxx-Included under Manipur.

Bibliography

Agrawal, A. N. (1975, 1979), *Indian Economy*, Vikas Publishing House, New Delhi.

Agrawal, P. C. (1968), *Human Geography of Bastar District*, Allahabad.

Agrawala, S. N. (1962), *Age at Marriage*, Kitab Mahal, Allahabad.

Apter, David (1965), *The Politics of Modernisation*, Chicago University Press, Chicago.

Aurora, W. G. (1972), *Tribe-Caste-Class Encounters*, Administrative Staff College of India, Hyderabad.

Ayyappan, A. (1960), *Tribe, Caste and Nation*, Manchester University Press, Manchester.

Aiyappan, A. (1937), Social and Physical Anthropology of the Nayadis of Malabar. Madras.

Amir-Ali, Hashim (1970), The Meos of Mewar. Delhi.

Archer, W.G. (1940), The Blue Grove: The Poetry of the Uraons. London.

Agrawal, D. P. (1971), The Copper Bronze Age in India. Delhi.

Allchin, B. and R. (1968), The Birth of Indian Civilization. Penguin.

Ayyangar, A. (1951), Report of the Criminal Tribes Act Enquiry Committee, 1949-50. Delhi.

Baden Powell, B.H. (1896), *The Indian Village Community*, London.

Bailey, F. G. (1960), *Tribe, Caste and Nation: A Study of Political Activity and Political Change in Highland Orissa*, Manchester University Press, Manchester.

Ball, Valentine (1880), *Jungle Life in India or the Journeys and Journals of an Indian Geologist*, Thos. De La Rue & Co., London.

Banerjee, Manoranjan (1964), *Primitive Men in India*, The Indian Publications, Ambala.

Barkataki, S. (1969), *Tribes of Assam*, National Book Trust, New Delhi.

Barton, R. F. (1949), *The Kalingas: Their Institutions and Custom Law*, University of Chicago Press, Chicago.

Beteille, Andre (1969), *Social Inequality*, Penguin, New Delhi.

Bhowmick, K. K. (ed.) (1971), *Tribal India: A Profile of Indian Ethnology*, The World Press, Calcutta.

Biswas, P. C. (1965), *Santals of Santal Parganas*, Bharatiya Adimjati Seva Sangh, New Delhi.

Bodding, Paul Olaf (1942), *Traditions and Institutions of the Santals*, A. W. Broggers Boktrykkeri, Oslo.

Bogue, D. J. (1969), *Principles of Demography*, John Wiley & Sons, New York.

Bose, N. K. (1972), *Some Indian Tribes*, National Book Trust, New Delhi.

Bradley-Birt, F. B. (1903), *Chotanagpur*, London.

Brewster, A. B. (1922), *The Hill Tribes of Fiji*, Seeley Service.

Bareja, J. D. (1961), Across the Golden Hieghts of Assam and NEFA. Shillong.

Barkataki, S. (1969), Tribes of Assam. New Delhi.

Besseignet, P. (1958), Tribesmen of the Chittagaong Hill Tracts. Dacca.

Burling, R., Rengranggri (1963), Family and Kinship in a Garo Village. Philadelphia.

Burling, R. (1965), Hill Farms and Paddy Fields. New Jersey.

Biswas, P. C. (1956), Santhals of the Santhal Parganas. Delhi.

Bhargava B. S. (1949), Criminal Tribes. Lucknow.

Bhomick, P. K. (1963), The Lodhas of West Bengal. Calcutta.

Blunt, B. A. H. (1946), Social Services in India. London.

Bonington, C. J., "The Bhantus, A Criminal Tribe in India."

Briggs, G. W. (1953), The Doms. Mysore.

Banerjee, N. R. (1965), The Iron Age in India, Delhi.

Burrow, T. (1959), The Sanskrit Language. London.

Carter, G. F. (1964), *Man and the Land–A Cultural Geography*, Rinehart and Winston, Inc., New York.

Chakrabarty, B. and C.R. Malakar (1962), *Demographic Data–An Imperative Need for the Welfare of the Tribal Population in India* (Mimeo), Indian Statistical Institute, Calcutta.

Chakraborti, M. and D. Mukherji (1971), *Indian Tribes*, Saraswati Press, Calcutta.

Chandrasekhar, S. (1954), *Hungary People and Empty Land*, George Allen and Unwin Ltd., London.

Chattoraj, A.K. (1968), "Santals of Santal Parganas: A Study in Human Geography", M.A. Dissertation, Department of Geography, Patna University.

Chaudhuri, G.N. (1978), "Impact of Industrialisation on Tribal Villages", Ph.D. Thesis (unpublished), Department of Anthropology, Ranchi University, Ranchi.

Chaudhury, Buddhadeb (ed.) (1982), *Tribal Development in India*, Inter-India Publications, New Delhi.

Chauhan, B.R. (1970), *Towns in the Tribal Setting*, National Publishing House, Delhi.

Cologan, J.F.R. (1884), *Hindu Tribes: Ethnological Section*, Government Printing Press, Calcutta.

Crooke, W. (1907), *Natives of Northern India*, Archibald Constable & Company Ltd., London.

Culshaw, W.J. (1949), *Tribal Heritage–A Study of the Santal*, Luther Worth Press, London.

Chatterjee, N. K. and P. Gupta (1963), Report on the Adittanalur Skulls. Delhi.

Clerk, J.D. (1959), The History of South Africa. Penguin.

Cooper, T.T. (1873), The Mishmi Hills. London.

Census of India 1981, series-I, New Delhi, 1981

Census of India 1991, series-I, New Delhi, 1991

Census of India 2001, series-I, New Delhi, 2001

Crooke, W. (1907), Natives of Northern India. London.

Chapekar, D.L. N. (1959), Thakurs of the Sahyadri. Bombay.

Culshaw, W.J. (1949), Tribal Heritage. London.

Dalton, E.T. (1872), *Descriptive Ethnology of Bengal*, Government of Bengal, Calcutta.

Dandekar, K. (1959), *Demographic Survey of Six Communities*, Gokhale Institute of Politics and Economics, Poona.

Das Gupta, N.K. (1963), *Problems of Tribal Education and the Santals*, Bharatiya Adimjati Sevak Samaj, New Delhi.

Das, Amal Kumar (1966), *Handbook on Scheduled Castes and Scheduled Tribes of West Bengal*, Tribal Welfare Department, Government of West Bengal, Calcutta.

Datta, Kalikinkar (1940), *The Santal Insurrection*, Calcutta University, Calcutta.

Deogaonkar, S.G. (1980), *Problems of Development of Tribal Areas*, Inter-India Publications, New Delhi.

Dhan, R.O. (1967), *These are My Tribesmen: The Oraon*, Lutheran Church Press, Ranchi.

Dube, S.C. (1977), *Tribal Heritage of India* (in 4 volumes), Vikas Publishing House Pvt. Ltd., New Delhi.

Datta, J.M. (1962), Demographic Notes on the Remains from Harappa'. Calcutta.

Dass, F.A.M. (1937), The Andaman Islands. Bangalore.

Das, A.K. and M.K. Raha (1967), The Rabhas of West Bengal. Calcutta.

Dunbar, G. (1938), Other Men's Lives. London.

Dutta, P. (1969), The Tangsas. Shillong.

Das, A.K. *et al.* (1966), The Malpaharias of West Bengal. Calcutta.

Datta-Majumdar, N. (1956), The Santal–A Study in Culture Change. Delhi.

Dave, P.C. (1960), The Grasias. Delhi.

Doshi, S.L. (1971), Bhils. New Delhi.

Dube, S.C. (1951), The Kamar. Lucknow.

Das, A.K. *et al.* (1966), Handbook on Scheduled Castes and Scheduled Tribes of West Bengal, Calcutta.

Drew, Fr. (1971), The Fummoo and Kashmir Territories. Delhi.

Elwin, V. (1959), India's North-East Frontier. Oxford University Press.

Elwin, V. (1961), A Philosophy for NEFA. Shillong.

Elwin, V. (1968), Myths of the North-East Frontier of India. Shillong.

Elwin, V. (1951), The Tribal Art of middle India, Oxford University Press.

Elwin, V. (1939), The Baiga. London.

Elwin, V. (1942), The Agaria. Calcutta.

Elwin, V. (1950), Bondo Highlander. Bombay.

Elwin, V. (1955), The Religion of an Indian Tribe. Oxford University Press.

Endle, S. (1938), The Kacharies. London.

Enthoven, R.E. (1992), The Tribes and Castes of Bombay, 3 Vols. Bombay.

Ehrenfels, U.R. (1952), Kadar of Cochin. Madras.

Elwin, Verrier (1944), *The Aboriginals*, Oxford Pamphlets on Indian Affairs, No. 14, London.

Furer-Haimendorf, C. von (1943), The Chechu. London.

Firth, R. (1950), *Primitive Polynesian Economy*, Humanities Press, New York.

Foster, I.L. and F. Alcocle (ed.) (1963), *Culture and Environment*, Routledge and Kegan Paul, London.

Fuchs, Stephen (1973), *The Aboriginal Tribes of India*, The Macmillan Co. of India, Delhi.

Forsyth, J. (1919), The Highlands of Central India. London.

Fuchs, S. (1960), The Gond and Bhumia of Eastern Mandla. Bombay.

Furer-Haimendorf, C. von (1946), The Naked Nagas. Calcutta.

Furer-Haimendorf, C. von (1955), Himalayan Barbary. London.

Furer-Haimendorf, C. von (1962), The Apa Tani and their Neighbours. London.

Furer-Haimendorf, C. von (1943), The Chenchus. London.

Furer-Haimendorf (1945), The Reddis of the Bison Hills. London.

Furer-Haimendorf (1948), The Raj Gonds of Adilabad. London.

Fuchs, S. (1967), 'Anthropometric Analysis of the Waghris'. In P.G. Shah: Denotified Communities in Western India. Bombay.

Ferreira, J.V. (1965), Totemism in India; Oxford University Press, Bombay.

Gait, E. (1826), A History of Assam. Calcutta.

Gurdon, P.R.T. (1907), The Khasis. London.

Glatter, A. (1969), Contributions to the Ethnography of the Chodris. Wien.

Grierson, G.A. (1927), The Linguistic Survey of India. Introductory. Calcutta.

Grigson, W.V. (1938), The Hill Marias of Bastar. London.

Ghurye, G.S. (1957), The Mahadeo Kolis, Bombay.

Gorer, G. (1967), Himalayan Village. 2nd ed. London.

Gunthrope, E.J. (1882), Notes on Criminal Tribes. Bombay.

Gordon, D.H. (1958), The Historic Background of Indian Culture. Bombay.

Guha, B.S. (1937), An Outline of the Racial Ethnology of India. Calcutta.

Guha, B.S. (1944), Racial elements in the population, London.

Ghurye, G.S. (1959), The Scheduled Tribes of India, Bombay.

Gadgil, D.R. (1972), *Planning and Economic Policy in India*, Gokhale Institute Studies No. 59, Gokhale Institute of Politics and Economics, Poona.

Grierson, G.A. (1968), *Linguistic Survey of India*, Vol. IV, Motilal Banarisidass, Delhi.

Hodson, T.C. (1908), The Meitheis of Manipur. London.

Hodson, T.C. (1912), The Naga Tribes of Manipur. London.

Hutton, J.H. (1921), The Angami Nagas. London.

Hutton, J.H. (1921), The Sema Nagas. London.

Hutton, J.H. (1951), Caste in India. Oxford University Press.

Hivale, S. (1946), The Pardhans of the Upper Narbada Valley. Bombay.

Haimendorf, Christoph Von Fiirer (1975), *Himalayan Traders: Life in Highland Nepal*, John Murray, London.

Harimohan (1973), *The Chero: A Study in Acculturation*, Bihar Tribal Research Institute, Ranchi.

Hodson, T.C. (1922), *The Primitive Culture of India*, The Royal Asiatic Society, London.

Houlton, John (1949), *Bihar: The Heart of India*, Orient Longmans Ltd., Calcutta.

Hunter, W.W. (1975), *The Annals of the Rural Bengal*, Cosmo Publication, Delhi.

Huntington, E. and S.W. Cushing. *Principles of Human Geography*, Wiley, New York, 1934.

Jones, Emrys (ed.) (1975), *Readings in Social Geography*, Oxford University Press, London.

Kaushic, S.D. (1970-71), *Human Geography*, Rastogi & Co., Meerut.

Kroeber, A.L. (1952), *The Nature of Culture*, Chicago Press, Chicago.

Krzywicki, L. (1934), *Primitive Society and Its Vital Statistics*, Mianowski, Macmillan, London.

Khatri, A.P. (1964), Rock Paintings at Adamgarh (Central India) and Their Age. Anthropos, Vol. 59.

Krishnaswamy, V.D.K. (1947), Prehistory in India. Ancient India No. 3, Delhi.

Karve, I. (1961), The Bhils of West-Khandesh. Bombay.

Katiyar, T.S. (1964), Social Life in Rajasthan. Allahabad.

Karan, P.P. and Jenkins, W.M. (1963), The Himalayan Kingdoms. New York.

Lal, M.M. (1968), The Tribal Village in Bihar: A Study in Unity and Extension, New Delhi.

Lang, Andrew (1898), The making of Religion, London.

Lyer, A.L.K. (1909-12), Cochin Tribes and Castes. 2 Vols. Madras.

Lyer, A.L.K. (1937), Travancore Tribes and Castes. 2 vols. Trivandrum.

Lyer, A.L.K. (1968), 'Social History of Kerala'. Vol: The Pre-Dravidians. Madras.

Luiz, A.A.D. (1962), Tribes of Kerala. New Delhi.

Lokanathan, P.S. (1963), Socio-economic Conditions of Primitive Tribes in Madhaya Pradesh. New Delhi.

Lawrence, W.R. (1967), The Valley of Kashmir. Srinagar.

Leuva, K.K. (1963), *The Asur: A Study of Primitive Iron-Smelters*, Bharatiya Adimjari Sevak Sangh, Delhi.

Lewis, W. Arthur (1966), *Development and Planning*, George Allen and Unwin, London.

Luiz, A.A.F. (1962), *Tribes of Kerala*, Bharatiya Adimjati Sevak Sangh, New Delhi.

MacBurney, C.B.M. (1960), The Stone Age of Northern Africa. Pelican.

Malik, S.C. (1964), 'Levels in Indian Prehistory' in Current Anthropology, June, p. 205.

Majumdar, D.N. (1944), *The Fortunes of Primitive Tribes,* Universal Publishers, Lucknow.

Majumdar, D.N. (1950), Race Realities in Cultural Gujarat. Bombay.

Mills, J.P. (1922), The Lhota Nagas. London.

Mills, J.P. (1926), The Ao Nagas. London.

Mills, J.P. (1937), The Rengma Nagas. London.

Mathur, K.K. (1967), Nicobar Islands. New Delhi.

Mamoria, C.B. (1957), Tribal Demography in India, Kitab Mahal, Allahabad.

Mandal, R.B. (1979), Introduction to Rural Settlements, Concept Publishing Company, New Delhi.

Minhas, B.S. (1974), Planning and the Poor, S. Chand & Co., New Delhi.

Mukherjee, R. (1940), Man and His Habitation: A Study in Social Ecology, Longmans Green & Co., London.

Myrdal, Gunnar (1968), Asian Drama (3 volumes), The Penguin Press, London.

Naik, T.B. (1956), The Bhils. Delhi.

Nanjundayya, H.V. and Lyer, L.K.A. (1928-36), Mysore Tribes and Castes. 4 vols. Mysore.

N.I.C.D. *Perspective on Tribal Development and Administration,* NICD, Hyderabad, 1974.

Nag, D.S. (1958), *Tribal Economy–An Economic Study of Baiga,* Bharatiya Adimjari Sevak Sangh, Delhi.

Orans, Martin (1965), *The Santals: The Tribe in Search of a Great Tradition,* Wayne State University Press, Detroit.

Panda, (Dr.) N.K.' 'Policies, Programmes and Strategies of Tribal Development, Kalpaz Publications, New Delhi, 20

Pareek, R.N. (1977), *Tribal Culture in Flux,* B.R. Publishing Corporation, New Delhi.

Parvathamma, C. (1984), *Scheduled Castes and Scheduled Tribes: A Socio-economic Survey,* Asish Publishing House, New Delhi.

Patel, J.L. (1974), *Changing Land Problems of Tribal India,* Progress Publishers, Bhopal.

Patel, S. (1991), *Tribal Education in India,* Mittal Publications, New Delhi.

Patel, M.L. (ed.) (1972), *Agro-Economic Problems of Tribal India*, Progress Publishers, Bhopal.

Pinney, Roy (1968), *Vanishing Tribes*, Arthur Barker Limited, London.

Prasad, Saileshwar (1974), *Where the Three Tribes Meet: A Study in Tribal Interaction*, Indian International Publications, Allahabad.

Prasad, A. (1973), *Chotanagpur: Geography of Rural Settlement*, Ranchi University, Ranchi.

Prasad, K.N. (1967), *The Economies of a Backward Region in a Backward Economy* (Two Volumes), Scientific Book Agency, Calcutta.

Prasad, Narmadeshwar (1961), *Land and People of Tribal Bihar*, Bihar Tribal Research Institute, Ranchi.

Parry, N.E. (1932), The Lakhers. London.

Playfair, A. (1909), The Garos. London.

Peter of Greece and Denmark (1960), A Study of Polyandry. The Hague.

Punekar, V.B. (1959), The Son Kolis of Bombay. Bombay.

Raghaviah, V. (1956), *Tribes of India*, Bharatiya Adimjati Sevak Sangh, New Delhi.

Rai, B.K. (1967), *Nature and Man: A Study of Interaction Between Man and Forest in Bihar*, Ph.D. Thesis (unpublished), Ranchi University, Ranchi.

Roy. N.R. (1953), Never too Late, Orient Book Company,Calcutta-12.

Redfield, Robert (1956), *Peasant, Society and Culture*, The University of Chicago Press, Chicago.

Richards, A.I. (1954), *Economic Development and Tribal Change*, Heffer, Cambridge.

Risley, H.H. (1891), *The Tribes and Castes of Bengal*, Government of India, Calcutta.

Roy, S.C. (1915), *The Oraon of Chotanagpur*, The Brahmo Mission Press, Calcutta.

Russell, R.V. and Hira Lal (1970), *Tribes and Castes of the Central Provinces of India*, Vol. 4, Rajdhani Book Centre, Delhi.

Randhawa, M.S. (1970), The Kumoon Himalyas. Delhi.

Rahelia, S.P. (1968), The Gaduliya Lohars of Rajasthan. New Delhi.

Roy, Sarat Chandra (1912), The Mundas and their Country. Calcutta.

Roy, Sarat Chandra (1915), The Oraons of Chota Nagpur, Ranchi.

Roy, Sarat Chandra (1917), A note on Totemism among the Asurs, J.B.O.R.S. III, Calcutta.

Radchiffe-Brown, A.R. (1922), The Andaman Islanders. Cambridge.

Ragaviah, V. (1962), The Yanadis. New Delhi.

Rivers, W.H.R. (1906), The Todas. London.

Sachchidanand (1964), Cultural Change in Tribal Bihar, Bookland, Calcutta.

Sarkar, S.N. (1965), Psycho-Dynamics of Tribal Behaviour, Bookland, Calcutta.

Sarkar, S.S. (1938), The Malers of the Rajmahal Hills, Calcutta Book Co., Calcutta.

Schilippe, Pierre de (1956), Shifting Cultivation in Africa: The Zande System of Agriculture, Routledge and Kegan Paul, London.

Sharma, R.C. (1972), Settlement of Geography of the Indian Desert, Kumar Brothers, New Delhi.

Shashi, S.S. (1977), The Gaddi Tribe of Himachal Pradesh: A Sociological Study, Sterling Publishers, New Delhi.

Sikidan, Sujit (1990), Economic Development of Tribal India, Asish Publishing House, New Delhi.

Singh, D.P. (1968), Cultural Change in an Inter-Tribal Market, Asia Publishing House, London.

Singh, K. Suresh (ed.) (1972), Tribal Situation in India, Indian Institute of Advanced Study, Simla.

Singh, L.R. (1965), The Terai Region of UP: A Study of Human Geography, Allahabad.

Sinha, V.N.P. (1976), Chota Nagpur Plateau: A Study in Settlement Geography, K.B. Publications, New Delhi.

Srivastava, S.K. (1958), The Tharus: A Study in Cultural Dynamics, Agra University Press, Agra.

Sshay, B.N. (1966), Changes in the Leadership Pattern Among the Maler and the Santal of Santal Parganas, Ph.D. Thesis, Ranchi University, Ranchi.

Sarkar, S.S. (1954), The Aboriginal races of India, Calcutta.

Sankalia, H.D. (1962), Prehistory and Protohistory in India and Pakistan, Bombay.

Sankalia, H.D., B. Subbarao and S.B. Deo (1958), The Excavations at Masheswar and Navda-toli. Baroda.

Shashi, S.C. (1971), Himachal. Delhi.

Swinson, A. (1969), North-west Frontier. London.

Shah, P.G. (1967), Denotified Communities in Western India. Bombay.

Sher Singh Sher (1966), The Sansis of Punjab. Delhi.

Sher Singh Sher (1966), The Sikligars of Punjab. Delhi.

Save, K.J. (1945), The Warlis. Bombay.

Shah, P.G. (1958), The Dublas of Gujarat. Delhi.

Shah, P.G. (1959), Naikas-Naikdas. Bombay.

Shah, P.G. (1964), Tribal Life in Gujurat. Bombay.

Sengupta, S. (1970), Social Profiles of the Mahalis, Calcutta.

Shaw, W. (1928), Notes on the Thadou-Kukis. J.A.S. of Bengal, v. 24.

Shukla, B.K. (1959), The Daflas of the Subansiri Region. Shillong.

Sinha, K. (1970), Meghalaya. Delhi.

Smith, W.C. (1925), The Ao Naga Tribes of Assam. London.

Stack, E. and Lyall (1908), The Mikirs. London.

Stevenson, H.N.C. (1943), The Economics of the Central Chin Tribes. Bombay.

Seligman, C.G. and B.Z. (1911), The Veddas. Cambridge.

Spittel, R.L. (1927), Wild Ceylon. Colombo.

Spittel, R.L. (1950), Vanished Trails. Oxford University Press.

Subbarayan, V. (1948), Forgotten Sons of India. Madras.

Turner, A.C. (1931), 'Some Ethnographic Notes on Miscellaneous Castes and Tribes', *Census of India*, Vol. I.

Trewartha, G.T. (1975), *Tribal Development: Retrospect and Prospect*, New Delhi.

Troisi, J. (1976), *The Santals – A Classified and Annotated Bibliography*, Manohar, New Delhi.

Thurston, E. (1909), The Castes and Tribes of South India. 7 vols. Madras.

Upadhyaya, V.S. (1965), *Tribal Rehabilitation Schemes: A Study of Directed Social Change in Chotanagpur*, Ph.D. Thesis (unpublished), Ranchi University, Ranchi.

Verma, K.K. (1977), *Culture, Ecology and Population*, National Publishing House, New Delhi.

Vidyarthi, L.P. (ed.) (1959), Anthropology and Tribal Welfare in India, Council of Social and Cultural Research, Bihar.

Von Eick Stedt, E. (1935), The Position of Mysore in India's Racial History, Mysore, p. 33.

Von Furer-Haimendorf, C. (1955), New Aspects of the Dravidian Problem. Vol. II, Wien.

Vidyarathi, L.P. (1963), The Maler. Calcutta.

Vidyarthi, L.P. and Makhan Jha (1978), Dimensions of Indian Civilisation: An Anthropological Perspective, Classical Publications, New Delhi.

Vidyarthi, L.P. and B.K. Roy. (1976), The Tribal Culture of India, Concept Publishing Co., New Delhi.

Vidyarthi, L.P. and K.N. Sahay (1976), Dynamics of Tribal Leadership in Bihar, Kitab Mahal, Allahabad.

Winick, Charls (1956), Dictionary of Anthropology, Philosophical Library, New York.

Waterfield, H.G. (1931), Note on Mohghias'. Census of India, Vol. I.

Weling, A.N. (1934), The Katkaris. Bombay.

Whitehead, G. (1921), In the Nicobar Islands. London.

Wood, R. (1953), The Hill Tribes of Assam. J.B.B. of R.A.S., Vol. 28.

Reports and Journals

Government of India. *Report of the Working Group on Tribal Development During the Sixth Plan*, New Delhi.

Government of India. *Report of the Working Group on Development of Scheduled Tribes During the Seventh Five-Year Plan*, New Delhi.

Government of India. *Report of the Working Group on Development of Scheduled Tribes During the Eighth Five-Year Plan*, New Delhi.

Government of India. *Report of the Working Group on Development of Scheduled Tribes During the Ninth Five-Year Plan*, New Delhi.

Government of India. *Report of the Working Group on Development of Scheduled Tribes During the Tenth Five-Year Plan*, New Delhi.

Guidelines for Tribal Sub-Plan, New Delhi.

Occasional Papers on Tribal Development.

Report of the Steering Group on Development of Backward Classes and Social Welfare for the Fifth Five-Year Plan, 1973.

Report of the Working Group on Development of Scheduled Tribes During Eight Plan, 1992-97.

Report of the Scheduled Areas and Scheduled Tribes Commission, Vol. I, 1960-61.

Report of the Study Team on Tribal Development Programmes, 1969.

Government of Orissa. *Scheduled Tribes and Scheduled Castes of Orissa,* 1989.

Sub-Plan for Tribal Regions of Orissa, 1974-79 (Draft), Bhubaneswar.

A Compendium of Circulars and Instructions on Sub-Plan and Integrated Tribal Development Projects of Orissa for Guidance of Field Officers (Vol. I & II).

Living Conditions of Scheduled Tribes, Scheduled Castes and Other Backward Classes in Orissa, 1963.

Adair, A.R. (1946), "The Kumarbhag Paharias", *Man in India,* Vol. 26, Nos. 3 & 4, September-December, pp. 207-14.

Banerjee, H.N. (1962), "Statutory Safeguards for Scheduled Tribes and Scheduled Castes", *Bulletin of the Cultural Research Institute,* Vol. I.

Behura, N.K. (1990), "Tribal Societies in Orissa", in *Tribes of Orissa,* Government of Orissa.

Bhowmick, P.K. (1986), "Reports on Scheduled Tribes: An Appraisal", in L.P. Vidyarthi (ed.), *Tribal Development and Its Administration,* Concept Publishing House, New Delhi.

Biswal, G.C. (1985), "Tribal Development and Education: Some Issues", *Vanyajati,* January, Vol. XXXII, No. 1.

Chakravarti, M. and C.S. Singhrole. "Problems of Tribal Education–A Key to Development", *Man in India,* Vol. 14, Nos. 1 & 2, pp. 91-96.

Choudhury, Budhadeb and Smita Choudhury (1982), "On Some Tribal Problems", in Budhadeb Choudhury (ed.), *Tribal Development in India: Problems and Prospects,* Inter-India Publications, New Delhi.

Danda, Ajit K. (1986), "Statutory Provisions Safeguarding Interests of Scheduled Tribes and Scheduled Castes", in L.P. Vidyarthi (ed.), *Tribal Development and Its Administration,* Concept Publishing Company, New Delhi.

Devi, Mahasweta. "You Just Cannot Do Without Them", *Yojana,* Vol. 28, Nos. 20 & 21.

Dube, S.C. (1968), "Approaches to Tribal Problems in India", in L.P. Vidyarthi (ed.), *Applied Anthropology in India*, Kitab Mahal, Allahabad.

Elwin, V. "Notes on the Juang", *Man in India*, Vol. XXVIII, Nos. 1 & 2.

Guha, B.S. (1939), "The Aboriginal Races of India", *Science and Culture*, Vol. 4, No. 12, pp. 677-83.

Haldipur, R.N. (1979), "Problems of Administration of Tribals of North East India", *Vanyajati*, April.

Jaiseal, N.K. (1974), "Barriers to Diffusion of Farm Innovations Among Tribal People", A Paper Presented in a Workshop on "Perspective on Tribal Development and Administration" in N.I.C.D., Hyderabad on 18-20 April.

"The Indian Aborigines and Their Administration", *Journal of the Asiatic Society*, Vol. 17, No. 1, 1951, pp. 19-44.

Lal, R.B. (1969), "A Brief Note on Socio-Cultural Aspects, Aspirations and Attitudes of the Tribals of Gujarat", *Quarterly Bulletin of the Tribal Research Institute*, Udaipur, Vol. VI, No. 2, June.

Lewis, I.M. (1968), "Tribal Society", in *International Encyclopaedia of Social Sciences*, Vol. 16, Macmillan, New Delhi.

Majumdar, D.N. (1988), "Significance of Women's Position in Tribal Society", *Economic and Political Weekly*, Vol. XXIII, No. 26, 25 June.

Mamoria, C.B. (1957), "Tribes in India: Their Classification", *The Modern Review*, Vol. 150, No. 4.

Mathur, Harimohan (1986), "Strengthening Administrative Capability for Development of Tribal Regions", in L.P. Vidyarthi (ed.), *Tribal Development and Its Administration*, Concept Publishing Company, New Delhi.

Mishra, R.K. (1974), "Some Problems of Developmental Administration in Tribal Areas in India", A Paper Presented in a Workshop on "Perspective on Tribal Development and Administration" in N.I.C.D., Hyderabad on 18-20 April.

Mishra, Rajalakshmi (1972), "Inter-Tribal Relations in Erumad", *The Eastern Anthropologist*, Vol. XXVI, No. 2.

Mohanty, Gopinath (1962-63), "Evaluation of Tribal Policy", *Adivasi*.

Mohapatra, Kulamani and Kiranabala Devi (1972-73), "Shifting Cultivation in Orissa", *Adivasi*, Vol. XIV, No. 4.

Naik, T.B. (1968), "What is Tribe? Conflicting Definitions", in L.P. Vidyarthi (ed.), *Applied Anthropology*, Allahabad.

Omvedt, Gail (1988), "Are Adivasis Subaltern", *Economic and Political Weekly*, September 24, Vol. XXIII, No. 39.

Patel, M.L. (1981), "Micro-Planning for Human Resource Development in Tribal Areas", *Economic Journal*.

Patel, M.L. (1982), "Agro-Economic Problems of Tribals of India", in Buuddhadeb Choudhury (ed.), *Tribal Development in India*, Inter-India Publications, New Delhi.

Pathy, E. (1976), "Tribal Studies in India: An Appraisal", *The Eastern Anthropologist*.

Patel, M.L. (1974), "Some Aspects of Educational Development of Tribals", *Bulletin of Cultural Research Institute*.

Paul, B.N. "Policy Measures of Tribal Agriculture", in M.L. Patel (ed.) (1972), *Agro-Economic Problems of Tribal India*, Progress Publishers, Bhopal.

Rath, M.K. and S.C. Das. (1982), "Constitutional Safeguards for Scheduled Tribes", in Buddhadeb Choudhury (ed.), *Tribal Development in India: Problems and Prospects*, Inter-India Publications, New Delhi.

Reddy, G.P. (1989), "Introductory Agriculture in a Tribal Community - The Case of Chenchus", in M.K. Raha and P.C. Coomar (eds.), *Tribal India: Problems and Prospects*, Vol. II, Gian Publishing House, New Delhi.

Reddy, T. Prabhakar (1989), "Tribal Land Alienation in Andhra Pradesh", *Economic and Political Weekly*, Vol. XXIV, No. 28, 15 July.

Rojora, S.C. (1986), "Tribal Society and Its Differential Profile", *Vanyajati*, January, Vol. XXXIV, No. 1, pp. 7-10.

Roy Burman, B.K. (1982), "Transfer and Alienation of Tribal Land", in Buddhadeb Choudhury (ed.), *Tribal Development in India: Problems and Prospects*, Inter-India Publications, New Delhi.

Sahoo, F.M. (1989), "Study of Tribal Cultures in Orissa", in B.C. Ray (ed.), *Tribals of Orissa: Changing Socio-Economic Profile*, Gian Publishing House, New Delhi.

Sengupta, P.N. (1959), "The Aborigines, Their Nutrition and Welfare", *Bulletin of the Bihar Tribal Research Institute*, Vol. 1, No. 1, pp. 56-66.

Sharma, B.D. (1977), "Administration for Tribal development", *Indian Journal of Public Administration*, Vol. XXIII, No. 3, July-September.

Sinha, S.P. (1986), "Tribal Development Administration", in L.P. Vidyarthi (ed.), *Tribal Development and Its Administration*, Concept Publishing Company, New Delhi.

Srikant, L.M. (1956), "The Integration of Aboriginal Population of India", *International Labour Review*, Vol. LXXIII, No. 3, March.

Velayuthan, K. Shanmuga (1979), "A Sub-Plan Approach to Tribal Development", *The Indian Journal of Social Work*, Vol. XI, No. 2, July.

Wadia, F.K. (1976), "Control of Shifting Cultivation in North Eastern Region", *Prajna*, Vol. 3, July-September.

INDEX

T